A SHORTER GUIDE TO THE HOLY SPIRIT

A SHORTER GUIDE TO THE HOLY SPIRIT

Bible, Doctrine, Experience

Anthony C. Thiselton

WILLIAM B. EERDMANS PUBLISHING COMPANY
GRAND RAPIDS, MICHIGAN

© 2016 Anthony C. Thiselton

Published 2016 by
Wm. B. Eerdmans Publishing Co.
2140 Oak Industrial Drive N.E., Grand Rapids, Michigan 49505

Printed in the United States of America

22 21 20 19 18 17 16   7 6 5 4 3 2 1

Library of Congress Cataloging-in-Publication Data

Names: Thiselton, Anthony C., author.
Title: A shorter guide to the Holy Spirit : Bible, doctrine, experience /
Anthony C. Thiselton.
Description: Grand Rapids, Michigan : Eerdmans Publishing Company, 2016. |
Includes bibliographical references.
Identifiers: LCCN 2015043610 | ISBN 9780802873491 (pbk. : alk. paper)
Subjects: LCSH: Holy Spirit. | Holy Spirit—Biblical teaching.
Classification: LCC BT121.3 .T453 2016 | DDC 231/.3—dc23
LC record available at http://lccn.loc.gov/2015043610

www.eerdmans.com

Contents

CONTENTS

PART III: Experience and Global Origins and Current Issues among Pentecostals

Preface

This shorter book on the Holy Spirit was specifically requested by Eerdmans. They kindly indicated that my larger book of 570 pages (2013) had been well received and appreciated. Indeed, the larger book received the "Award of Merit in the Category of Theology/Ethics" by *Christianity Today* for 2014. But many urged their preference for a shorter book. The publishers therefore contracted with me to write a second book on the same subject with a maximum of 80,000 words. I enjoyed writing this, not least because it gave me the opportunity to fill in some gaps and also to write a more doctrinal and less historical section. The most glaring omission was the explosion of Pentecostalism in the two-thirds world as a global phenomenon.

I have resisted the temptation simply to repeat passages from the earlier book. I have seldom consulted it while writing the present book. The section on the Old Testament, for example, is significantly expanded. Some New Testament material may overlap, but Part II concerns themes of the Christian *doctrine* of the Holy Spirit, rather than a previously detailed *historical* account of writers on the Holy Spirit. Part III is new, on the experience of the Holy Spirit. This includes the origins and global expansion of Pentecostalism; the Spirit, "modern," and "Pentecostal" hermeneutics; and the essential inspiration of the Holy Spirit in prayer and worship.

I have been impressed by the self-awareness of Pentecostals, their worldwide numbers and witness, and their seriousness, living commitment, and joy in worship. As before, I hope that my writing aims at mutual respect and common ground. I have been honest, however, about certain disagreements and reservations, and in this volume I offer a critique of some worship in charismatic renewal, especially as cited by those who have been directly involved in it from within the charismatic movement, such as Tom Smail, as well as others.

One feature of the book may be potentially embarrassing. I know that many Pentecostals and charismatics find personal testimony more convincing than argument. Hence in trying to distinguish "current but traditional" hermeneutics from claims for a "Pentecostal hermeneutics," I have explained the former simply by testifying to my own exploration of, and writing on, hermeneutics since the 1970s. But personal testimony may at times look like self-advertisement. This has never been my aim. I have simply expounded how I perceived the Spirit to be leading me, in order to ask: is the Holy Spirit active only in "Pentecostal hermeneutics"? The Holy Spirit presumably inspires many to engage in interpreting Scripture properly and to God's glory. For an Englishman to write in such a personal style is probably more painful than it might be for some American colleagues, where personal profiles may seem less outrageous. But in fact the personal mode covers only a short half of a chapter.

The shorter compass of the book inevitably brings casualties. I had planned to write more on Roman Catholic theology, but I have included, in effect, only Congar. For more I must refer readers to the historical and contemporary sections of the larger work. I do, however, refer to the recent Anglican and Pentecostal Consultation of April 2014, which aimed at deeper mutual ecumenical understanding.

It is my sincere hope that this smaller book will facilitate greater mutual understanding on this crucial subject. I have always believed in the importance of understanding rightly the work of the Holy Spirit, since my master's degree in 1964. Like many Greeks and Romans of old, I send out this book with some trepidation, but with much hope. Throughout, my wife Rosemary has been a tireless support, indeed a fellow worker for the Gospel. She has done virtually all the typing and has provided many suggestions for corrections and greater clarity. I pray for God's blessing on this book.

ANTHONY C. THISELTON, FBA,
Emeritus Professor of Christian Theology,
University of Nottingham, UK

Abbreviations

ANF	*Ante-Nicene Fathers*
BDAG	W. Bauer, F. W. Danker, W. F. Arndt, and F. W. Gingrich, *A Greek–English Lexicon of the New Testament and Other Early Christian Literature,* 3rd ed. (Chicago: University of Chicago Press, 2003)
EKKNT	Evangelisch-katholischer Kommentar zum Neuen Testament
HR	E. Hatch and H. A. Redpath, *A Concordance to the Septuagint,* 2nd ed. (Grand Rapids: Baker Academic, 1998)
ICC	International Critical Commentary
JBL	*Journal of Biblical Literature*
JPT	*Journal of Pentecostal Theology*
JPTSup	Journal of Pentecostal Theology Supplement Series
JSNT	*Journal for the Study of the New Testament*
JTS	*Journal of Theological Studies*
LCC	Library of Christian Classics
NCB	New Century Bible
NICNT	New International Commentary on the New Testament
NIDB	*New Interpreter's Dictionary of the Bible*
NIDOTTE	*New International Dictionary of Old Testament Theology and Exegesis*
NIDPCM	*New International Dictionary of Pentecostal and Charismatic Movements*
NIGTC	New International Greek Testament Commentary
NPNF	*Nicene and Post-Nicene Fathers*
NTS	*New Testament Studies*
PG	*Patrologia Graeca,* ed. J-P. Migne
PL	*Patrologia Latina,* ed. J-P. Migne
SBLDS	Society of Biblical Literature Dissertation Series

SBT	Studies in Biblical Theology
SJT	*Scottish Journal of Theology*
SNTSM	Studiorum Novi Testamenti Societas Monographs
TDNT	*Theological Dictionary of the New Testament*
TDOT	*Theological Dictionary of the Old Testament*
WUNT	Wissenschaftliche Untersuchungen zum Neuen Testament
WUNT/2	Wissenschaftliche Untersuchungen zum Neuen Testament, 2. Reihe

PART I

The Spirit in the Biblical Writings

CHAPTER 1

The Spirit in the Old Testament

This first chapter will be devoted to the Old Testament. But we must also take note of developments in Judaism, which constitutes a smaller second chapter. The Spirit in Judaism presents features of similarity to and contrast with the New Testament and Christian doctrine.

(1) Of the many characteristics of the Spirit of God in the Old Testament, one of the most distinctive is the otherness of the Spirit from humankind. The theological term for this is normally the "transcendence" of the Spirit. The Spirit does indeed also work within, and this extends to his being *immanent as well as transcendent.* Indeed in one specific sense C. F. D. Moule declares, "The Holy Spirit is most characteristically experienced as God immanent in man . . . the voice of God addressing himself from within man."[1] But the indwelling of the Spirit is possible only because he comes from God. In crude terms, he first comes *from outside* humankind.

In their introduction to *Presence, Power, and Promise,* Firth and Wegner call the Spirit in the OT "the energizing force in the lives of people to accomplish God's mission on earth."[2] Thus the OT often uses such phrases as "the Spirit of the Lord rushed on him" (Judg. 14:6); "the Spirit of the Lord came mightily upon David" (1 Sam. 16:13); "the Spirit of the Lord shall rest upon him" (Isa. 11:2); and "the Spirit (NRSV, a spirit) entered me" (Ezek. 2:2). To repeat: the Spirit of God comes upon human beings from without; the Spirit is not a latent inner human capacity.

---

1. C. F. D. Moule, *The Holy Spirit* (London: Mowbray, 1978), p. 81.
2. David G. Firth and Paul D. Wegner, "Introduction," in their edited volume, *Presence, Power, and Promise: The Role of the Spirit in the Old Testament* (Nottingham: Apollos, 2011), pp. 1-21, here p. 15.

The practical consequences of this attribute can readily be seen in the popular and sometimes careless way in which people often speak today of "spirituality." In popular usage the term can mean the religious aspect of *human aspiration,* as if this naturally flows from the capacities of humankind. In previous years, people often described the work of the Spirit on humanity as empowerment or godliness; today they often use the less precise, and potentially misleading, term "spirituality." On the contrary, the Spirit of God in the OT is precisely *God* in action.

In this sense the Spirit of God stands in contrast to all that is merely human, finite, or of this world. As Gordon Fee has shown, the Spirit is the presence and power of God himself, not some impersonal force.[3] Often in the OT, the presence of God occurs in synonymous parallelism with the Spirit of God. For example, the Psalmist asks, "Where can I go from your Spirit? Or where can I flee from your presence?" (Ps. 139:7). Similarly, "Do not cast me from your presence, and do not take your Holy Spirit from me" (Ps. 51:11). Haggai exclaims, "I am with you. . . . My Spirit abides among you" (Hag. 2:4-5). One possible danger is that of seeking the Spirit as if to do this were somehow different from seeking *God.*

The Spirit of God means more than heightened human capacities or even superhuman forces; again the Spirit contrasts with all that is merely human. One classic passage implies this: "The Egyptians are human, and not God; their horses are flesh, not spirit" (Isa. 31:3). In this context *flesh* denotes all that is merely creaturely, fallible, and weak, in contrast to God.

Another clear example of this principle occurs in Ezek. 37:7-14, in which God declares, "I will put my Spirit within you, and you shall live." The community of Israel was as dead and withered as "dry bones" (v. 11); they had no prospect of deriving any life from their own capacities. Dead people can contribute nothing at all to life. Hence God promises to put his Spirit within them, as if from "outside." *God alone* can raise the community to restored life as restored people.

Ezekiel also reveals the vision of the transcendent God on his sovereign throne. The Spirit, who animates the "living creatures" around the throne, is active, living, and dynamic (Ezek. 1:12, 20). Writers have likened Ezekiel's picture of the enthroned God to the imagery of apocalyptic "throne-visions" that portray the transcendence of God. God is awesomely "from Beyond," and this is true of God's Spirit. The Spirit of God also lifts

---

3. Gordon Fee, *God's Empowering Presence: The Holy Spirit in the Letters of Paul* (Milton Keynes: Paternoster, 1995 / Peabody, MA: Hendrickson, 1994).

up the prophet and carries him away (Ezek. 3:14; 8:3; 11:1). Various other OT passages corroborate this emphasis of the Spirit and creation of life and order. Job declares, "The Spirit of God has made me, and the breath of the Almighty gives me life" (Job 33:4). The Psalmist asserts, "By the word of the Lord the heavens were made, and all their host by the breath (Heb. *rûaḥ*) of his mouth" (Ps. 33:6).

(2) A second characteristic of the Spirit is that he is the source of life, creation, and creativity. In Gen. 1:2 the KJV/AV and RSV translate the Hebrew, "The Spirit of God was moving over (KJV, moved upon) the face of the waters." The NIV translates this verse, "The Spirit of God was hovering over the waters," which accords with C. K. Barrett's comment, "The word *merachepheth* suggests the brooding or hovering of a bird."[4] He compares the Spirit with a bird's hovering over its nest, prior to giving creative birth. It is a pity that the NRSV translates this, "A wind from God swept over the face of the waters." Admittedly the Hebrew noun *rûaḥ* can mean both *Spirit* and *wind,* but the former seems to fit the context of the creation narrative more appropriately, especially since the Spirit of God brought order out of chaos. On the other hand Richard Averbeck argues that the Hebrew *rûaḥ* can mean here both wind and Spirit shaping creation.[5]

The Hebrew phrase *tohû wā-bohû,* traditionally translated "formless and void" or something comparable, denotes *an unproductive waste.* Many still disagree about the right translation, and Robert Hubbard argues that this means formless and empty, or simply "an unproductive and uninhabited place," one that is not "chaotic."[6] Walter Kaiser writes, "It was God himself who brought the creative power of the work of the Holy Spirit to show order, design, and functionality to an earth that emerged at its first appearance as 'empty and vacant'."[7] It seems to relate to a future parallel with the descent of the dove at the baptism of Jesus, when he saw "the Spirit descending like a dove on him" (Mark 1:10) — the Spirit here is One of order, rather than, as is sometimes argued, One who brings chaos in place of institutional order. The Spirit creatively ushered in the new era of Jesus Christ as Messiah.

---

4. C. K. Barrett, *The Holy Spirit and the Gospel Tradition* (London: SPCK, 1958), p. 18.

5. Richard E. Averbeck, "Breath, Wind, Spirit and the Holy Spirit in the O.T.," in Firth and Wegner, eds., *Presence, Power, and Promise,* pp. 25-37, here p. 34.

6. Robert L. Hubbard, "The Spirit and Creation," in Firth and Wegner, eds., *Presence, Power, and Promise,* pp. 71-91, here pp. 83.

7. Walter C. Kaiser, "The Pentateuch," in Trevor J. Burke and Keith Warrington, eds., *A Biblical Theology of the Holy Spirit* (London: SPCK, 2014), pp. 1-11, here p. 5.

One well-known writer on the Spirit, Jürgen Moltmann, calls his book on this subject *The Spirit of Life*.[8] Formulating the theme that the Spirit comes from outside us, not in origin from within us, Moltmann observes, "Experiences [of the Spirit] 'happen' to us and 'befall' us."[9] He elsewhere states, "The experience of God's Spirit is not limited to the human subject's experience of the self."[10] In the NT this experience of receiving life is related to rebirth in John and resurrection in Paul. Daniel Block refers to "*Rûaḥ* as the agent of animation" in the prophets.[11] God "gives breath to the people on it (the earth) and Spirit to those who walk in it" (Isa. 42:5). He breathed into humankind "the breath of life" (Gen. 2:7). Psalm 104:29-30 declares, "When you take away their breath, they die and return to dust. When you send forth your Spirit, they are created." The context of Ezek. 34–39 is national renewal and revival: "I will cause *rûaḥ* (Spirit) to enter you, and you shall live" (Ezek. 37:5). The dried-up scattered bones of the long-dead corpse come together, and the new corporate community receives life.

(3) A third characteristic of the Spirit of God is the empowerment of the individual, especially for leadership, but specifically for the benefit of the *community* of God's people. Often the Spirit of God is given *temporally for a specific task,* which will also benefit others. One classic example is the gift of God's Spirit to the judges. The Spirit is given to Othniel (Judg. 3:7-11), to Ehud (Judg. 3:12-30), to Deborah (Judg. 4:1-24), to Gideon (Judg. 6:11–8:35), and to several others. They delivered Israel from oppression in the power of the Spirit. But the narrator stresses that these feats of deliverance could never have been done in their own strength. Thus all have some handicap, as their contemporaries would have perceived it. Ehud was left-handed; Deborah was a woman; Gideon had to reduce the size of his army; Samson abused his gift. But the basic principle is still true today: God's gift is given for a God-given task, and leads to victory and success, even if humans alone do not have this capacity.

Such gifts were not only for warfare. Bezalel is given the gift of skill and craftsmanship (Exod. 31:2-5). John Levison observes, "This is more than a momentary event."[12] Richard Hess explains that this "emphasizes

---

8. Jürgen Moltmann, *The Spirit of Life: A Universal Affirmation* (London: SCM, 1982).

9. Moltmann, *The Spirit of Life*, p. 22.

10. Moltmann, *The Spirit of Life*, p. 34.

11. Daniel I. Block, "The View from the Top: The Holy Spirit in the Prophets," in Firth and Wegner, eds., *Presence, Power, and Promise*, pp. 175-207, here pp. 191-201.

12. John R. Levison, *Filled with the Spirit* (Grand Rapids: Eerdmans, 2009), pp. 52-58.

that every area of the person is full of God's presence. No area is with-held. And so every part of the skill and understanding becomes divinely endowed with the full presence of divinity."[13] The seventy elders receive the gift of good administration to relieve Moses of the task (Num. 11:16-25). Eugene Merrill comments, "Num. 11:16-30 is replete with references to the spirit or 'God's Spirit' (seven times in vv. 17, 25, 26, 29), all in the context of the instalment of seventy elders empowered to assist Moses in the leadership of the community."[14] In Isaiah the Spirit brings peace and justice (Isa. 32:15-16). Zechariah declares, "Not by might, nor by power, but by my Spirit, says the Lord of hosts" (4:6); i.e. not by brute force. This is clearest of all in messianic prophecies.

The Spirit of God anoints the messianic figure: "The Spirit of the Lord shall rest on him, the Spirit of wisdom and understanding, the Spirit of counsel and might" (Isa. 11:1-2). Admittedly the NRSV usually uses the lower-case initial letter "spirit," and this is possible in some instances. But we have consistently used the initial capital for "Spirit," because all of our main examples so far seem to us to refer to the Spirit of God, not to human capacities. The Hebrew *rûaḥ* leaves interpreters free to make their own judgments about the English. Hilary Harlow explains, "The *rûach* of God is the means by which he [the messianic figure] executes judgment . . . and restoration."[15]

(4) A fourth characteristic of God's Spirit is his gift of prophecy and inspiration. Montague calls him "the instigator and the animator of proph-ecy."[16] An early example is that of Balaam in Num. 22–24. We read in Num. 24:2 that "The Spirit of the Lord came upon him," and he uttered his or-acle as "one who heard the words of God." In a later OT writing the false prophet Zedekiah challenges the prophet Micaiah: "Which way did the Spirit of the Lord pass from me to speak to you?" (1 Kings 22:24). Micaiah declared that God had put a lying spirit in Zedekiah's mouth, and that King Ahab would die in battle. He asserted, "Whatever the Lord says to me, I will speak" (22:14). The claims of false prophets to be inspired by the Spirit

13. Richard S. Hess, "Bezalel and Oholiab: Spirit and Creativity," in Firth and Wegner, eds., *Presence, Power, and Promise,* pp. 161-72, here p. 165.

14. Eugene H. Merrill, "The Samson Saga and Spiritual Leadership," in Firth and Wegner, eds., *Presence, Power, and Promise,* pp. 281-93, here p. 285.

15. Hilary Harlow, "The Spirit of Yahweh in Isaiah 11:1-9," in Firth and Wegner, eds., *Presence, Power, and Promise,* pp. 220-32, here p. 224.

16. George T. Montague, *The Holy Spirit: The Growth of a Biblical Tradition* (Eugene, OR: Wipf & Stock, 1976), p. 45.

of God were difficult to cope with. *This is still very much an urgent matter in the face of such claims today.* Moberly discusses the Micaiah passage over some twenty pages in his definitive book on true and false prophecy. The prophets were to provide guidance to the kings of Israel and Judah with regard to a military campaign. Zedekiah and other prophets tell King Jehoshaphat what he wants to hear, and he suspects their authenticity as they rubber-stamp his wishes. So he seeks out Micaiah. The narrative raises "the possibility that the 400 prophets are speaking less than the truth . . . (and) we are given to know exactly what Micaiah has to face."[17]

False prophecy, in other words, was a recurrent danger and demanding problem throughout the history of Israel. Deuteronomy and Jeremiah witness to this. Too many, even today, glibly claim to be God's spokesmen who speak on his behalf. In Deuteronomy, however, stern words are uttered about this, especially in 18:19-22. In 18:20 God declares, "Any prophet . . . who presumes to speak in my name a word that I have not commanded the prophet to speak — that prophet shall die." Deuteronomy 18:22 again warns us against speaking a word that the Lord has not spoken. Jeremiah 23:32 speaks of those "who lead my people astray by their lies . . . when I did not send them or appoint them." Even today the problem is still with us. History is littered with self-proclaimed prophets, to whom patently God did not speak, but to whom people listened with respect and obedience. To claim prophetic inspiration has always been a heavy responsibility, both for oneself and for the people who may be led astray.

This probably explains why the true OT prophets were often reluctant to claim openly that the Spirit of God was inspiring them. Amos has no reference to the Spirit's inspiration, and even seems deliberately to play down his role as God's prophet. J. E. Fison writes, "There is all the difference in the world between 'hearing the word of the Lord' and working yourself up into an ecstasy of mystical rapture."[18]

Daniel Block heads one of his sections, "*Rûach* as agent of prophetic inspiration."[19] He, like Moberly, discusses false prophecy, in his case in Ezekiel 13. God instructs Ezekiel, "Mortal, prophesy against the prophets of Israel who are prophesying; say to those who prophesy out of their own imagination: 'Hear the Word of the Lord'" (Ezek. 13:2). The great prophet

---

17. R. W. L. Moberly, *Prophecy and Discernment* (Cambridge: Cambridge University Press, 2006), p. 113, see also pp. 109-29.

18. J. E. Fison, *The Blessing of the Holy Spirit* (London: Longmans, Green, 1950), p. 67.

19. Block, "The View from the Top," pp. 184-88.

resisted all self-induced experiences of "prophetic inspiration." Ezekiel declared, "Alas for the senseless prophets who follow their own spirit, and have seen nothing" (Ezek. 13:3). Isa. 32:5-6 condemns the same folly. More positively, the prophets regard the Spirit as agent of divine empowerment. Block cites a range of biblical passages, from the anointing of David in Isaiah to the figure who will administer justice to the nations (Isa. 42:1-4), and Daniel's ability to solve mysteries (Dan. 4:5–5:29).

(5) A fifth characteristic of the Spirit is that his status might be called "more than personal" — that is to say, the Spirit cannot be *less* "personal" than conscious or self-conscious creatures such as humankind; but the Spirit far exceeds what "personal" means when we apply the term to human beings. In the same way, God is not less "personal" than humankind, but his personhood far exceeds any notion of human beings as "personal." We shall address this question more fully when we consider the NT evidence, as well as some historical thinkers. Meanwhile, we have noted already that in the OT the "Spirit of God" occurs in synonymous parallelism with "God." This means that even on the basis of the OT we should exercise extreme caution in calling the Spirit "it," as if he were merely one created object among others, or in describing the Spirit like an impersonal force of energy or wisdom. Many argue, in response, that the OT uses the term "Holy Spirit" only three times (Psalm 51:11, Isa. 63:10-11), and that consequently he is not a person distinct from God. But the very fact that he is the Spirit *of God* should invite us to be cautious in too hastily speaking of him as if he were an "it." In Dan. 4:8 he is the Spirit of the holy God.

Some argue from time to time that since the Hebrew word *rûaḥ,* "spirit," is feminine, we should refer to the Spirit of God as "She." But, as James Barr has pointed out, an accident of grammar does not indicate gender at all.[20] In the NT *pneuma,* "spirit," is neuter (just as *child* is neuter), and *paraklētos,* "Paraclete," is masculine. The Spirit, like God, is *beyond gender,* just as he is "more" than personal, but not "less" than personal. The Spirit of God can be "grieved" (Isa. 63:10-14). In our larger book on the Holy Spirit we have multiplied examples of personal action. He is, unlike a "thing," omnipresent, as in Ps. 139:7: "Where can I go from your Spirit?" He is also all-knowing, as in Isa. 40:13: "Who has directed the Spirit of the Lord?" We shall return to this more fully when we consider the NT.

This becomes especially important in messianic passages in the OT.

---

20. James Barr, *The Semantics of Biblical Language* (Oxford: Oxford University Press, 1961), pp. 39-40, 96.

In Isa. 42:1, 5, the Servant of the Lord is "My chosen, in whom my soul delights; I have put my Spirit upon him." Similarly in Ezekiel 37, the Spirit comes from without; he is not merely some strengthened capacity within. This becomes clearer in the light of two distinct traditions in the OT and Judaism. According to the "prophetic" tradition, the Messiah will be the kingly but earthly Son of David who will bring in the Kingdom of God through his being anointed by the Spirit of God. In the "apocalyptic" tradition, however, the world has so far fallen into sin that *only God* can redeem it, through the *divine* person of the Messiah. Once again, the *Spirit* of God and *God-in-action* work in parallel, just as the Messiah is *human, but also* anointed by the Spirit, and represents *God himself.*

Other prophecies look forward to fulfilments which far exceed the limits of the immediate situation. For example, Joel 2:28 promises, "I will pour out my Spirit on all flesh" (i.e. on all kinds of people, on everyone without distinction). We shall note under the NT that such language as "pour out" does not depersonalize the Spirit.

(6) The Spirit of God is *Derived from Another*, that is, he is *One who can be Shared out among Participants*. A classic example appears, as we have noted, in Num. 11:25. Here Moses was overburdened with administration, and the Lord "took some of the Spirit (NRSV, spirit) that was on him and put it on the seventy elders; and when the Spirit rested upon them, they prophesied." Similarly, Joshua derives the Spirit from Moses through Moses' laying on of hands (Deut. 34:9), and Elisha from the Spirit given to Elijah (2 Kings 2:13-15).

The importance of this will become clearer in the NT, when Paul stresses that our experience of the Holy Spirit is *derived from Christ,* just like our adoption as sons and daughters, and our dying and being raised with Christ. Resurrection in the NT is by the Holy Spirit (Rom. 8:11), because we are in Christ. The OT pattern of participation in a derived Gift anticipates the possibility of this.

(7) The Spirit of God is known by a name or term which in linguistic terms is a homonym. "Homonym" is a term in linguistics that denotes a word which can have more than one meaning. Such words are common. For example a "bank" may denote the dry borders of a river, or an institution in which financial accounts are stored. In the same way the Hebrew *rûaḥ*, like the Greek *pneuma*, may denote either the Spirit of *God,* or the spirit within *human beings.* Van Pelt counts 387 occurrences of *rûaḥ* in the OT, and comments, "Since *ruach* has such a broad range of meanings, it is difficult to capture its semantic breadth with a single term

or phrase."[21] Some refer to the latter as the "anthropological" meanings of spirit. Clearly the OT uses both meanings, and they easily cause confusion and debate.

This problem has been long recognized. Brown, Driver, and Briggs, authors of the standard Old Testament Hebrew–English lexicon, allocate some four columns of their lexicon to *rûaḥ*.[22] They list some nine meanings, each subdivided, including (i) as breath or wind; (ii) as wind of heaven or air; (iii) as spirit or disposition; (iv) as spirit of the living being; (v) as spirit as the seat of emotion; (vi) occasionally mind or mental act; (vii) as an act or attitude of moral character; (viii) as spirit or Spirit of God. On the face of it, anthropological uses are more numerous than theological ones. But breath may include breath of God, especially when it denotes his anger (Exod. 15:8, 10). Often it clearly denotes a wide range of different meanings: the "east," "north," or "west wind" (Exod. 10:13; 14:21; Prov. 25:23; etc.). It may sometimes denote "animation" or "vivacity" (1 Kings 10:5). In Josh. 5:1 it denotes "courage," although NRSV renders it literally as "spirit." The human spirit can depart at death (Psalm 78:39, NRSV, "wind"; Isa. 38:16). Often the word refers to the human spirit as such (Job 17:1). There are too many biblical references to cite.

On the other hand, we firmly reject any notion that biblical writers in the OT or NT share the mind–body dualism of the ancient Greeks, or in later years of Descartes and Locke. The Hebrew people, like the NT writers, held a unitary view of the human person. Even to speak of "two components" of the person can be misleading. The Hebrew word *nepeš* is often translated "soul," but in some contexts it also denotes a corpse or dead body (Num. 9:6, 7, 10). Pannenberg speaks of biblical and modern concepts of the human being, in which "the soul and body (are) constitutive elements of *the unity of human life that belong together,*" as "a *psychosomatic unity.*"[23] In Paul, Käsemann's view of the body makes this abundantly clear.

(8) An eighth feature of the Spirit of God is the way in which the Spirit of God sustains all life. Psalm 104:29 reminds us, "When you take away their breath, they die and return to dust. When you send forth your Spirit, they are created." The Psalmist elsewhere asks, "Where can I go

---

21. M. V. Van Pelt and Walter C. Kaiser, "*ruach,*" in *NIDOTTE,* pp. 1073-78, here p. 1073.

22. Francis Brown, S. R. Driver, and C. A. Briggs, *Hebrew and English Lexicon,* rev. ed. (Lafayette: Associated Publishers, 1980), pp. 924-26.

23. Wolfhart Pannenberg, *Systematic Theology,* 3 vols. (Edinburgh: T&T Clark / Grand Rapids: Eerdmans, 1994), 2.182 (my italics).

from your Spirit?" (139:7). This is not the purely immanent spirit or world-soul of the Stoics. The OT simply asserts that the Spirit of God sustains all life. This will become clearer when we consider Paul on this subject. We considered numerous passages under our section (2) above. These included "the breath of life" in Gen. 2:7; Ps. 104:29-30; and Ezek. 34–39, which concerns national renewal and revival: "I will cause *rûaḥ* to enter you, and you shall live" (Ezek. 37:5).

(9) It goes almost without saying that the Spirit is invisible and intangible: hence he is known from his effects. But this does not mean, as some philosophers used to maintain, that his activity cannot be subject to the modern principles of verification or falsification. The visibility of the Spirit's work is seen from what effects and changes his invisible work brings about. In the same way the invisible wind can be seen in the shaking of trees (Isa. 7:2), and in the separation of chaff from wheat (Isa. 41:16). Even if the Spirit himself cannot be seen, the *effects* of his action are evident.

Nevertheless this does raise one particular danger, as Karl Barth warns us. It is all too easy to focus on the *phenomena* of the Spirit, at the expense of asking what *purpose* lies behind the phenomena, and what *consequences* follow. He applies this especially to prophecy.[24] As is often said, we should not be distracted from seeking *the Giver,* by obsessively seeking *the gift.*

(10) Firth and Wegner suggest at least "one good reason for God not [yet] to reveal the Trinity" in the OT.[25] For Israel polytheism or belief in multiple deities was a long-standing problem. The *Shema* of Deut. 6:4 needed to be thoroughly learned before the people of God could be introduced to Trinitarian theology and faith. This is not as radical as it might seem. The NT and the Church Fathers clearly teach that all Persons of the Trinity act together to bring about the will of God. The NT shows that creation involves Christ as well as the Father and the Spirit (Col. 1:15; Heb. 1:2); that "God was in Christ" in our redemption (2 Cor. 5:19); and that resurrection occurs by an act of God in Christ through the Holy Spirit (Rom. 8:11). This serves to remind us that the Old Testament is *not a finished* revelation, but looks forward to fulfilment and completion in the New, and that retrospectively the NT shows why this partial revelation does not cause a problem (Heb. 1:1-2).

---

24. Karl Barth, *The Resurrection of the Dead* (London: Hodder & Stoughton, 1933), p. 80.

25. Firth and Wegner, "Introduction," p. 19.

CHAPTER 2

The Literature of Intertestamental Judaism

The purpose of this chapter is quite different from that of my larger book. In the larger book on the Holy Spirit, I considered major Jewish sources from after the latest OT writers until the first century A.D. by carefully distinguishing their respective dates, cultural backgrounds, and purposes. My purpose in this smaller book is different. It is less academic and "objective." I still take for granted that there was much interpenetration between what used to be called "Palestinian" Judaism and "Hellenistic" Judaism, as Martin Hengel, Howard Marshall, and others have urged. But for the sake of this distinctly shorter book, and its mainly Christian readers, I focus more narrowly and more briefly on major similarities and differences between developments in Judaism and a biblical theology of the Old and New Testaments, as most Christians understand these. For more detailed questions about Jewish literature, readers are referred to the larger book. First we trace the main points of affinity and contrast with the Christian Bible.

1. The Main Points of Affinity, Which Are Greater Than the Contrasts

(1) The intertestamental Jewish writings maintain the OT theme that the Spirit of God inspires both the Scriptures and prophecy. This applies to the OT prophets in the Dead Sea Scrolls (mostly first century B.C.–first century A.D.). For example, 1QS 3.7-8 (*The Manual of Discipline*) suggests that the Spirit inspired the OT prophets when it comments on Neh. 9:30: "You . . . warned them by your Spirit through the prophets; yet they would

not listen." Similarly the same passage comments on Zech. 7:12: "the words that the Lord of hosts had sent by his Spirit through the former prophets."

In the Apocryphal Books, Jub. 31:12 recounts, "And the Spirit of prophecy came down into his mouth" (where "came down" suggests that this is not merely the human spirit). Jubilees 25:14 and 31:12 speak of "the Spirit of prophecy" (NRSV, regularly, "spirit").

In Greek-speaking Jewish literature, Philo of Alexandria (c. 20 B.C.–A.D. 50) regards the Spirit as inspiring the OT (*On the Life of Moses,* 1.175; 1.277; 2.191; *On the Virtues,* 217-19; *On Dreams,* 2.252; *On the Special Laws,* 4.49; and elsewhere). The prophet can be completely overborne by the Spirit. The Greek-speaking, pro-Roman, Jewish writer Josephus (c. A.D. 37–100) shares the same view (Josephus, *Antiquities,* 4.199; 8.4.3). Schlechter insists, "To them (the Rabbis) the whole of the Torah (was) . . . dictated by the . . . Spirit," citing a number of rabbinic passages.[1]

A standard treatment of the Spirit in Judaism has been offered by John Levison (2002).[2] This updated an earlier treatment by Erik Sjöberg and, less directly, by Eduard Schweizer in Kittel's *TDNT.*[3] Schweizer refers to "the typically Jewish idea that the Spirit is the Spirit of prophecy" in the context of the background to Luke.[4] Max Turner and Robert Menzies undertook studies of Jewish literature as background to the Holy Spirit in Luke, especially in relation to the charismatic and Pentecostal movements, respectively.[5] Turner cites such standard sources as 1 Enoch 91:1 and 4 Ezra 14:22 in the Pseudepigrapha, and Sir. 48:4 and Jub. 71:12 in the Apocrypha. He also cites the Dead Sea Scrolls, e.g. 1QS 8.16.

A problem arises, however, in Turner's citations from the Targums. These were Aramaic paraphrases of the Hebrew OT, mainly used in synagogue services. Admittedly some texts date from before the NT, but the earliest traditions were oral, not written, and the written text of the Baby-

---

1. S. Schlechter, *Some Aspects of Rabbinic Theology* (London: Black, 1909), p. 120; he cites Gen. Rab., 85.2; *Sifre,* 33a; *Sanhedrin,* 99B; and others.

2. John R. Levison, *The Spirit in First-Century Judaism* (Leiden: Brill, 2002).

3. Erik Sjöberg, *"Pneuma, pneumatikos, pneō, empneō, pnoē, ekpneō, theopneustos:* C.III. *Rûaḥ* in Palestinian Judaism," in *TDNT,* 6.375-89; Schweizer provided the latter part of the *"Pneuma, pneumatikos"* entry (*TDNT,* 6.389-455), covering the Spirit in Gnosticism, the New Testament, and the post-apostolic fathers.

4. Eduard Schweizer, *"Pneuma, pneumatikos, pneō, empneō, pnoē, ekpneō, theopneustos:* E.II. Luke and Acts," in *TDNT,* 6.404-15, here 407.

5. Max Turner, *Power from on High: The Spirit in Israel's Restoration and Witness in Luke–Acts* (Sheffield: Sheffield Academic Press, 2000), esp. pp. 82-138; and Robert Menzies, *Empowered for Witness: The Spirit in Luke–Acts* (Sheffield: Sheffield Academic Press, 1994).

lonian Targum Onqelos dates only from the mid-second century A.D. The Palestinian Targum Pseudo-Jonathan dates from a little later. It is possible that they reflect earlier traditions, but we cannot be entirely certain about individual texts. They are therefore not always reliable as influences on the NT writers. The most that we can say is that Turner cites numerous examples of Targumic comments on passages in Genesis and elsewhere that ascribe prophecy to the Spirit; he uses examples from the Jacob and Rebekah stories, among others.[6] Nevertheless, the theme that the Spirit inspires Scripture and prophecy cannot be doubted.

(2) Closely related to this is a second theme that the Spirit inspires study of the law and is the source of wisdom and holiness. The Greek Wis. Sol. 9:17 reads: "Who has learned your counsel, unless you have given wisdom and sent your Holy Spirit from on High?" Paul takes this up in 1 Cor. 2:6-15, especially vv. 10-13, which is almost a quotation. God is a "Spirit of Truth" (1QS 4.20-21). Philo believes that the Spirit inspired the Scriptures and their reading (*On the Life of Moses*, 2.191; 1.277). It is unnecessary to belabor the point.

(3) The Spirit is personal or suprapersonal, and radiates God's presence and activity. Sjöberg writes, "There are many instances of the Spirit speaking, crying, admonishing, sorrowing, weeping, rejoicing, comforting."[7]

(4) The Spirit will equip a Messianic figure to bring salvation to God's people. In the nationalistic and apocalyptic Psalms of Solomon, the author builds up the picture of a warrior-messianic figure who will restore his people: "God will make him mighty by means of his holy Spirit, and wise by . . . the spirit of understanding" (Ps. Sol. 17:42). He will "shepherd his flock" (14:45) and lead them (v. 46). 1QS 9.11 speaks of the priestly messiah of Aaron and the kingly messiah of Israel.

2. The Main Points of Contrast and Difference

(1) The most striking and glaring contrast with the NT is that often in Jewish literature the Spirit of God is a reward for holiness and obedience, whereas in Paul and the apostolic Church the Spirit of God is the cause

---

6. Turner, *Power from on High,* p. 87; he discusses Gen. 27:5, 42; 30:26-27, 33; 43:14; etc.

7. Sjöberg, "*Rûaḥ* in Palestinian Judaism," 6.386.

of holiness and obedience. Sjöberg writes, "The gift of the Spirit is especially viewed as a reward for a righteous life."[8] Rabbi Acha declared, "He who sacrifices himself for Israel will receive . . . the Holy Spirit" (Numbers Rabbah 15:20). We may also compare Rabbi Nehemiah commenting on Exod. 15:1, "He who undertakes a commandment in faith is worthy that the Holy Spirit should rest on him" (Mekilta Exodus 15:1, a Tannaitic Midrash on Exodus 15). Sjöberg also cites Genesis Rabbah 91:6 (on Gen. 41:1), and other sources. These stand in utter contrast to Gal. 3:1-5, where Paul asks with rhetorical irony: "Did you receive the Spirit by doing the works of the law or by believing what you heard?" (v. 2). We may grant that the *intention* was to urge the case for purity and holiness. Even some Christian holiness groups, like the extreme "Radical" Reformers, verged towards the edge of this abyss. Luther exclaimed that this undermined his theme of justification by grace through faith alone. It utterly undermined the free sovereign grace of God in Christ.

(2) Although we cannot draw an over-sharp line between the transcendence and immanence of God, who is both beyond the world and within it, the Jewish writings, especially those influenced by Greek speculations, tended to stress the *immanence* of the Spirit at the expense of his otherness. Wisdom 12:1 begins, "Your immortal spirit is in all things." This is not strictly wrong. It expresses "panentheism" rather than pantheism. To be fair, Montague stresses: "Probably in the view of the rest of the Bible, the breath of life never ceases to be God's"; it is only "on loan to man during his earthly life (Wis. 15:16)."[9] Yet Paul carefully distances himself from a one-sided emphasis on immanence in 1 Cor. 2:10-13. In contrast to a Stoic notion of the Spirit as the "soul" of the world, he calls the Holy Spirit the One who *comes forth from God* (2:12). The Greek construction here could be translated literally, "the Spirit, the out-of-God One" (NRSV, "the Spirit that is from God"). We must urge again that this emphasis in Judaism is largely due to the influence of Hellenistic ideas in Diaspora Judaism, where sheer numbers of Jews outnumbered those in the Holy Land.

(3) In the same vein the Spirit of God was sometimes *insufficiently distinguished from sheer rationality*, in both God and humankind. Again, the line is blurred, because reason and order indeed come from God. Only in certain revivalist circles is the Spirit of God ever associated with chaos or

---

8. Sjöberg, "*Rûaḥ* in Palestinian Judaism," 6.383.

9. George Montague, *The Holy Spirit: The Growth of a Biblical Tradition* (Eugene, OR: Wipf & Stock, 1976), p. 102.

confusion. The Spirit at creation explicitly brought order out of chaos. But if reason or reasonableness is regarded as the Spirit himself, rather than as *effects* of the Spirit, we have crossed the line which separates God from all that is human and created.

Nevertheless, this trend remains a tricky one to define, because the Spirit bears a close relation to Wisdom in both the OT and Judaism. We may, however, say that Paul maintains a sharp contrast between human wisdom and the Wisdom of God in Christ in 1 Cor. 1:18-2:5: "In the Wisdom of God, the world did not know God through wisdom" (1:21). We must not, however, overstate the contrast; we merely note a divergent trend. We have already encroached on some NT issues, so it is time to turn to the NT writers themselves. We conclude that out of a possibly longer list, at least four characteristic features of the Spirit of God are shared by Judaism and the NT on the basis of the OT, but at least three offer points of difference and contrast, largely because of Greek influences.

CHAPTER 3

The Holy Spirit in the First Three Gospels

Mark, probably the earliest of the gospels, has just six references to the Holy Spirit. Some argue that Mark has only three. Matthew has eleven references to the Spirit, and Luke has seventeen or eighteen, depending on the manuscript readings. Although Matthew and Luke include the part played by the Holy Spirit in the birth narratives, Mark and the threefold tradition of the synoptic gospels stress the action and person of the Spirit in the baptism of Jesus.

(1) The Holy Spirit as Agent in the baptism of Jesus. In Mark 1:10-11, just as Jesus was coming out of the water, John the Baptist "saw the heavens torn apart and the Spirit descending like a dove on him. And a voice came from heaven, 'You are my Son, the Beloved; with you I am well pleased.'" Matt. 3:16 is a close parallel, and Luke relates, "the Holy Spirit descended upon him in bodily form like a dove" (3:22). Luke also recounts the voice from heaven. The key theme here is that *the Holy Spirit anointed Jesus for appointment to his messianic work and office.* Through the centuries this theme has consistently featured as essential for understanding the person and work of the Holy Spirit, as well as of Jesus Christ.

Some argue convincingly that in this special sense the gift of the Holy Spirit even *precedes* the coming of Jesus. Certainly the gift of the Spirit at the baptism of Jesus demonstrates the unity of Jesus Christ and the doctrine of the Holy Spirit.[1] At least one writer, Rogers, links the baptism of Jesus with an anticipation of the doctrine of the Trinity. He writes, "The baptism of Jesus is primarily to be understood as an intratrinitarian event

---

1. John D. Zizioulas, *Being as Communion* (New York: St. Vladimir's Seminary Press, 1997), pp. 107, 110-11, 129.

. . . It is an event in which the Spirit bears witness to the love between the Father and the Son . . . The Father expresses his love ('this is my Son, my beloved, with whom I am well pleased')."[2]

A number of NT scholars would dissent from this interpretation, although Moltmann also took this Trinitarian approach earlier, and Pannenberg adopts this approach.[3] The very least that we can say is this: the Father, the Son, and the Holy Spirit all participate in this single purpose and event. *The Father* calls Jesus his beloved Son and commands that we hear him; *the Spirit* descends upon Jesus, and anoints him for his messianic work; *Jesus* undergoes baptism, pleases his Father and accepts his will. Thereafter Jesus is clearly and explicitly led by the Holy Spirit. We discuss this passage further under Doctrine (Part II), when we consider the Spirit and the Trinity.

Many associate the baptism of Jesus with the promise of John the Baptist that Jesus "will baptize you with the Holy Spirit and fire" (Luke 3:16). Warrington interprets this correctly when he states, "the Spirit burns," in the sense that he purifies and conveys holiness.[4] Many Pentecostals regard this verse, along with 1 Cor. 12:13, among those verses which point to "the baptism in the Holy Spirit." We discuss this in Part III. Michael Welker comments, "The faith grounded by the Spirit through this public installation of the Christ and the hope grounded through the action of the Spirit, are concretized within specific spectra of experience and expectation."[5] The baptism of Jesus also looks back to Isaiah 11 and 42.

Craig Keener sees the baptism of Jesus as of critical importance for Matthew. He argues that Matt. 3:16, when the Spirit descended upon Jesus, is "critical to Matthew's Gospel" because of its foundation for Jesus' later mission; he observes, "12:28 ('By the Spirit of God . . . I cast out demons') is central in a large measure because Matthew defines Jesus' Spirit-empowerment contextually in terms of the Isaiah quotation."[6]

---

2. Eugene F. Rogers, *After the Spirit: A Constructive Pneumatology* (London: SCM / Grand Rapids: Eerdmans, 2006), pp. 136-63, here pp. 136-37.

3. Jürgen Moltmann, *The Trinity and the Kingdom of God* (London: SCM, 1981), p. 72.

4. Keith Warrington, "The Synoptic Gospels," in Trevor J. Burke and Keith Warrington, eds., *A Biblical Theology of the Holy Spirit* (London: SPCK, 2014), pp. 84-103, here p. 95.

5. Michael Welker, *God the Spirit* (Minneapolis: Fortress, 1994), p. 189.

6. Craig S. Keener, *The Spirit in the Gospels and Acts: Divine Purity and Power* (Grand Rapids: Baker Academic, 1997), pp. 102-3.

(2) Many nineteenth-century writers explicitly called this the messianic anointing of Jesus. Smeaton rightly calls it "the anointing of Christ," "the *unction* of the Spirit," and the *empowerment* by the Spirit.[7] Luke adds "in bodily form" to show that it was an objective, visible experience, and not merely projected subjectively by the mind, as if it were purely a vision. But he qualifies this by adding that it was "like it," i.e. not quite "bodily" in the sense of "physical," but real, objective, public, and visible. The dove is not here a symbol of peace, but a symbol of the new creation, or a new era. Turner calls it "a metaphorical way of referring to the inception of a specific new activity."[8] Turner goes further in evaluating Luke's theological assessment of the baptism of Jesus. He writes, "Jesus experiences a Spirit-given new creation sonship with a depth . . . fundamentally changed by the Jordan experience."[9] All four Gospels regard the baptism of Jesus as a decisive event (cf. John 1:32-34). It signals the fulfilment of what Turner calls "Jesus' installation as Son of God, king of Israel." Hence this constitutes a public event.

(3) Matthew and Luke recount ways in which the initiative of the Holy Spirit featured in the birth narratives of Jesus. Matthew asserts, "She (Mary) was found to be with child from (Greek, *ek*) the Holy Spirit" (Matt. 1:18). Luke recounts the appearance to Mary of the angel Gabriel, who announces, "The Holy Spirit will come upon you, and the power of the Most High will overshadow you; therefore the child to be born will be holy; he will be called Son of God" (Luke 1:35). Luz rightly comments, "This refers to the creative intervention of God, and not to the Spirit as a second partner for Mary."[10] Welker calls this event "Jesus' self-abasement in solidarity with sinful human beings," as indeed his baptism was.[11] He further comments, "Jesus *demonstrates* the power that he already has in relation to Satan by the very act of declining a spectacular moral or political seizure of power."[12] We discuss the Virgin Birth in greater detail in chapter 9, on Jesus and the Spirit in terms of Christian doctrine.

---

7. George Smeaton, *The Doctrine of the Holy Spirit* (London: Banner of Truth, 1958 [1882]), pp. 118-20 (my italics).

8. Max Turner, *Power from on High: The Spirit in Israel's Restoration and Witness in Luke–Acts* (Sheffield: Sheffield Academic Press, 2000), p. 47.

9. Turner, *Power from on High*, p. 199.

10. Ulrich Luz, *Matthew 1–7: A Commentary* (Edinburgh: T&T Clark, 1990), p. 120.

11. Welker, *God the Spirit*, p. 190.

12. Welker, *God the Spirit*, p. 187 (his italics).

(4) The first three gospels tell us that immediately after the baptism of Jesus the Holy Spirit "drove" Jesus (Mark 1:12) into the wilderness to be tempted or *tested for his messianic vocation*. Matthew uses the gentler form "led" (Matt. 4:1), while Luke says that Jesus went into the wilderness "full of the Holy Spirit" (Luke 4:1). The lesson for us is that sometimes, often even, *the Holy Spirit provokes conflict and testing*. Would temptation have been real for Jesus? Yes, indeed! Robinson reminds us that if the pull of temptation had not been genuine, Jesus would not have been truly human.[13] So also Bishop Westcott argued, "Only One who is sinless has experienced the greatest intensity of temptation, for only such a person has not yielded before the last and greatest strain."[14]

But could Jesus have been tempted to do *wrong?* Each of the three classic messianic temptations were enticements to bring in the Kingdom, i.e. to achieve what was ultimately God's will, *but not in God's way.* To command that stones become bread (Matt. 4:3; Luke 4:3) was a way of impressing and winning followers or disciples by a spectacular miracle, but this was *not* how God willed this to be achieved. It was not the way of the cross. Similarly Jesus was tempted to throw himself down from the high ground on which the Temple was built, into the deep valley of *Gē Hinnom*, far below (Matt. 4:5-6; Luke 4:9). This, again, would win the crowds to his cause by a spectacular miracle. But it was not God's will to win followers other than by the word of God and the cross. Third, Jesus was tempted to bring in the Kingdom of God by using the devil's tools, i.e. to achieve it by brute force (Matt. 4:9; Luke 4:6-7). But Jesus asserted, "Worship the Lord your God, and serve *only him.*" Jesus proved that he would obey only God, and he would obey him in every detail. He would use no shortcut to fulfil his Father's will. All this came into the open at the specific instigation of the Holy Spirit. (Incidentally, the difference of chronological sequence in Matthew and Luke is due to the evangelists as narrators using "narrative time," i.e. what best served the purposes of the narrative, rather than clock time).

The biblical accounts make it clear that temptations or testing was not limited to these three model examples. The devil left Jesus only "until an opportune time" (Luke 4:13). Similarly the anointing by the Holy Spirit continued throughout his messianic ministry. Thus, "Jesus, filled with the power of the Spirit, returned to Galilee" (Luke 4:14).

13. J. A. T. Robinson, *The Human Face of God* (London: SCM, 1973).

14. B. F. Westcott, *Epistle to the Hebrews: The Greek Text* (New York: Macmillan, 1903), on 4:15.

(5) In his first synagogue sermon Jesus quoted from Isaiah, "The Spirit of the Lord is upon me, because he has anointed me to bring good news to the poor . . . release to the captives . . . the year of the Lord's favor" (Luke 4:18-19, quoting mainly Isa. 61:1). The preaching of Jesus was in the power of the Holy Spirit. Lampe comments, "The reading of the prophecy and the announcement of its fulfilment in the mission of Jesus serve as a prologue to the whole of the rest of St. Luke's work."[15] He regards preaching and prayer as the two outstanding gifts of the Spirit to Jesus.

(6) The action of the Holy Spirit also concerns the "mighty works" of Jesus. These include exorcisms and miracles of healing. These phenomena stand in continuity with the rabbinic writings. Levison places these acts in the context of "doing good."[16] He is right to select the famous passage, "if it is by the Spirit of God that I cast out demons, then the kingdom of God has come to you" (Matt. 12:28). The important point here is that exorcisms are associated with the coming of *the Kingdom of God*. Luke's parallel has "finger of God" in place of "Spirit," which may look back to Exod. 8:19, in relation to which Jesus brings the new exodus. Turner endorses the link with both the intertestamental writings and the new exodus theme.[17]

Welker comments, "It is striking that in Jesus' pre-Easter activity, the demonic powers are not removed in one blow, but are 'driven out' in a multitude of individual, concrete actions of liberation."[18] The background, he says, is sober and realistic. Again, the presence of the Kingdom as part realised and part yet to come influences how exorcisms are viewed by the evangelists.

Luke includes the "rebuke" of the wind and the waves (Luke 8:22-25); the healing of the Gerasene demoniac (8:26-39); the restoration of Jairus' daughter (8:40-42, 49-56); and the healing of the woman with a hemorrhage (8:43-48). There are many more. In this shorter volume, we have tried to avoid too many controversial issues. However, we find two distinct views about the importance of miracles and exorcisms for Jesus. Dunn regards Jesus as a "charismatic figure," and Turner and Stronstad

15. Geoffrey W. H. Lampe, "The Holy Spirit in the Writings of St. Luke," in D. E. Nineham, ed., *Studies in the Gospels* (Oxford: Blackwell, 1967), pp. 159-200, here p. 171.
16. John R. Levison, "The Holy Spirit in the Gospels," in Johnson T. K. Lim, ed., *Holy Spirit: Unfinished Agenda* (Singapore: Armour, 2015), pp. 52-56, here p. 53.
17. Turner, *Power from on High,* pp. 231 and 244-50.
18. Welker, *God the Spirit,* p. 202.

broadly support him.[19] On the other hand Barrett, Fison, Lampe, Levison, Warrington, and Congar tend to emphasize what they call the *kenōsis*, or "self-emptying," of the Spirit during the earthly ministry of Jesus, which places much less emphasis on the miracles and exorcisms.

Dunn calls Jesus "an ecstatic."[20] Stronstad stresses vocation and prophecy, and allows room for a more "charismatic" emphasis.[21] Barrett, however, considers the question, "Why do the Gospels say so little about the Spirit?" He concludes, "Jesus acted under the necessity of a divine constraint. *Lack of glory and a cup of suffering were his Messianic vocation, and part of his poverty was the absence of all the signs of the spirit of God.* They would have been inconsistent with the office of a humiliated Messiah."[22] In precisely the same way, Fison speaks of the "self-effacement" of the Holy Spirit.[23] What Fison calls self-effacement, Welker calls self-abasement.[24]

Dunn can find support in Luke 4:18-19, and he insists rightly that Jesus relied on God in trust and on the Holy Spirit for his deeds of power. Yet Barrett and Fison are correct in their christology. Each side must be carefully qualified by the other. The exorcisms and miracles of Jesus are best understood as signs of the inbreaking of the Kingdom of God. They should not be regarded as "normal," even if they always remain possible for almighty, sovereign God, on particular occasions.

(7) One often puzzling saying is the pronouncement of Jesus about blasphemy against the Holy Spirit. Mark recounts the charge of some of the teachers of the law that Jesus was driving out demons by the prince of demons. Jesus replies, "People will be forgiven for their sins and whatever blasphemies they utter; but whoever blasphemes against the Holy Spirit can never have forgiveness, but is guilty of an eternal sin" (Mark 3:28-29). I wrote in our Doctrine Commission Report: "The saying stands as a warn-

---

19. James D. G. Dunn, *Jesus and the Spirit: A Study of the Religious and Charismatic Experience of Jesus and the First Christians as Reflected in the New Testament* (London: SCM, 1975), p. 68.

20. Dunn, *Jesus and the Spirit,* pp. 54, 68-92.

21. Roger Stronstad, *The Charismatic Theology of Saint Luke* (Peabody, MA: Hendrickson, 1984); idem, *The Prophethood of All Believers: A Study in Luke's Charismatic Theology* (Sheffield: Sheffield Academic Press, 1999), pp. 18-27 and elsewhere.

22. C. K. Barrett, *The Holy Spirit and the Gospel Tradition* (London: SPCK, 1947), p. 158 (my italics).

23. J. E. Fison, *The Blessing of the Holy Spirit* (London: Longmans, Green, 1950), pp. 11, 22, 72, 93, 107-8, 138-40, 199-200.

24. Welker, *God the Spirit,* p. 190.

ing against the wilful and deliberate manipulation of good and evil, when evil is called 'good' and good is called 'evil.' If a person were to manipulate all moral value and truth with such wilful cynicism, there is no way out of the vicious circle which has been erected."[25] How could repentance be possible, if evil has been redefined as good?

This is a serious saying of Jesus, but pastorally has needlessly troubled many enquirers. But it is a hypothetical warning to be understood *not at all* as a general statement, *divorced from any context.* It specifically addresses those who wilfully distort and reverse good and evil, undermining all moral values, thereby excluding all possibility of repentance. Pastorally, if anyone is worrying about this saying, this is a sign that the Holy Spirit is still working in their heart, and that they need not fear it.

In broader terms, the context relates to the overcoming of Satan by Jesus in the coming of the Kingdom of God. Mark 3:23 reads, "How can Satan cast out Satan?" and v. 27 continues, "no one can enter a strong man's house and plunder his property without first tying up the strong man," i.e. Jesus has begun the binding of Satan. Welker comments, "The superior power . . . overwhelms the demonic powers . . . Jesus' action of driving out demons by the Spirit of God means that God's rule has come."[26]

(8) Dunn and others regard the special intimacy of Jesus with his Father as a prominent feature of the Holy Spirit's activity. The special Aramaic word *Abba* ("Father") in Mark 14:36 is uniquely on the lips of Jesus, until Paul shows how it becomes the special privilege of all Christians to derive the same intimate word from Jesus by the Holy Spirit (Rom. 8:15-16; Gal. 4:6). In a wider sense God is the Father of all humankind as Creator and Provider (Deut. 32:6; Mal. 2:10; Ps. 103:13; Jer. 3:19; Hos. 11:3). But in a more important theological sense, God is Father of those who derive their sonship from Christ, and thus share it.

In *The Central Message of the New Testament* Jeremias argued that this term signified utter trust and intimacy, to such an extent that most Jews would have thought it irreverent to use it. He writes, "It was something new, something unique and unheard of, that Jesus dared . . . to speak with God as a child speaks . . . simply, intimately, securely."[27] Unfortunately,

25. Doctrine Commission of the Church of England, *We Believe in the Holy Spirit* (London: Church House Publishing, 1991), p. 184.

26. Welker, *God the Spirit*, pp. 213-14.

27. Joachim Jeremias, *The Central Message of the New Testament* (London: SCM, 1965), p. 21.

perhaps, counterexamples to Jeremias's argument have been found. But Dunn and many others insist that his argument remains largely true, even if with much less exaggeration. Similarly Dunn links this with Jesus' experience of the Holy Spirit.[28]

(9) The first three Gospels anticipate Acts in stressing the guidance of the Holy Spirit in moments of crisis. A classic example occurs in Mark 13:11. Here the disciples are warned about times of trial concerning which Jesus urges, "Do not worry beforehand about what you are to say; but say whatever is given you at that time, for it is not you who speak, but the Holy Spirit." R. T. France warns us that this is not an encouragement for "lazy preachers."[29] Henry Swete comments, "It guarantees to Christian confessors, in the moment of need, the presence of an Advocate within."[30] On the promise for the future, we may offer a last quotation from Levison. He writes, "This is not a vague promise of joyful inspiration . . . it is rather a promise to a desperate, persecuted, and betrayed people who stand before governors and kings in the service of the gospel."[31]

(10) Luke writes that the Holy Spirit may be received as the result of prayer: "The Father will give the Holy Spirit to those who ask him" (Luke 11:13). We may note that praying for the Spirit is still primarily addressed to God as Father. The context is that of persistence in prayer. The partial parallel in Matt. 7:7-11 stresses the generous Fatherhood of God. In connection with the gift of the Spirit to the disciples, Luke records the "exultation" of Jesus in the Spirit (as Turner calls it) in Luke 10:21.[32]

(11) As we might expect, Matthew and Luke include sayings relating to the Holy Spirit after the Resurrection of Jesus. Matt. 28:19 recalls the Great Commission, "Make disciples of all nations, baptizing them in the name of the Father and of the Son and of the Holy Spirit." Many scholars consider that this saying comes only from later reflection or revelation about the Spirit. One strong argument is that Jesus would not have invoked the name of the Trinity. But *Didachē* 7:1 and 3 urges baptism "in the name of the Father, and of the Son, and of the Holy Spirit," possibly before

28. Dunn, *Jesus and the Spirit,* pp. 62-66; and Joachim Jeremias, *New Testament Theology,* vol. 1 (London: SCM, 1971), pp. 61-68.

29. Richard T. France, *The Gospel of Mark: A Commentary on the Greek Text* (Grand Rapids: Eerdmans, 2002), p. 517.

30. Henry B. Swete, *The Holy Spirit in the New Testament* (London: Macmillan, 1921), p. 122.

31. John R. Levison, "The Holy Spirit in the Gospels," p. 55.

32. Turner, *Power from on High,* p. 264.

the end of the first century.[33] This may reflect very early tradition. Arthur Wainwright supports this view.[34]

The saying of Jesus in Luke is more indirect. In Luke 24:49, Jesus says, "I am sending upon you what my Father promised . . . you [will] have been clothed with power from on high." Most writers understand this as a promise of the gift of the Holy Spirit, as fulfilled at Pentecost.

Other uses of *spirit* in the first three (or synoptic) gospels usually refer either to the psychological spirit within a person, or to demonic or "supernatural" beings. These are not relevant to teaching or theology about the Holy Spirit of God.

33. K. Lake, *Apostolic Fathers* (Greek and English; Cambridge, MA: Heinemann, 1912), pp. 318-21.

34. Arthur Wainwright, *The Trinity in the New Testament* (London: SPCK, 1962), pp. 238-41.

CHAPTER 4

The Holy Spirit in the Pauline Epistles

Some tend to pit Paul against Luke–Acts, as if they show quite different theologies and experiences of the Holy Spirit. But is this justified? Any difference between the two sets of biblical writings should certainly not be exaggerated. We should expect some differences of emphasis. For the Pauline epistles specifically contain the *explicit teaching* of the apostle Paul on the Christian life in the churches, whereas the Acts of the Apostles often takes the form of *narrative,* which may simply be descriptive rather than prescriptive.

It is not always clear how narrative should be interpreted for today. Certainly it is not the case that the Acts narrative necessarily constitutes an early model which must be imitated in every respect, as if it were a model or blueprint for future action. Many regard Acts as providing a unique historical sketch of the earliest period of the Christian church, which is not necessarily to be replicated today. Even if some scholars date Luke–Acts later than the major Pauline epistles, the *function* of narrative in Acts still remains a matter of debate, and will be discussed when we consider the Acts of the Apostles. Sometimes more extreme Pentecostals and Charismatic Renewal Christians, but by no means all, accuse mainstream churches of giving privilege to the Pauline writings over against Luke–Acts. But we shall see that certain differences depend on Acts presenting narrative for a wider readership, while Paul usually represents explicit instruction for the Christian churches. This involves hermeneutics and interpretation, and we return to this later, when we consider Acts, and in the pertinent chapter in Part III.

We shall begin by selecting some of the primary and clearest themes or principles in Paul. Here we cannot easily avoid following the initial sequence of the chapter on Paul in our larger book.

1. Fundamental Features of the Holy Spirit in the Pauline Writings

(1) The work of the Holy Spirit is Christ-centered. Paul exclaims, "No one can say 'Jesus is Lord' except by the Holy Spirit" (1 Cor. 12:3). He had earlier expressed this theme in Galatians: "God has sent the Spirit of his Son into our hearts, crying, 'Abba! Father!'" (Gal. 4:6). Dunn cites Rom. 8:9-11 ("Anyone who does not have the Spirit of Christ does not belong to him") together with 1 Cor. 12:4-6, and comments, "Paul's experience of Christ and the Spirit were one, and . . . Christ was experienced through the Holy Spirit."[1] When he has expounded the work of the Holy Spirit in conveying the wisdom of God and revelation to us, Paul concludes, "We have the mind of Christ" (1 Cor. 2:16).

Occasionally people accuse Pentecostals and sometimes charismatic believers of approaching the Holy Spirit independently of Christ. But Pentecostal scholars are as adamant as others on the Christocentric nature of the Holy Spirit in Paul. For example, Gordon Fee, perhaps the most scholarly of Pentecostals, observes, "The Spirit is none other than the Spirit of Christ."[2] The Pentecostal writer Frank Macchia similarly writes: "The Spirit . . . binds us to Christ through the proclaimed gospel."[3] To cite two final examples, Kärkkäinen declares, "Paul's pneumatology is christologically founded . . . It is only through the Spirit that the believer is able to confess that 'Jesus is Lord' (1 Cor. 12:1-3) . . . It is the gift of the Spirit that makes one a Christian (Rom. 8:9)."[4] Amos Yong agrees, placing this verse within a Trinitarian framework.[5]

We see one of the passages which comes very near to associating

---

1. James D. G. Dunn, *Baptism in the Holy Spirit* (London: SCM, 1970), p. 148.

2. Gordon D. Fee, *God's Empowering Presence: The Holy Spirit in the Letters of Paul* (Milton Keynes: Paternoster, 1995 / Peabody, MA: Hendrickson, 1994), p. 545.

3. Frank D. Macchia, *Baptized in the Spirit: A Global Pentecostal Theology* (Grand Rapids: Zondervan, 2006), p. 72.

4. Veli-Matti Kärkkäinen, *Pneumatology: The Holy Spirit in Ecumenical, International, and Contextual Perspective* (Grand Rapids: Baker Academic, 2002), p. 32.

5. Amos Yong, *Spirit–Word–Community: Theological Hermeneutics in Trinitarian Perspective* (Burlington, VT: Ashgate, 2002), p. 227.

the Holy Spirit with Christ in a Trinitarian framework in 1 Cor. 12:4-7. In these verses "the same Spirit," "the same Lord," and "the same God" work to achieve the same end. In contrast stand "varieties of gifts . . . varieties of services . . . and varieties of activities." The Holy Trinity is the unifying bond of the gifts of the Spirit, service to Christ as Lord, and activities initiated by God. The practical lesson consists not only in the Trinitarian frame, but also in the warning that if a work or gift of the Spirit is not like Christ, and glorifying to Christ, we must doubt its genuineness. All three persons work toward the one goal.

One passage has caused needless concern. In 2 Cor. 3:17 Paul declares, "The Lord is the Spirit." The mistake is to regard "is" as signifying identity. Jesus Christ and the Holy Spirit are not the same person, even if each is a manifestation of the one God. A host of scholars from Vincent Taylor to George Hendry rightly insist that "is" should be understood as "denotes in Scripture" or "signifies."[6]

(2) The second principle is that according to Paul, every Christian receives the Holy Spirit, whether or not they "deserve" the Spirit. Ultimately we cannot be "in" Christ, or belong to him, without the gift of the Holy Spirit. One of Paul's most pointed statements occurs in Rom. 8:9: "Anyone who does not have the Spirit of Christ does not belong to him." A second passage comes from Galatians: "Because you are children, God sent the Spirit of his Son into our hearts, crying 'Abba! Father' " (Gal. 4:6). This was certainly predicted by Old Testament prophets, for example, when Joel prophesied that God "will pour out my Spirit upon all flesh" (Joel 2:28; quoted in Acts 2:17). Dunn argues that Rom. 8:9 rules out the possibility both of a non-Christian's possessing the Spirit, and of a Christian's *not* possessing the Spirit.[7]

This may seem to be either obvious or purely unapplied theology. It is neither. For a genuine heartfelt desire for greater holiness can lead us wrongly to expect that if we can reach a new level of purity of life, God will then grant us a "greater" experience of the Holy Spirit. Gradually, however, this can lead into the well-intentioned but mistaken assumptions shared by some rabbinic writings, most of the "Radical Reformers," and some in the Holiness revival movements, that the Holy Spirit is granted

---

6. Vincent Taylor, *The Person of Christ in New Testament Teaching* (London: Macmillan, 1958), p. 54; George Hendry, *The Holy Spirit in Christian Theology* (London: SCM, 1966), p. 24.

7. Dunn, *Baptism in the Holy Spirit,* p. 95.

at two distinct levels. The so-called "higher" level comes to be thought of as contingent on passionate longing for holiness and a certain degree of achieving it. This is precisely why Martin Luther complained that Thomas Müntzer and the other "Radical Reformers" had unwittingly undermined the Pauline doctrine of justification by sheer sovereign grace through faith alone. This principle, then, does remain highly relevant to the teaching and practice of today's Church.

(3) Third, it may again seem obvious that God gives special gifts of the Holy Spirit to chosen individuals, but always for the good of the whole Church, not for the individual alone. Paul asserts: The Spirit allots his gifts "to each one individually, just as the Holy Spirit chooses" (1 Cor. 12:11). Special gifts are "for the common good" (1 Cor. 12:7). We can see this from the diversity of gifts of the Holy Spirit described in 1 Cor. 12:4-26 and 14:2-40. Paul is aware of the danger that especially "gifted" people may lead the "less gifted" to imagine that they are somehow second-class Christians. Hence he states, "The members of the body that seem to be weaker are indispensable" (1 Cor. 12:22). Similarly, he rebukes the "gifted": "The eye cannot say to the hand, 'I have no need of you,' nor again the head to the feet, 'I have no need of you'" (1 Cor. 12:21). He declares, "If all were a single member, where would the body be?" (1 Cor. 12:19). Every Christian belongs to the body of Christ, and we should honor those who seem to be less "gifted" in spectacular ways, just as the body depends equally on those parts which perform its lowliest but necessary functions (1 Cor. 12:22-24).

This still has an important application today. There is always the danger that people with the more spectacular gifts will be seen as the standard model of what all other Christians should be. But Paul insists that the allocation of gifts is not our choice, but God's alone (1 Cor. 12:24, 28-30). Some strain to manifest certain spectacular gifts, when God may have chosen them to be treasurers, administrators, welcomers, washers-up, or visitors to the elderly or sick. It is God who chooses; our part is to trust and obey. Again, all gifts are "for the common good" (1 Cor. 12:7), and "just as the Spirit chooses" (v. 11).

(4) A fourth feature is that the Holy Spirit will be the future agent and guarantor of our resurrection with Christ and our future. According to Rom. 8:11 it was through the Holy Spirit that God raised Christ from the dead. This matches Paul's understanding of the resurrection as a cosmic event. When Christ rose from the dead, this did not apply to him alone, but it constituted a universal event in which, in principle, the whole people of God were raised.

Thornton expresses this vividly. When Jesus was crucified, he says, "The hope of Israel went down into the grave," but "when Christ rose, the Church rose from the dead."[8] If one cannot date one's first coming to faith by secular clock-time or calendar, in theological terms Thornton has rightly pinpointed the decisive date! Meanwhile, Paul regards the gift of the Holy Spirit as a pledge, guarantee, foretaste, or earnest (AV/KJV; Greek *arrabōn*) of the resurrection which we share with Christ.

The same word occurs in 2 Cor. 1:22, where it is usually translated "deposit" or "down payment." A store will sometimes require a deposit for what it will keep for you until full payment is made and received. In this sense it is also a *guarantee.* It is also a *first installment* of what will be given more fully in the future. To judge what the gift of the Holy Spirit amounts to, it would be premature to make our assessment now, in advance of when the fuller gift of the Spirit will be given and received without measure.

This opens out into a broader question about the relation between the Holy Spirit and the future. Hamilton correctly writes, "The gift of the Spirit in the present is to be understood as only the beginning of the harvest proper, which will occur in . . . the future age."[9] Similarly Fison declares, "The Holy Spirit is the key to the doctrine of the End."[10] Several writers have made special studies of Paul's concept of inheritance, which necessarily points to something stored up for believers in the future, which will one day become theirs.[11] In Rom. 8:19 Paul speaks of creation's waiting with eager longing (*apokaradokia*) for the revelation of the children of God. Here the Greek word carries with it the notion of stretching out the head, or in today's language, creation "cranes its neck" for this revelation in the future. Similar passages occur in Gal. 4:7 ("then also an heir"); Rom. 4:13 ("the promise that he would inherit the world"); 1 Cor. 6:9 ("inherit the kingdom of God," repeated in 15:50; cf. also Eph. 5:5).

A climax of all this comes in Paul's description of our resurrection "body" as "spiritual" (1 Cor. 15:44). Here spiritual does not mean immaterial. When he uses the word spiritual (*pneumatikos*), Paul usually means "under the control and influence of the Holy Spirit." This is especially the case in 1 Corinthians, where "spiritual people" denotes those who are led

---

8. Lionel S. Thornton, *The Common Life in the Body of Christ*, 3rd ed. (London: Dacre, 1950), p. 282.

9. Neil Q. Hamilton, *The Holy Spirit and Eschatology in Paul* (Edinburgh: Oliver and Boyd, 1957), p. 19.

10. J. E. Fison, *The Blessing of the Holy Spirit* (London: Longmans, Green, 1950), p. 4.

11. James Hester, *Paul's Concept of Inheritance* (Edinburgh: Oliver and Boyd, 1968).

by the Holy Spirit (1 Cor. 3:1; 12:1, and elsewhere). A "spiritual body" is a mode of being which is animated, sustained, and characterized, by the Holy Spirit. It is dynamic and ongoing, for the experience of the Spirit is ever new and ever fresh. Because it is characterized by the Spirit, it will not merely be static perfection. Certainly life dictated by the Spirit can never be dull or boring! Who knows what new things might occur?

In more general terms, Jerry Sumney comments in a recent essay, "This eschatological gift imparts the ability to perceive reality from a different perspective. Believers are able to see beyond the evaluations of the world . . . The Spirit gives the ability to see things in eschatological perspective, and so to recognize that the cross is a demonstration of God's wisdom (1 Cor. 1:18–2:16)."[12]

(5) A fifth feature of the Holy Spirit is his inspiring preaching and prophecy. This becomes clear in Paul's earliest epistle. In 1 Thess. 1:5, Paul writes, "Our message of the gospel came to you not in word only, but also in power and in the Holy Spirit." This is Paul's first mention of the parallel between word and Spirit. Toward the end of this epistle, Paul explains, "Do not quench the Spirit" as "Do not despise the words of prophets" (1 Thess. 5:19-20). "Prophecy" occurs in Rom. 12:6; 1 Cor. 12:10; 13:2; 14:6; and the verb "to prophesy" in 1 Cor. 11:4, 5; 14:1, 3, 4-5, 24, 31, and 39. It is generally agreed that "to build up" (*oikodomeō*) and "to encourage" (*parakaleō*) constitute its main purpose or function. Nevertheless it also conveys gospel truths to "the outsider" (NRSV; 1 Cor. 14:16). For this and many other strong reasons, Hill, Müller, and Gillespie have convincingly argued that there is a strong overlap between prophecy and preaching. Indeed they define "prophecy" as normally "applied preaching."[13] "Teaching" would more readily mean communicating basic theological principles.

Without doubt, the effects of the two modes of proclamation are the same in most cases. Moreover, Paul regards himself as one of the prophets.[14] Yet clearly Paul rejects uttering "Thus says the Lord" in favor of persuasive argument. Pannenberg asserts, "If . . . the preacher desires to convince his audience (by the) power of judgment, then the Holy Spirit becomes effec-

---

12. Jerry L. Sumney, "The Holy Spirit in Paul," in Johnson T. K. Lim, ed., *Holy Spirit: Unfinished Agenda* (Singapore: Armour, 2015), pp. 67-70, esp. p. 67.

13. David Hill, *New Testament Prophecy* (London: Marshall, 1979), pp. 110-40, 183-213; Ulrich B. Müller, *Prophetie und Predigt im Neuen Testament* (Gütersloh: Mohn, 1975); Thomas W. Gillespie, *The First Theologians: A Study in Early Christian Prophecy* (Grand Rapids: Eerdmans, 1994).

14. K. O. Sandnes, *Paul — One of the Prophets?* (Tübingen: Mohr Siebeck, 1991).

tive through his words and arguments. *Argumentation* and the operation of the Spirit are not in competition with each other. *In trusting in the spirit, Paul in no way spared himself thinking and arguing.*[15] Bornkamm, Stowers, and Jewett confirm this verdict at length and convincingly.[16]

A survey of historical theologians confirms this. Hilary of Poitiers (c. 312-68) writes that "prophecy" means "our understanding of doctrine." Ambrose of Milan (c. 339-97) restricts the term to "prophets in Scripture."[17] Cyril of Jerusalem (c. 315-87) is still mindful of the dangers of "spontaneous" prophecy from Montanist days. By contrast, "the Holy Spirit spoke the Scriptures."[18] Thomas Aquinas (c. 1225-74) devotes much discussion to prophecy. It is primarily an intellectual gift; imagination may confuse us.[19] He points out that Paul insists, "The spirits of the prophets are subject to the prophets" (1 Cor. 14:32).[20] Under this heading he classifies *preaching* as the *usual* meaning of *prophecy,* while any different form is "exceptional."

It is well known that Martin Luther described the "prophecies" of Karlstadt and Müntzer, the left-wing radicals, as "satanic." They claimed to hear the Spirit but in reality heard "the Arch-Devil."[21] He insisted that prophecy must remain under the Word of God. The Enthusiasts, he claimed, have turned the gospel upside down, and undermined justification by grace through faith. When we examine some of the actual pronouncements of Müntzer, clearly they are at variance with Scripture.[22] John Calvin asserts, "The prophet is, so to speak, God's messenger to men."[23] But John Owen, like Luther, while discussing the prophetic gift

---

15. Wolfhart Pannenberg, *Basic Questions in Theology* (London: SCM, 1971), 2.35, my italics.

16. Günther Bornkamm, *Early Christian Experience* (London: SCM, 1969), pp. 29-46, esp. pp. 30-35; Stanley K. Stowers, *The Diatribe and Paul's Letter to the Romans* (Chico: Scholars, 1981); Robert Jewett, *Romans: A Commentary* (Minneapolis: Fortress, 2007), pp. 23-46.

17. Ambrose, *On the Holy Spirit* 1.3.32 (Eng. *NPNF,* ser. 2, 10.103).

18. Cyril of Jerusalem, *Catechetical Lectures,* 16.4 (Eng. *NPNF,* ser. 2, 7.115-57).

19. Thomas Aquinas*, Summa Theologiae,* 60 vols. (London: Eyre & Spottiswoode / New York: McGraw-Hill, 1964-81), Ia, Qu. 173, arts. 2 and 3.

20. Aquinas, *Summa,* Qu. 173, art. 3, reply to obj. 4.

21. Martin Luther, *Treatise against the Heavenly Prophets,* in *Luther's Works,* 55 vols. (St. Louis and Philadelphia: Concordia and Fortress, 1955-86), cited in Regin Prenter, *Spiritus Creator: Luther's Concept of the Holy Spirit* (Philadelphia: Muhlenberg, 1953), p. 248.

22. Thomas Müntzer, *Collected Works* (Edinburgh: T&T Clark, 1988).

23. John Calvin, *The First Epistle of Paul to the Corinthians* (Grand Rapids: Eerdmans, 1960), p. 263.

of the Holy Spirit, warns his readers against "unduly pretending unto supernatural agitations from God, when they were really acted by the devil." He further warns us against "the deceits and abuses which have abounded in all ages of the Church and the pretence of the name and work of the Holy Spirit."[24] In authentic prophecy, he continues, the Spirit exposes the wickedness of the world. John Wesley (1703-91) emphasizes a renewed and living experience of the Holy Spirit, but he also warns his readers, "How many have resisted this Scripture . . . to the destruction of their souls! How many have mistaken the voice of their imagination for this witness of the Spirit of God."[25] At the beginning of the twentieth century H. B. Swete reaffirmed the main patristic view.

In light of this, it appears that the narrower "enthusiastic" or "exceptional" view of the gift of prophecy came into prominence largely with the nascent Pentecostal movement in the early decades of the twentieth century, and with the beginning phases of the renewal movement in the 1960s and 1970s.

(6) As in the Old Testament, the Holy Spirit constitutes the power and presence of God himself. As we have noted, the most detailed study on this theme is that done by the Pentecostal New Testament scholar Gordon Fee. William Atkinson comments, "God's Spirit can trace God's deepest thoughts. The Spirit is not a creature (1 Cor. 2:10)."[26] Paul maintains the Old Testament emphasis on the transcendence of the Spirit of God. Powell observes, "(The Spirit) does not belong to him whose native sphere is that of *bāśar* (flesh)."[27] Similarly Fison relates "Holy" in the words, "the Holy Spirit," to "the living God of the Hebrews."[28] This carries with it the concept of the Spirit as personal or supra-personal. Meanwhile, we may note that these six features do not exhaust Paul's theology of the Spirit. We must now consider some of the gifts of the Spirit, and explore other themes, such as the personhood of the Holy Spirit.

(7) Paul's preference for personal language about the Holy Spirit underlines the Spirit's personal or supra-personal nature. Trevor Burke, alluding to Ben Witherington, writes, "It is remarkable how Paul prefers not

---

24. John Owen, *The Holy Spirit* (Grand Rapids: Kregel, 1954), p. 15.

25. John Wesley, Sermon 10, sect. 2, from the *Christian Classics Ethereal Library,* http://www.ccel.org/ccel/wesley/sermons.

26. William Atkinson, "1 Corinthians," in Trevor J. Burke and Keith Warrington, eds., *A Biblical Theology of the Holy Spirit* (London: SPCK, 2014), pp. 146-59, here p. 149.

27. C. H. Powell, *The Biblical Concept of Power* (London: Epworth, 1993), p. 26.

28. Fison, *The Blessing of the Holy Spirit,* p. 43.

to describe the 'Spirit' in inanimate or impersonal terms (e.g. wind, water, and fire); rather he stresses . . . the personal nature of the Holy Spirit, where verbs of personal agency are employed to describe this activity."[29]

Some writers express skepticism on this point. Bultmann, for example, claims that since Paul often speaks of the Holy Spirit as if he were merely a fluid or a liquid that can be "poured out," this use of what Bultmann calls "dynamistic thinking" contradicts the personal status of the Holy Spirit.[30] Certainly Paul does use such dynamistic language (Rom. 5:5; 2 Cor. 1:22; 5:5; 1 Thess. 4:8), but Bultmann totally misunderstands what Ian Ramsey in Britain has called the use of models and qualifiers.[31] "Personal" words alone are Paul's main model, but if they are not *qualified,* we might think of the Holy Spirit as a person in exactly the same sense as human beings are persons. By qualifying this personal language by other kinds of language, Paul shows that he is not using "personal" in the normal sense of the term. This is why the word "supra-personal" is preferable as a term for both God and the Holy Spirit. Nevertheless, the Holy Spirit is certainly not sub-personal. As we have commented elsewhere, to call the Spirit "it," or to demote him to the status of a mere force, borders on blasphemous thoughtlessness. It militates against regarding the Spirit as God himself. These models should not be understood in isolation from each other; they *together* communicate the personhood of the Holy Spirit in a distinctive way. To borrow Ramsey's examples, God may be called "wise," but he is also "infinitely wise"; God may be called the "cause" of the universe, but he is also its "first cause." That is to say, God is uniquely supra-personal.

Thus the Spirit searches and understands (1 Cor. 2:10-11); he bears witness (Rom. 8:16); he comes alongside to help (*synantilambanetai*); he intercedes (Rom. 8:26-27); and so on. Lindsay Dewar calls *synantilambanetai* "a strongly personal word."[32]

(8) An eighth feature is that Paul takes up the traditional view that the Holy Spirit makes possible the sanctification of the Christian and the

---

29. Trevor Burke, "Romans," in Burke and Warrington, eds., *A Biblical Theology of the Holy Spirit,* pp. 129-45, here p. 139.

30. Rudolf Bultmann, *Theology of the New Testament* (London: SCM, 1952), pp. 155-56.

31. Ian T. Ramsey, *Religious Language: An Empirical Placing of Theological Phrases* (London: SCM, 1957), pp. 49-89.

32. Lindsay Dewar, *The Holy Spirit in Modern Thought* (London: Mowbray, 1952), p. 71.

Church. In 1 Thess. 4:3, Paul writes, "This is the will of God, your sanctification." He does not immediately refer to the Holy Spirit, but in v. 8 he ties his exhortations to God's gift of the Holy Spirit. In 1 Corinthians the Holy Spirit's indwelling of the Christian as his holy temple is both individual and corporate. The whole congregation is referred to in 1 Cor. 3:16: "Do you not know that you (plural) are God's temple and that God's Spirit dwells in you?" In 1 Cor. 6:19, Paul asks, "Do you not know that your body is a temple of the Holy Spirit within you, which you have from God?" In both cases "Do you not know?" signals a familiar truth, perhaps a pre-Pauline one. The second reference refers more to personal lifestyle. But in both verses the very presence of the Holy Spirit sanctifies the temple.[33] This theme played a major part in the theology of the Reformers, especially Calvin.

2. Particular Gifts of the Holy Spirit in 1 Corinthians 12–14, Romans 12:4-8, and Ephesians 4:4-13

1 Corinthians 12–14, Rom. 12:4-8: and Eph. 4:4-13, each expounds the gifts of the Holy Spirit in the context of the unity of purpose of the one body or the one Spirit, and the diversity of functions of its "limbs" or members. This similarity of context and content is striking.

The metaphor of the body and limbs (*melē*) assumes a closer relation than the word "member" suggests. One can be a "member" of a golf club, a political party, or an automobile club, without the organic and intimate connection which Paul has in mind here. He borrows this analogy from Livy and other Greco-Roman authors, who used it to suggest that slaves, as members of a single political state, should not rebel against the Senate or their masters. Paul reverses the point of the metaphor, to show that most ordinary, weak, or disabled people are needed by one another for the healthy functioning of the body of Christ. It is the reverse of an elitist metaphor.

Moltmann refers this to our present-day church. He writes, "Our regular, mainline, church services display a wealth of ideas . . . in their sermons, but are poverty-stricken in their forms of expression. . . . [They are]one big mouth and a lot of little ears."[34] Paul regards "the limbs of

---

33. Anthony C. Thiselton, *The First Epistle to the Corinthians: A Commentary on the Greek Text* (Grand Rapids: Eerdmans, 2000), pp. 315-18, 674; Albert L. A. Hogeterp, *Paul and God's Temple* (Leuven: Peeters, 2006), pp. 197-386.

34. Jürgen Moltmann, *The Spirit of Life: A Universal Affirmation* (London: SCM, 1982), p. 185.

Christ" as serving God through one another, including the weakest among the limbs. He stresses that the whole body needs the weakest, the most ordinary, and even the disabled (1 Cor. 12:14-26; Rom. 12:3; Eph. 4:12-13). He concludes, "The eye cannot say to the hand, 'I have no need of you.' . . . On the contrary, the members of the body that seem to be weaker are indispensable, and those members of the body that we think less honorable we clothe with greater honor, and our less respectable members are treated with greater respect" (1 Cor. 12:21-23).

Some writers, such as Gordon Fee and Jean Héring, stress the *variety* of the functions of the limbs whereas others, such as Dale Martin and Margaret Mitchell, stress the *unity* of the Spirit or the body. But Paul emphasizes both the unity and the diversity. The gifts are different, but all have the same purpose, namely to build up the whole body. The body would not be a body if it did not have a variety of limbs. Within the one body God calls us to specific tasks. Moltmann, again, writes, "Call and endowment, *klēsis* and *charisma,* belong together and are interchangeable terms."[35] If God gives us a task, he will provide the *charisma,* or free gift, for us to perform it in his freely given strength.

In the light of this Paul expounds "varieties of gifts . . . for the common good" (12:4, 7). No one is expected to process all of these gifts; this is why we need every Christian, who together possess these gifts. We shall now enumerate the nine gifts in 1 Corinthians 12, comment on their meaning, and then consider other gifts in Paul.

(1) The meaning of the "utterance of wisdom" *(logos sophias)* is hotly debated, as is "utterance of knowledge." They both serve the common good, but the difference between the two is not clear to most commentators. The term "utterance" translates the Greek *logos,* which usually means articulate speech or rational communication. It denotes a stretch of language or often a sentence rather than a single word. The deeper question concerns the difference between word of *knowledge* and word of *wisdom.* The context in 1 Corinthians suggests that the term *wisdom* reflects the many uses of the term which are peculiar to this epistle. Wisdom occurs eleven times in 1 Corinthians, but much less in other Pauline epistles. In 1 Cor. 1–2 Paul speaks of the wisdom of God as that which concerns both the wisdom that Christ revealed upon the cross and God's purposes for the world, as the term denotes in Romans. Certainly the term appears to relate to the *proclamation of the gospel,* rather than to some individualistic

---

35. Moltmann, *The Spirit of Life,* p. 180.

utterance of personal guidance to some particular individual. Origen tended to regard the utterance of wisdom as fundamentally relating to the gospel, and described utterance of knowledge as "inferior to it."[36]

(2) Utterance of knowledge must be different from utterance of wisdom because the second gift is given "to another" (1 Cor. 12:8). Knowledge (gnōsis) occurs ten times in this epistle alone. In 1 Cor. 8:1-3 and 7-11 the term is not wholly positive, and it regularly stands in contrast to love. Knowledge can inflate, while love builds up (8:1). Hence the verb "coming to know," as denoting a continuous process, is usually much more positive. Today the term might be equivalent to "knowledge of basic Christian truth," or even to the affirmations of a creed. Conzelmann translates it "theology." In this sense, it constitutes a gift of the Holy Spirit, but it remains capable of being divorced from practice, which may then, if abused, lead to self-confidence and pride.[37]

Mark Cartledge describes more popular understandings of both terms in the so-called third wave charismatic renewal movement modeled after the style of John Wimber. These descriptions seem very remote indeed from the context of 1 Corinthians, and from anything that would command a scholarly consensus.[38]

(3) In v. 9, faith cannot be the faith that mediates justification by grace, because it is given "to another," i.e., to some but not all believers. Virtually all commentators emphasize this point. Paul uses "faith" in various ways. Sometimes he speaks of "the obedience of faith" (Rom. 1:5). Sometimes faith denotes the acceptance of the common apostolic understanding of the faith (1 Thess. 1:8). Sometimes faith is the trustful faith of Abraham (Rom. 4:5). In our present verse it cannot mean any of these things. It probably denotes the confident, daring, optimistic trust in God, which lifts the spirits of a church community when the congregation passes through disappointment or difficult times. Such faith may reenergize a flagging congregation and redirect them in the ways of God. It must not be seen in terms of modern Western individualism, but as a gift for the benefit of the whole church.

(4) The same verse (v. 9) appears to speak of gifts of healing (NRSV).

---

36. Origen, *Against Celsus*, 3.46 (*ANF*, 4.483).

37. Thiselton, *The First Epistle to the Corinthians*, pp. 938-44; and idem, *The Holy Spirit — In Biblical Teaching, through the Centuries, and Today* (Grand: Rapids: Eerdmans / London: SPCK, 2013), pp. 84-89.

38. Mark J. Cartledge, *Speaking in Tongues: Multi-Disciplinary Perspectives* (Milton Keynes: Paternoster, 2006), p. 209.

But in Greek "of healing" is in the plural (*iamatōn*), which almost certainly denotes "kinds of healing." In English "fruits" or "cheeses" generally denote *generic* plurals. Thus Edwards explicitly translates the Greek "kinds of healings."[39] Paul uses this word elsewhere only at 12:28 and 30. In 2 Cor. 12:7-9 God does not heal him from his "thorn in the flesh" (NEB, "sharp physical pain"). Max Turner places this gift among "signs and wonders."[40] But the Pentecostal writer Donald Gee insists (surely correctly) that "kinds of healings" "should not preclude . . . the work of medical healing."[41] Similarly the pietist expositor Bengel insists that "healings" may include both the miraculous and "natural remedies."[42] Similarly Collins argues, "Paul does not claim for himself the gift of healing."[43]

The pastoral issue today concerns *the expectation* of *automatic* healing, often conditional on faith. Such an expectation of universal healing for all can cause immense distress, doubt, and damage if healing does not occur. Even the Pentecostal writer David Pets argued in his 1993 PhD thesis that God does not automatically heal everyone who has faith. Paul does not provide a universal guarantee of healing in this passage. On the other hand, he does assert God's ability to heal *when, whether, and where* God chooses, and by *whatever means* he chooses.

(5) Effective deeds of power translates the next gift, in v. 10 *(energēmata dynameōn)*. This is translated by the NRSV and NJB as "the working of miracles"; and by the NIV as "miraculous powers." More helpfully, the RV margin renders the Greek literally as "workings of powers." As this implies, the paraphrase "miracles" is not in the Greek at all. We have no right to impose onto Paul in the first century a "dualist" or "two-story" contrast between the "natural" and "supernatural" worlds, which only came to govern much of modern thought since the eighteenth century with deism and the Enlightenment. Paul regarded the one, single universe as firmly under the control of God, whether he governed by regular means or less usual means. Hence "effective deeds of power" does not exclude "the miraculous," but leaves God's sovereign acts unspecified. Keener's

39. T. C. Edwards, *A Commentary on the First Epistle to the Corinthians: Greek Text*, 3rd ed. (London: Hodder and Stoughton, 1885), p. 316.

40. Max Turner, *The Holy Spirit and Spiritual Gifts: Then and Now* (Carlisle: Paternoster, 1996), p. 252.

41. Donald Gee, *Spiritual Gifts in the Work of the Ministry Today* (Springfield, MO: Gospel Publications, 1963).

42. J. A. Bengel, *Gnomon Novi Testamenti*, 3rd ed. (Stuttgart: Steinkopf, 1866), p. 652.

43. R. F. Collins, *First Corinthians* (Collegeville: Glazier, 1999), p. 454.

impressive and recent two-volume work on miracles also merits careful examination. He concludes, "Paul anticipated noticeable miraculous phenomena in the Christian communities" (1 Cor. 12:9-10, 28-30; Gal. 3:5)."[44] Thus Paul's reference to "effective deeds of power" here could include what many call "the miraculous," although we must be cautious about the over-translation of the term in v. 9. It is often wiser and more accurate to speak of the "providential."

"Effective" takes up Karl Barth's exposition of Paul's treatment of power in 1 Corinthians. The general meaning, he says, designates *effective action.*[45] Calvin doubts that the phrase here means power to effect miracles, although it may denote power (Latin, *virtutem*) exercised against demons.[46] The Greek, he says, means "effective working." Thielicke sees it as an effective power against all "ungodly forces."[47] Walter Hollenweger, respected for his work on Pentecostals, warns us of the natural/supernatural distinction which is now outdated. He warns that it is irresponsible to describe the supernatural as a breach of natural laws.[48]

(6) The sixth gift, prophecy, has been already considered above. It includes preaching the gospel, even if it also signifies more than this. In our chapter above on the Old Testament, we warned against the notion of false prophecy with special reference to Deut. 18:19-22 and Jer. 23:32. Paul would be aware of such warnings, and thus he stresses the need for all prophecy to be tested and carefully evaluated (1 Cor. 14:37-38; 1 Thess. 5:20-21). However, we should not lose sight of what has been called "normal" prophecy (i.e., preaching and applying the gospel) in favor of "exceptional" prophecy, for which "testing" is at least as urgent.

Bittlinger quotes here the well-known catchphrase, "Prophecy is not in the first instance foretelling, but rather forth-telling."[49] In Paul the terms "prophecy" and "prophesy" are almost, but not entirely, exclusive to this

44. Craig S. Keener, *Miracles: The Credibility of New Testament Accounts,* 2 vols. (Grand Rapids: Baker Academic, 2011) 1.30-31.

45. Karl Barth, *The Resurrection of the Dead* (London: Hodder & Stoughton, 1933), p. 18.

46. John Calvin, *The First Epistle of Paul to the Corinthians* (Grand Rapids: Eerdmans, 1960), p. 262.

47. Helmut Thielicke, *The Evangelical Faith,* 3 vols. (Grand Rapids: Eerdmans, 1974-82) 3.79.

48. Walter Hollenweger, *Der 1 Korintherbrief: eine Arbeithilfe zur Bibelwoche* (Kingmünster: Volksmissionarisches, 1964), p. 26.

49. A. Bittlinger, *Gifts and Graces: A Commentary on 1 Corinthians 12–14* (London: Hodder and Stoughton, 1967), p. 42.

epistle (cf. 1 Thess. 2:15; 5:20; Rom. 11:3; 12:6; Eph. 4:11). Hill, following Friedrich, regards the work of prophecy as "admonition and comfort, the call for repentance and promise," and in pastoral contexts also praise and blame.[50] These features, together with exhortation and encouragement, constitute what we should call a *sermon* in today's language. Any contrary view seems to depend on whether it detracts from the Spirit's work if the sermon is prepared. On the contrary, the Holy Spirit works as much through the mental preparation of the preacher as in his or her delivery. I have discussed prophecy at length in my larger commentary.[51]

(7) The seventh gift, "discernment of spirits" *(diakriseis pneumatōn),* probably denotes "discerning what is of the Holy Spirit." G. Dautzenberg and H. Merklein regard this gift primarily as that of interpretation, but Wayne Grudem has effectively criticized this.[52] He regards "spirits" as both beneficial and demonic agencies, and the gift may relate to the testing of prophecies. The Greek *diakrinō* may mean "evaluate." Jewett, Fuchs, and Hoyle confirm this critical capacity. Augustine, following Chrysostom, calls this "the gift of discernment from God."[53] With the completion of the New Testament canon after Paul's death, the use of this gift may have become more occasional than before. But evil can always masquerade as good, and deception needs to be exposed. (Incidentally, the difficult verses about the prohibition of women speaking in 14:34-36 may possibly refer to the assessment of prophecy between wife and husband. This suggestion is speculative, but there is no MS evidence of a non-Pauline interpolation.)

(8) We come next to "various kinds of tongues" (v. 10). Elsewhere I distinguish six views of the meaning of "tongues" that have been suggested. These include: angelic speech; power to speak known foreign languages; the use of archaic liturgical speech; tongues as "ecstatic speech"; the release of praise and longings buried in the unconscious or subsconscious; and such language released in the "sighs too deep for words" in Rom. 8:26. Each of these six "explanations" is backed by one or more scholarly names, which we shall not enumerate here. They are available, however, in my commentary.[54] The last three suggestions overlap somewhat.

---

50. Hill, *New Testament Prophecy,* pp. 120-21, 131; G. Friedrich, "*prophētēs, prophētis, prophēteuō, propheteia, prophētikos, pseudoprophētēs,*" in *TDNT,* 6.781-862, here 6.855.

51. Thiselton, *The First Epistle to the Corinthians,* pp. 956-65, 1087-94.

52. Wayne Grudem, *The Gift of Prophecy in 1 Corinthians* (Lanham, MD: University Press of America, 1982), pp. 58-60.

53. Augustine, *On the Trinity,* 3.9.18.

54. Thiselton, *The First Epistle to the Corinthians,* pp. 970-89.

The two main categories remain the power to speak known foreign languages and "ecstatic" speech. The latter can be subdivided into unintelligible speech as such; the liberating release of unconscious longings; and specific reference to "sighs too deep for words" in Romans 8:26.

The Greek term *genē glōssōn* tells us at once that utterances in tongues need not be restricted to one particular understanding of tongues alone. Indeed many assert that one "kind" of tongues appears in Acts 2, while another kind appears in Paul. Proponents of such a distinction often assume that Acts refers to the knowledge of other languages, and many of the church fathers understood tongues-speech in this way. Even in Acts 2, however, we are faced with several problems. Why did some think that tongues-speakers were drunk on alcohol? (Acts 2:13). Why are "tongues" not cited as a specific gift for missionary outreach? Why did Greek-speaking Jews from the Diaspora need languages other than Greek?

Various answers have been given to each question. For example, some of the visiting Jews might have come from rural areas, such as the Parthians, Medes, Mesopotamians, and Arabs. Most agree that this was a miracle of hearing, not a miracle of speaking (Acts 2:8, 11). Further, in the early days of Pentecostalism some missionaries discovered that "tongues" were not intelligible to a native audience. Some argue, moreover, that tongues-speech does not exhibit an intelligible linguistic structure. The difficulties seem great, and evidence is usually anecdotal rather than clearly and firmly documented. Meanwhile the third explanation about archaic liturgical language remains purely speculative.

Many object to the term "ecstatic." These include Robert Gundry, Max Turner, and Christopher Forbes. They argue that this view too readily depends on supposed parallels in Greco-Roman religions. But Paul implies that in tongues-speech *the mind is inactive* (1 Cor. 14:15, 19). In any case, this approach does not exclude the fifth and sixth suggestions, namely that of liberation from the conscious mind, or the sighs of Rom. 8:26.

A thorough study of the unconscious in Paul and its relation to tongues has been convincingly and extensively undertaken by Gerd Theissen.[55] Paul often speaks of the "secrets of the heart," which will be revealed by God. Bultmann, Stendahl, Jewett, and Käsemann also emphasize this dimension. In human life the "censor" can hold prisoner those things which may be too sinful, too wonderful, or too life-changing to face in our

---

55. Gerd Theissen, *Psychological Aspects of Pauline Theology* (Edinburgh: T&T Clark, 1987), pp. 74-114, 292-341.

conscious mind. Käsemann compares tongues to "sighing for redemption from bodily temptation" (cf. Luther's *Anfechtung*), and he regards tongues-speech as longing for liberty.[56]

The Pentecostal writer Frank Macchia regards the "sighs" of Rom. 8:26 as a plausible indication of Paul's view.[57] Some dissent from this view, but almost every view on this subject has its critics. One of the sanest observers in this field is Krister Stendahl. He writes that tongues are "not suited for evangelism or publicity . . . Those who are not professional in the shaping of words are free to express freely their overwhelmed praise to their Lord"; on the other hand, "Few human beings can helpfully live with high-voltage religious experience over a long period of time."[58] It certainly makes sense to understand how such liberation can constitute a gift of the Holy Spirit for a specific period of time. Frank Macchia and Veli-Matti Kärkkäinen have reported how nowadays only a minority of Pentecostals actually practice tongues-speech.

(9) The last of the nine gifts recounted in 1 Cor. 12:8-10 is "the interpretation of tongues" *(hermēneia glōssōn)*. What this signifies depends largely on which of the above six understandings of tongues we accept. There is a *prima facie* case for tongues being unintelligible, if they are not interpreted. The traditional view is that this gift denotes the making intelligible of what would otherwise be unintelligible.

There is one other important issue. In 1 Cor. 14:13 the older versions sometimes translate *"someone* should pray for the power to interpret." The word "someone" is entirely lacking in Greek, and the NRSV is correct to translate "one who speaks in a tongue should pray for the power to interpret." The speaker-in-tongues should pray that he or she can make his or her utterance intelligible to the community. That would amount to the utterance eventually becoming equivalent to prophetic communication. The notion that tongues-speech should be temporary in public worship seems to confirm this. This is not at all to restrict a private use of tongues (1 Cor. 14:2-5, 20-25). I first drew attention to this point in 1979.[59]

---

56. Ernst Käsemann, "The Cry for Liberty in the Church's Worship," in his *Perspectives on Paul* (London: SCM, 1971), pp. 122-37, here p. 132.

57. Frank D. Macchia, "Groans Too Deep for Words," *Asian Journal of Pentecostal Studies* 1 (1998), pp. 149-73.

58. Krister Stendahl, "Glossolalia — The New Testament Evidence," in his *Paul Among Jews and Gentiles* (London: SCM, 1977), pp. 109-24, here pp. 111, 113, 122-23.

59. Anthony C. Thiselton, "'The Interpretation of Tongues': A New Suggestion in the Light of Greek Usage in Philo and Josephus" *JTS* 30 (1979), pp. 15-36.

Throughout this list of gifts in 1 Cor. 12: 8-10 Paul has used the word *charisma* or *charismata,* in contrast to the Corinthians' favored word *pneumatika.* As Sumney comments, "Paul changes the word . . . to emphasize that the one who is empowered with ability from the Spirit receives it as a gift from God, not as something they deserve or have attained."[60] This section inevitably overlaps with our review of Pentecostalism in Part III.

3. Particular Gifts in 1 Cor. 12:27-31 and in Rom. 12:4-8 and Eph. 4:4-13

(1) In 1 Cor. 12:27 Paul takes up the imagery of the body and limbs. He then (v. 28) adds within this context that "God has appointed in the church first apostles, second prophets, third teachers; then deeds of power, then gifts of healing, forms of assistance, forms of leadership, various kinds of tongues." To emphasize that these gifts are far from universal for all Christians he adds, "Are all apostles? Are all prophets . . ." (v. 29), and he applies this question to each of the gifts of the Holy Spirit (v. 30). The much-disputed question of whether love (13:1-13) constitutes a gift or "fruit" is difficult to decide, but it differs from the "gifts" in that it is enjoined as a universal, not individual, gift and quality of life.

The adjectives "first" *(prōton),* "second" *(deuteron),* and "third" *(triton)* may denote degrees of importance or indispensability, or they may simply be numbers which check off a list. In favor of the second is that Paul is not elitist. On the other hand, apostolicity, preaching, and teaching are vital to the foundation of the church, whereas the other gifts are helpful but, some would say, not vital. F. F. Bruce sets these three offices above the others.

"Apostles" for Paul denote more than the Twelve (as the term may have meant in Luke–Acts). Apostles are commissioned by Christ and are witnesses of the resurrection (Rom. 15:15-16; 1 Cor. 4:9; 15:7-8; Eph. 3:5). Contrary to Roman and Anglo-Catholic views, this implies that they are not only "foundational" for the Church, but perhaps have no successors. They are "sent" in the power of the Spirit. As E. Best and J. Crafton urge, they hold a crucial but humble office, to be "windows" to Christ himself. B. Holmberg rightly calls attention to their collegial ministry with coworkers.

---

60. Sumney, "The Holy Spirit in Paul," in Lim, ed., *Holy Spirit: Unfinished Agenda,* p. 69.

"Prophets" have been discussed above in 1 Cor. 12:10. But "teachers" *(didaskaloi)* have the task and vocation, in Danker's words, "to provide instruction in a formal or informal setting."[61] Today most wish to avoid clericalism, but we urgently need more of a *teaching ministry* in the Church as a whole. I have been astonished to hear at the church door after preaching some members of the congregation say "We really *learned* something today," as if this came as an unexpected surprise! Part of the marks of a bishop or elder is that the bishop must be "an apt teacher" (1 Tim. 3:2).

We have already discussed works of power and gifts of healing. The next new terms are "forms of assistance" and "forms of leadership" (NRSV). But those translations are rather vaguer than the Greek. The first, *antilēmpsis,* means literally a coming to the aid of someone. In English this would be a personal assistant, who is to give *administrative support.* Again, this gives the lie to any notion that the Holy Spirit works only spontaneously: a spontaneous administrator would be a disaster! The second word is *kybernēseis.* In the papyri this often retains its meaning as "pilot" or "guide."[62] What best does justice to this term in modern English is "the gift of strategic vision." The last gift is "kinds of tongues," which we discussed above.

Paul stresses in vv. 29-30 that these gifts are not given to all. God makes the definitive choice about to whom he gives a specific gift. He points out how foolish it is to pine away for a gift that God is not pleased to give.

Love (1 Cor. 13:1-13) appears as a "gift of the Spirit," if we take seriously the exhortation in v. 31 to "strive for the greater gifts" and understand chapter 13 as explicating the verse. But there are two crucial differences. First, *all,* not just some, should cultivate love. Second, because God does not restrict his choice, we are enjoined to "strive for" or "seek" (*zēloute*) these "greater" *charismata.* Love is more valued than angelic tongues (13:1), and without love, Christian speech becomes "a resonating jar or a reverberating symbol" (v. 1, my translation). It eclipses "prophecy," "knowledge," and "every kind of faith" (v. 2).

I have translated 13:4-7: "Love patiently; love shows kindness; does not burn with envy; does not brag — is not inflated with its own importance. It does not behave with ill-mannered impropriety . . . it does not

---

61. Danker, BDAG, pp. 240-41.

62. J. M. Moulton and G. Milligan, *The Vocabulary of the Greek Testament* (London: Hodder & Stoughton, 1952), p. 363.

become exasperated into pique. . . . It never tires of support, never loses faith, never exhausts hope, never gives up."[63] I translate v. 8 "love never falls apart." In vv. 9-13 it is clear that love survives to eternity, when gifts of preaching, prophecy, healing, and much else will have become obsolete. Once again, in the sense in which love is enjoined at the end of chapter 12, it may be viewed as a gift of the Spirit; in the sense that it is not too restricted to some, and may be sought, it may not constitute a "gift" (charisma) in the same sense as those enumerated in 12:8-10 and 27-29. Moreover it is also not a mere emotion alone, for emotions cannot be commanded. It constitutes a *settled state of mind, heart, and action,* and it sometime involves emotion additionally.

(2) In Rom. 12:4-8, as we have noted, the "gifts" spring from the analogy of the body and limbs (v. 4), as in 1 Corinthians, especially 1 Cor. 12:14-26. In 12:5, the Greek for "individually" is *to kath' heis allēlōn melē,* which means essentially "one by one." In point of fact, in both epistles Paul uses "freely given gifts" (charismata), and *prophecy* and *teaching* are identical. The main new words are "ministry" (diakonia), "exhortation" (parakalōn), and "generosity" and "compassion" (ho eleōn en hilarotēti). The word *diakonia* does denote ministry, and traditionally has been understood as social or administrative service. This meaning is accepted by Danker, although following the work of John Collins, it has been understood in the context of the church to mean deputy or intermediary, probably of presbyters or elders.[64] The dating of developments remains uncertain. The word *eleos* denotes kindness or compassion, while *hilarotēs* may mean cheerfulness or graciousness.[65]

(3) In Eph. 4:4-13 the unity of the body and of the Holy Spirit is underlined (v. 3) by repetition of "*one* Spirit" and the addition of "one Lord, one faith, one baptism, one God" (vv. 5-6a). This time the gifts are from the ascended Christ *through* the Spirit. The list of gifts in v. 11 replicates those of Rom. 12 and 1 Cor. 12, with the addition of "*evangelists*" (euangelistas) and "pastors" (Greek, *poimenas,* "shepherds"). Together these gifts are to equip the church for ministry and for "building up the body of Christ" (v. 12). The ultimate aim is to build "to the measure of the full stature of Christ" (v. 13). Christlikeness is the final goal of the gifts.

---

63. Thiselton, *The First Epistle to the Corinthians,* p. 1026.
64. Danker, BDAG, pp. 230-31.
65. Danker, BDAG, p. 473.

4. Other Themes in the Pauline Epistles

(1) Uses of the word *pneuma*, "spirit," that may or may not refer to the Holy Spirit. A notorious example of occasional ambiguity occurs in Rom. 12:11. The AV/KJV translates the Greek *tō pneumati zeontes* as "fervent in the spirit," assuming that "spirit" denotes here the human spirit. But the RSV has "be aglow with the Spirit," while the NRSV (to my mind, regrettably) returns to "be ardent in spirit." Both uses can claim to reflect the OT, and there is no decisive way to decide which translation accurately conveys Paul. I would argue that "spiritual" *(pneumatikos)* and Spirit *(pneuma)* usually denote either *of the Holy Spirit,* or *Holy Spirit,* but this alone cannot decide the matter. Similarly, in Rom. 1:4 the NJB has "according to the spirit of holiness." Again, we cannot be certain. In 2 Cor. 4:13 most English versions translate "the spirit of faith," while Furnish refers the verse to the Holy Spirit from whom faith comes.[66]

A number of Pauline passages do employ *pneuma* to refer to the human spirit. One which is notorious for a different reason is 1 Thess. 5:23: "May the God of peace himself sanctify you entirely; and may your spirit and soul and body be kept sound and blameless." Some nineteenth-century theologians saw a "trichotamous" view of human nature here, as if the human person consisted of three "parts," namely body, soul, and spirit. But this is emphatically *not* Paul's meaning. I have translated it "May you be sound and blameless through and through."[67] We may compare Mary's "My soul magnifies the Lord, and my spirit rejoices in God" (Luke 1:46-47), which is Hebrew poetic parallelism, not an allusion to physiology. On the other hand, Paul's exhortation in 2 Thess. 2:2 not to be alarmed "either by spirit or by word or by letter" is more ambiguous, and may refer to an evil spirit or false prophecy. The dichotomy "absent in body . . . present in spirit" in 1 Cor. 5:3 more clearly refers to the human spirit, but not definitely. It could possibly mean "by the action of the Holy Spirit."

Other references may be clearer anthropological references to the human spirit. In 1 Cor. 14:14 there is a contrast between "my spirit prays" and "my mind is unproductive." A "spirit of power" and a "spirit of cowardice" appear in 2 Tim. 1:7. References would become tedious to trace in full.

---

66. Victor P. Furnish, *2 Corinthians* (New York: Doubleday, 1984), p. 258.

67. Anthony C. Thiselton, *1 & 2 Thessalonians through the Centuries* (Oxford: Blackwell, 2011), p. 162, cf. pp. 163-75.

(2) Baptism in the Holy Spirit? The lone allusion to the concept in Paul occurs in 1 Cor. 12:13: "In one Spirit we were all baptized into one body — Jews or Greeks." We do not question that in Pentecostal traditions and in the charismatic renewal movement the term itself is often applied to a deep experience of God and of renewal that may occur subsequent to coming to Christian faith. Nor do we deny that many experiences of this kind are authentic. But *Paul does not use the term in this way,* and certainly not in 1 Cor. 12:13. Virtually every serious New Testament specialist, including Dunn and Fee, regards v. 13 as baptism into the *one united Church* in which Jew and Gentile are coequal in status, and that this baptism into the one community occurs through the agency of the Holy Spirit. Dunn describes this as "the initiatory and incorporative significance of the metaphor"; it means "to become a Christian and to become a member of the Body of Christ."[68]

Admittedly "Baptism in the Holy Spirit" has been identified by Dayton, Macchia, and Kärkkäinen and others as one of the key distinctive elements of Pentecostalism.[69] What is in question is not the validity of this experience, but whether there is genuine biblical terminology for it. Macchia calls it "an empowerment for ministry distinct from regeneration or initiation into Christ."[70] But unquestionably this is *not Paul's point in 1 Cor. 12:13,* and the phrase does not appear elsewhere in Paul. This use of the term (mainly beginning after 1904) must be justified, if at all, from some other part of Scripture. These comments must be considered in the light of further reflections on Pentecostalism and hermeneutics in our Part III.

No one questions the fact of *repeated* endowments of the Holy Spirit, especially for specific tasks. Mainline churches follow Paul in understanding special endowments for special needs or situations, including that of a step of more serious consecration. But such endowments may be *many.* They are not dignified into the status of what has popularly been called "the second blessing." Asked whether they believe in a second blessing, many biblical Christians respond, "Yes — and a third, a fourth, a fifth, and so on to the nth degree!"

---

68. Dunn, *Baptism in the Holy Spirit,* p. 129.

69. Donald W. Dayton, *The Theological Roots of Pentecostalism* (Metuchen, NJ: Scarecrow, 1987), p. 22; Frank B. Macchia, *Baptized in the Spirit,* p. 19; and Veli-Matti Kärkkäinen, *Spiritus ubi vult spirat* (Helsinki: Luther Agricola Society, 1998), p. 198.

70. Macchia, *Baptized in the Spirit,* p. 20.

CHAPTER 5

The Holy Spirit in Acts

In the Acts of the Apostles the Holy Spirit is seen throughout as *the guide and leader of an expanding missionary Church.* This is the overall theme. But Acts recounts a succession of particular events which have come to dominate the discussion of writers. The most important are easy to identify. The first is the pouring out of the Holy Spirit on the day of Pentecost (Acts 2:1-13), and its interpretation by Peter (2:14-36, 38-41). The second is the public descent of the Holy Spirit on the Samaritans (Acts 8:4-25). The third concerns the gift of the Spirit to Cornelius and the Gentiles (Acts 10:1-48). The fourth is the pouring of the Holy Spirit on the Ephesians in Acts 19:1-5, which has parallels with the gift of the Spirit to the Samaritans. Closer to the general purpose of Acts is Reeves's comment: "The expansion of the gospel is . . . directed by the spirit (Spirit)."[1]

1. The Pattern of Acts: Under the Guidance of the Holy Spirit

It is clear that Acts progresses in terms of the expansion of the gospel and the church. First, Acts 1:15–8:7 is centered on the area around Jerusalem; second, Acts 8:8–11:18 moves to Samaria and the coastal region; third, Acts 11:19–15:35 is centered on Antioch and the mission which the church there commissioned Paul and Barnabas to undertake; fourth, Acts 15:36–19:20 follows Paul's mission around the Aegean Sea, including Greece; finally, the fifth stage comes in 19:21–28:31, which traces the advance of the gospel

1. Keith Reeves, "The Holy Spirit in Luke/Acts," in Johnson T. K. Lim, ed., *Holy Spirit: Unfinished Agenda* (Singapore: Armour, 2015), pp. 62-66, here p. 65.

to Rome. For Luke, the whole narrative moves from Jerusalem to Rome, his two key cities. All the while this journey reflects the purpose of God, and the leading of the Holy Spirit, and the proclamation of Christ.

The Holy Spirit ensures that this expansion cannot be stopped. Ronald Williams subtitles his commentary on Acts, "Nothing Can Stop the Gospel."[2] The Spirit empowers the Church, and the Word of God denotes the content of the gospel. The Church faces setbacks and difficulties; but through the Spirit these were regularly turned to advantage. One striking example comes in Acts 8:1: "A severe persecution began against the church in Jerusalem, and all except the apostles were scattered throughout the countryside of Judea and Samaria." So what began as the disaster of persecution resulted in the positive "scattering" of Christian believers to Judea and Samaria. Thus the second stage of God's five-stage plan was reached: the gospel was proclaimed to the Samaritans. These became the Church's first non-Jewish or half-Jewish converts.

This is not the only incident of its kind. The internal dispute between Greek-speaking Christian widows and Aramaic-speaking Christian widows (Acts 6:1) led to the appointment of Greek-speaking Stephen and six others, "and the word of God continued to spread, and the number of the disciples increased greatly in Jerusalem" (6:7). There followed both Stephen's long defense and his final martyrdom (6:9–7:60). But his speech proved to be a turning point for the Church. Stephen expounded the history of Israel from a Christian viewpoint. He explained that the narrative of Abraham amounted to God's call of grace to move on, and that God has always acted in continuity with his promises (7:2-19). He raised up Moses and redeemed Israel from Egypt, when "He led them out" (7:36). This eventually led to moving the place of worship of the tabernacle (7:44-50). Yet in spite of God's goodness, the people persecuted the prophets and "opposed the Holy Spirit" (7:51). In the end they killed the Righteous One, Jesus (7:52). Stephen's theology paved the way for Samaria, Paul, and the admission of the Gentiles on an equal basis with the Jews. The God of Abraham and Moses, he argued, is not static, not local, as if tied to Jerusalem and the Temple, but is so much greater.

Other narratives make a similar point. When they were first arrested, Peter and John gave an account of the resurrection of Jesus, and "Many of those who heard the word believed; and they numbered

---

2. Ronald R. Williams, *The Acts of the Apostles* (London: SCM, 1953).

about five thousand" (Acts 4:4). When Ananias and Sapphira kept back part of their gift and lied "to the Holy Spirit" (5:3), at Peter's rebuke, they died, and "fear seized the whole church and all who heard of these things" (5:11). Acts 11:19 repeats what occurred in 8:1; "Those who were scattered because of the persecution that took place over Stephen traveled as far as Phoenicia, Cyprus, and Antioch." This is not an accidental doublet; Luke wishes to emphasize the recurrent cycle and principle of expansion.

2. The Barrier-breaking Event of the Day of Pentecost

Arie Zwiep calls the three events of Pentecost, the mission to the Samaritans, and the outreach to Cornelius and the Gentiles "barrier-breaking."[3] They marked a new stage in God's unfolding of his divine purposes for the world, in fulfilment of the prophets (Joel 2:28-29). Peter appeals to the inspiration of the Holy Spirit in the Psalms (Acts 1:16-21; 4:25-26). Pentecost took place some fifty days after the Passover (Lev. 23:15-16; Deut. 16:9-10; cf. Exod. 23:14-17; 34:18, 22-24). The festival was second in importance of the three Jewish festivals, and was celebrated like a holiday with joy in Jerusalem. Hence many Diaspora Jews visited Jerusalem for the festival. Welker sums up the significance of the event. He writes, "The pouring out of the Spirit not only comes on individual persons and groups of people in a surprising manner . . . The Spirit also influences people by coming from their proximate and their distant environments, inasmuch as the Spirit at the same time enlists the services of other people with them."[4] He several times refers to the effects of the Holy Spirit's outpouring as a "field of force" in which "*God effects a world-encompassing, multilingual, polyindividual testimony to Godself.*"[5]

On the day of Pentecost, the Christians were "all together in one place" (Acts 2:1). The signs of the pouring out of the Holy Spirit were audible ("a sound like the rush of a violent wind," 2:2), and also visible ("divided tongues, as of fire," 2:3). Fire serves as an image of judgment and purification (Isa. 5:24; 1 Enoch 14:8-13; Luke 3:16). Wind and fire ac-

---

3. Arie W. Zwiep, *Christ, the Spirit and the Community of God* (Tübingen: Mohr Siebeck, 2010), p. 116.
4. Michael Welker, *God the Spirit* (Minneapolis: Fortress, 1994), p. 228.
5. Welker, *God the Spirit*, p. 235 (his italics).

companied a theophany to Ezekiel (Ezek. 1:4; contrast this with Elijah's theophany in 1 Kings 19:11-12). The heart of the corporate experience was that "all of them were filled with the Holy Spirit, and began to speak in other languages, as the Spirit gave them ability" (Acts 2:4). Each phrase is important. "All of them were filled" translates the Greek *eplēsthēsan pantes,* i.e., filled completely, and not just some, but all. "Other languages" translates *heterais glōssais.* Many, indeed probably most, see this as a reversal of Babel.

As we observed in the previous chapter on Paul, the traditional view is that "other languages" are known languages of the world. John Chrysostom argued for this view.[6] A strong defender of this interpretation today is Don Carson, who calls this "*xenoglossia* — real, human languages never learned by the speakers."[7] He insists that this is a miracle of speech, not simply of hearing. He dismisses the charge of drunkenness (Acts 2:13) as being due simply to the commotion generated by such large numbers.

Nevertheless, strong arguments have been mounted against this view. H. B. Swete and others argue that virtually the whole crowd would have known enough colloquial Greek, or even a dialect of Aramaic, to understand what was communicated.[8] Moreover, the Pentecostal writer Janet Everts Powers insists that Luke's bestowal of "tongues" was not a "missionary gift": the apostles "preach in the vernacular, not tongues."[9] The charismatic renewal scholar Max Turner agrees, for "it is Peter's preaching which communicates the gospel."[10] Finally, Montague, against Carson, concludes, "It would seem . . . that this was a miracle of hearing."[11]

Far more important than the shape of the phenomenon of Pentecost is its theological significance. Dunn offers some wise words about whether the experience of Pentecost can ever be repeated. In one important sense, he explains, Pentecost is *initiatory,* and in this sense "Pentecost can never

---

6. John Chrysostom, *Homilies on Acts,* Homily 4 (Eng. *NPNF,* ser. 1, 11.28-29).

7. Donald Carson, *Showing the Spirit* (Grand Rapids: Baker, 1987), p. 138.

8. H. B. Swete, *The Holy Spirit in the New Testament* (London: Macmillan, 1909), p. 73.

9. Janet Everts Powers, "Missionary Tongues," *JPT* 17 (2000), pp. 39-55, here p. 40.

10. Max Turner, *The Holy Spirit and Spiritual Gifts Then and Now* (Carlisle: Paternoster, 1996), p. 223.

11. George T. Montague, *The Holy Spirit: The Growth of a Biblical Tradition* (Eugene, OR: Wipf & Stock, 1976), p. 281.

be repeated — the new age is here, and cannot be ushered in again . . . but in another sense," he continues, "the experience of Pentecost can and must be repeated in the experience of all who would become Christians."[12] In the sense in which he explains this, Dunn is right. But the *initiatory* nature of the experience is decisive. This is why Peter uses apocalyptic language: "portents in the heavens above and signs in the earth below, blood, and fire . . . The sun shall be turned to darkness and the moon to blood" (Acts 2:19-20).

In addition to this, the event of Pentecost is a *corporate* or *communal* event, not an individual one. Our modern Western individualism too often skews our hermeneutics or procedures of interpretation. Gaventa, Zwiep, and many others rightly stress this. Dale Bruner calls it "a communal . . . baptism with the Holy Spirit . . . this paradigmatic announcement of the baptism of the Holy Spirit."[13]

Equally important is that the gift of the Holy Spirit comes *from above.* It does not merely come from within, as if it were a religious aspiration of human beings. Max Turner and Hans von Baer regard Pentecost as the empowering of the Church for witness, which the Church may begin "when the Holy Spirit has come upon you" (Acts 1:8). If we regard the event as *initiatory,* it constitutes incorporation into Christ, rather than something to be experienced as "a second blessing."

Before we leave this subject, we should return to note the variety of views about Pentecost in relation to speaking in tongues. We discussed six views of the meaning of "tongues" in Paul, and noted that "tongues" in Acts are usually regarded either as the ability to speak foreign languages or as some version of *glossolalia.* Among viable views of the latter, some rightly regard tongues as the *release of unconscious longings for God,* or other forms of worship, intimacy, or praise. Pentecostals and many in the renewal movement, from at least the time of the classic Pentecostalism of Charles Parham in 1901 and William Seymour in 1905, have regarded tongues as "initial evidence" (to use the technical phrase) of "baptism in the Spirit." Contrary to this view, Welker argues, "It is undisputed that the descent of the Spirit is not necessarily bound up with the gift of speaking in tongues."[14]

12. James D. G. Dunn, *Baptism in the Holy Spirit* (London: SCM, 1970), p. 53.
13. F. Dale Bruner, *A Theology of the Holy Spirit* (Grand Rapids: Eerdmans, 1970), p. 157.
14. Welker, *God the Spirit,* p. 265.

This phenomenon is set out, for example, in McGee's book *Initial Evidence*.[15] Arguably Edward Irving held this view in the early nineteenth century. Charles Parham believed, "Holy Spirit baptism [is] evidenced by speaking in tongues."[16] Seymour initially accepted this but later had doubts and reservations about it. Today, however, this "classic Pentecostal" doctrine is not universally held among Pentecostals. Cartledge sees the influence of this doctrine as waning today, where tongues are often seen as an intimate or intense expression of praise and prayer.[17] In the conference of Pentecostals held in 2006, Veli-Matti Kärkkäinen reported that some forty percent of Pentecostals do not now claim to speak in tongues, while, as we have noted, Frank Macchia equates tongues with "sighs too deep for words" in Rom. 8:26. Some among the "Third Wave" renewal movement do speak in tongues. Nevertheless Max Turner, a scholarly advocate of renewal, speaks today of a spectrum of views, ranging from the "initial evidence" view even to the "cessationist view," which restricts tongues to the apostolic age. He himself firmly retains the view that Acts 2 speaks of "tongues" as foreign languages, as Carson does.[18] Yet in the same volume Neil Hudson concludes, "Speaking in tongues continues to be a marker of Pentecostalism," and also of "the charismatic renewal movement, which began in 1960."[19] Today Robert Menzies remains a scholarly adherent of the classical "initial evidence" view in Pentecostalism.[20] We shall consider this issue again in Part III.

It is probable that a final evaluation of the Acts account of the day of Pentecost cannot be completed until we have considered the three further examples of "tongues" in Acts and have compared Luke's view with that of other NT writings, and specialist studies of the theology of Luke–Acts.

15. Garry B. McGee, ed., *Initial Evidence: Historical and Biblical Perspectives on the Pentecostal Doctrine of Spirit Baptism* (Eugene, OR: Wipf & Stock, 1990), pp. 41-95, 219-34.

16. James R. Goff, Jr., "Initial Tongues in the Theology of Charles Fox Parham," in McGee, ed., *Initial Evidence,* pp. 57-71, here p. 69.

17. Mark J. Cartledge, *Charismatic Glossolalia: An Empirical-Theological Study* (Burlington, VT: Ashgate, 2002), pp. 215-16.

18. Max Turner, "Early Christian Experience and Theology of Tongues," in Mark J. Cartledge, ed., *Speaking in Tongues* (Milton Keynes: Paternoster, 2006), pp. 1-33, here p. 5.

19. Neil Hudson, "Strange Words and Their Impact on Early Pentecostals," in Cartledge, ed., *Speaking in Tongues,* pp. 111-46, here p. 137.

20. Robert Menzies, "Evidential Tongues: An Essay on Theological Method," *Asian Journal of Pentecostal Studies* 1 (1999), pp. 111-23.

3. The Next Key Event: The "Puzzle" of the Samaritans

As Reeves writes, "The next outpouring of the Spirit comes on the Samaritans when Peter and John, representatives of the gospel, lay their hands on the Samaritans" (Acts 8:17).[21] James Dunn calls this event "The Riddle of Samaria."[22] Bruner calls it "the Samaritan puzzle."[23]

The key to what is often believed to be a puzzle or riddle is that all four events in Acts of the pouring out of the Holy Spirit are what Zwiep calls "barrier-breaking" events. At Pentecost the barrier to be broken was that between the old age and the new, achieved by the inbreaking of the Holy Spirit, given initially to Jewish Christians. Geoffrey Lampe calls the gift of the Spirit to the Samaritans "a turning-point in the missionary enterprise."[24] The great missionary expansion in Acts fulfilled the word of Jesus: "You will be my witnesses in Jerusalem, in all Judea and Samaria, and to the ends of the earth" (Acts 1:8). There had always been hostility between Jews and Samaritans. Hence the Jews would require visible evidence that the Samaritans had received the Spirit. Welker points out that the expectation of "new tongues" was anticipated, or alluded to, in Mark 16:17; Acts 10:46; 19:6; 1 Cor. 12:10, 28; and 13:8.[25]

Philip had traveled to the city of Samaria to proclaim Christ there (Acts 8:5). But in the initial stage "the Spirit had not [yet] come upon any of them" (8:16). Hence Samaria was a "bridge to be crossed."[26] In this sense the Samaritans constituted a broadly halfway house between Jews and Gentiles. The visit to Samaria of Peter and John, together with the laying on of hands, displayed *the unity of the Church,* and the solidarity of the new community in Samaria with the church of the Jerusalem founding apostles. In this sense, Acts recounts a second barrier-breaking event of first importance. Today and in tradition we speak of the Church as "one, holy, catholic, and apostolic church"; these are the marks of the one, united church. This signals the second major step for the advance of the Church, also driven and led by the Holy Spirit.

---

21. Reeves, "The Holy Spirit in Luke/Acts," in Lim, ed., *The Holy Spirit: Unfinished Agenda,* p. 65.

22. Dunn, *Baptism in the Holy Spirit,* pp. 35, 55-72.

23. Bruner, *A Theology of the Holy Spirit,* p. 175.

24. G. W. H. Lampe, *The Seal of the Spirit* (London: Longmans, Green, 1951), pp. 70-72.

25. Welker, *God the Spirit,* p. 265.

26. Bruner, *A Theology of the Holy Spirit,* p. 175.

4. Other Barrier-Breaking Events: Cornelius and the Gentiles

The advance of the gospel to the Gentiles was such a momentous step that the Council of Jerusalem had to debate the terms on which the Gentiles could be admitted to the Church (Acts 15:1-29). *All of this reflects the prior event of Acts 11:5-18.* Peter, Paul, and Barnabas had to press the case on behalf of the Gentiles (Acts 15:2-5, 7-11, 12; Gal. 2:1-15). Clearly James and some Pharisaic Christians had doubts, while Galatians implies that Peter may have vacillated before joining Paul and Barnabas. But Peter also recounted the Cornelius episode as evidence. He explores the state of affairs in Acts 11:2-18.

While Peter was in Joppa he received a vision in which a sheet came down from heaven which contained "four-footed animals, beasts of prey, reptiles, and birds of the air" (Acts 11:5-6). Three times Peter, the Jew, was commanded, "Kill and eat" (11:7). But he replied, "'By no means, Lord; for nothing profane or unclean has ever entered my mouth'" (v. 8). Each time the heavenly voice declared "What God has made clean, you must not call profane" (v. 9). That very moment three men arrived from Caesarea, sent by Cornelius. The Holy Spirit told Peter to go with them, while the Spirit brought home to him that the vision means that he was to make no distinction between them (the Gentiles) and us (the Jews, 11:12). The climax of the narrative is now recounted: "As I began to speak, the Holy Spirit fell upon them just as it (he) had upon us at the beginning. . . If then God gave them the same gift that he gave us when we believed in the Lord Jesus Christ, who was I that I could hinder God?" (vv. 15, 17). Critics were silenced, saying, "Then God has given even to the Gentiles the repentance that leads to life" (v. 18).

In the event of Acts 11 there is no mention of baptism or the laying on of hands. It constitutes a third barrier-breaking event, which may be seen as a decisive milestone in "catching up" on the part of the Gentiles what the Jewish Christians had already experienced. Luke–Acts emphasizes that the Holy Spirit decisively directs each new stage of the expansion of the Christian Church and the gospel to a new constituency. God conspicuously sets his seal of approval on it, in the way that he expressed his approval of his Son's mission in the gospels. Lindsay Dewar calls this event "plainly unique — a Gentile Pentecost."[27]

The three events of Pentecost, the gift of the Spirit to the Samaritans,

---

27. Lindsay Dewar, *The Holy Spirit in Modern Thought* (London: Mowbray, 1952), p. 54.

and "the Gentile Pentecost," constitute the first three decisive stages of outreach and mission, sealed by the gift of the Spirit. The fourth and fifth stages are less clearly "staged" in the same sense, but they concern the gift to the disciples of John the Baptist at Ephesus, and the gift of the Spirit to Paul. These are not so much sequential stages, but rather decisive events.

5. Further Barrier-Breaking Events:
The Disciples at Ephesus and Paul's New Stage of Ministry

Acts 19:1 recounts how Paul came to Ephesus where he found "some disciples." But when he asked them, "Did you receive the Holy Spirit when you became believers?" they replied, "No, we have not even heard that there is a Holy Spirit" (19:2). Welker states that Pentecost is "no once-and-for-all event."[28] As we proceed, we find that he refers simply to the repeated events of Acts 8:17 and 19:6.

Here is a prima facie problem. If the "Paul" of Acts is the Paul of the epistles, he clearly teaches that no one can become a believer without the Holy Spirit (Rom. 8:9-10). There could be only three possible explanations: (i) either the Paul recorded in Acts is not the true Paul; or (ii) the Holy Spirit was at work but unknown as such; or (iii) this "becoming a believer" was not true Christian conversion to Christ in faith, because they were John's disciples. The explanation follows in the next verses, and excludes the necessity for considering (i) and (ii). When Paul asked into what the disciples were baptized, they replied, "Into John's baptism" (19:3). Clearly they had been disciples of John the Baptist, but not fully, if at all, of Jesus Christ.

Not everyone agrees with what to me is an obvious understanding of the event. Turner, for example, insists that the Holy Spirit is given here *after* faith.[29] But in what or in whom was their faith? Acts 19:1-7 was not an "exception," as many charismatic renewal or Pentecostal writers claim. Luke recounts, "They were baptized in the name of the Lord Jesus. When Paul had laid his hands on them, the Holy Spirit came upon them, and they spoke in tongues and prophesied" (19:5-6). As with Peter and John in Samaria, the coming to faith in Christ and receiving the Holy Spirit were a

---

28. Welker, *God the Spirit*, p. 229.
29. Max Turner, *Power from on High: The Spirit in Israel's Restoration and Witness in Luke–Acts* (Sheffield: Sheffield Academic Press, 2000), p. 362.

single event, but Paul, like Peter and John, ensured that the gift of the Spirit was seen as the one gift from God within the one, new, universal Church. There could be no fragmentation or splinter groups within the Church. The event may be more accurately described as "catching up" than as "barrier-breaking," except in relation to the expression of the one universal Church.

In the case of Paul in Acts, the Holy Spirit was given to Paul by God *prior* to his baptism. Acts 9:17 recounts how God sent Ananias "so that you (Paul) may regain your sight and be filled with the Holy Spirit." The next verse (v. 18) recounts how "he got up and was baptized." Gone are the days when people usually regarded Acts as structured in the first half around Peter, and in the second half around Paul. This is not to deny that in broad terms these two figures do represent the two centers of gravity in the missionary enterprise of salvation history. But most follow Gaventa in seeing the steady missionary expansion as reflecting the purpose of God. In this sense the gift of the Spirit to Paul represents both the norm for Christian experience, and a marker of the progress of God's purposes for the Church in history.

Pentecost and the three other barrier-breaking events should not blind us to the overall plan of Acts, in which the Holy Spirit is the driver and guide in the steady expansion of the Church. In Acts 13:2 it is the Holy Spirit who said, "Set apart for me Barnabas and Saul (Paul) for the work to which I have called them." Afterward the church at Antioch prayed and laid hands on them, commissioning them in the name of the Spirit and the church to undertake the first missionary journey.

This is close to being an ordination for Paul and Barnabas, even if there may be differences. Paul was no mere itinerant freelance evangelist; he was commissioned by the Holy Spirit and the Church to be a missionary–pastor, who worked collegially with many coworkers and revisited where he had evangelized. Turner may be correct to regard this as a gift of empowerment, but only in the broader context that we have outlined. Certainly in Acts, as Turner, Menzies, and others have argued, there are instances of prophecy, empowerment, and miracles — but again, only within the key context of the expansion and mission of the Church. Further, in Paul's ministry in Acts, as well as in the epistles, we see that the Holy Spirit gave him the gift of rational, persuasive argument, rather than the simple declaration, "Thus says the Lord." We have referred in this respect to evidence from Bornkamm, Stowers, Pannenberg, and others, and from Hill, Müller, and Gillespie, on preaching and prophecy. All this is expounded with further detail in our larger book on the Holy Spirit.

CHAPTER 6

The Holy Spirit in the Johannine Writings

John's Gospel was written probably to complement the first three gospels. If he seems perhaps to speak less about the Holy Spirit than the others, especially Luke, this is because he shines the spotlight on Christ, makes Christ alone the center of his picture, and especially integrates his theology of the Holy Spirit with Christology. In addition to this, Burge observes, "John integrates the Spirit into his ecclesiology and eschatology."[1] If there is less of the Spirit, however, this receives compensation in the five passages in John 14–16 about the Holy Spirit as the Paraclete who points to, and deputizes, Jesus Christ (John 14:17, 26; 15:26; 16:7, 13). It is also crucial and correct that, to quote Burge again, "For John, the Spirit is never an impersonal power."[2]

John includes various episodes about the Holy Spirit. In chapters 1–12, often called the Book of Signs, John recounts the descent of the Spirit "like a dove" at Jesus' baptism, and adds a key verb: "He on whom you see the Spirit descend *and remain* is the one who baptizes with the Holy Spirit" (John 1:33). John, like the first three gospels, includes John the Baptist's references to the Spirit. John the Baptist gives a witness or *testimonium* about the Spirit. He would be doubtless looking back to such OT and pseudepigraphic passages as Isa. 11:2; 32:15; Ezek. 36:26-27; 37:14; Jub. 1:23; Test. Jud. 24:1-3. Craig Keener writes, "Fire naturally symbolized future judgment. . . . John warned that the coming judge would be incomparably

---

1. Gary M. Burge, "The Gospel of John," in Trevor J. Burke and Keith Warrington, eds., *A Biblical Theology of the Holy Spirit* (London: SPCK, 2014), pp. 104-15, here p. 104.
2. Burge, "The Gospel of John," p. 111.

powerful. . . . The identity of this coming judge . . . John announces [in] John 3:11-12."[3]

However, the most sustained teaching about the Holy Spirit comes in the so-called Book of Passion. He gives four blocks of teaching about the Spirit using the word "Paraclete" (John 14:15-17, 26; 15:26-27; 16:5-15). Intriguingly, Hans Windisch suggested that these chapters would still flow if these Paraclete verses were removed, and that they therefore represent a distinctive block of teaching. But this is sheer speculation, and cannot be proved from any evidence. Most scholars reject his theory. According to Danker, the Paraclete (*paraklētos*) means "mediator, intercessor, helper," or "one who appears in another's behalf."[4] He not only witnesses to Christ; in John 14:18 Jesus declares, "I will not leave you orphaned, I am coming to you." In other words, he is Christ's alter ego. At the very least, as Swete declares, "The Spirit was sent to reveal the Son."[5] Dunn comments, "The Spirit . . . continues the presence of Jesus" (John 15:26; 16:27-28).[6]

To return to the Book of Signs, John speaks of the Holy Spirit in the life of Jesus. Not only, as we noted, does the Spirit "remain" on Jesus, Jesus also gives the Spirit "without measure" (John 3:34). But because the work of the Holy Spirit in the fourth gospel is to witness to Christ alone, Fison repeats that the Spirit *effaces himself and advertises Jesus:* "He will not speak on his own (*aph' heautou,* lit. 'of himself') . . . He will glorify me" (John 16:13-14).[7] The Holy Spirit does have a broader ministry also. Montague insists, "While Luke is interested in the charismatic explosion of the Spirit in tongues, prophecy and healing, John is more interested in the relation of the Spirit to power over sin . . . founded on a word of Jesus."[8] In John 1–12 we find various confessions of Jesus Christ. He is "Lamb of God" and "Son of Man" (John 1:29, 51); "Son of God" (5:19-24), and "Bread of Life"

3. Craig S. Keener, *The Spirit in the Gospels and Acts: Divine Purity and Power* (Grand Rapids: Baker Academic, 1997), p. 96.

4. Danker, BDAG, p. 766.

5. Henry B. Swete, *The Holy Spirit in the New Testament* (London: Macmillan, 1921), p. 153.

6. James D. G. Dunn, *Jesus and the Spirit: A Study of the Religious and Charismatic Experience of Jesus and the First Christians as Reflected in the New Testament* (London: SCM, 1975).

7. J. E. Fison, *The Blessing of the Holy Spirit* (London: Longmans, Green, 1950), p. 137 (my italics).

8. George T. Montague, *The Holy Spirit: The Growth of a Biblical Tradition* (Eugene, OR: Wipf & Stock, 1976), p. 363.

(6:35), while in John 13–21 we reach a climax in Thomas's confession, "My Lord and my God" (20:28).

The sovereignty of the Holy Spirit finds expression in the words "the Spirit blows where it (he) chooses" (John 3:8). His character is revealed as "the Spirit of truth" (14:17; 15:26; 16:13). This term occurs also in the Dead Sea Scrolls (1QS 3.17-19; 4.23-24). The Spirit guides the Church into all truth (16:13a). In 6:63 the Holy Spirit is the giver of life. In 4:24 "God is Spirit" (not "a" spirit; NRSV correctly leaves out the article but translates with the lower-case "spirit"). Clearly in John the Spirit is derived from Christ and is emphatically *not* an impersonal force. In his conversation with the woman of Samaria, God, like his Spirit, transcends any given physical location (4:21). Worship should be "in Spirit and truth" (4:24; NRSV again translated with the lower case here). In 7:38 when Jesus speaks at the Festival of Booths, he promises that "out of the believer's heart shall flow rivers of living water." John comments, "He said this about the Spirit, which believers in him were to receive" (7:39).

When we discussed the Old Testament, we stressed the transcendence of the Spirit. In Jesus' dialogue with Nicodemus, John emphasizes that the new birth is "from above," i.e., from beyond. Moltmann, among others, insists that "from above" (*anōthen,* John 3:3, 7) is correct; the interpretation (and translation) "born again" should be rejected.[9] Even more dramatically, in the second part of John, the Holy Spirit comes forth or "proceeds" from God the Father (*to pneuma . . . ho para tou patros ekporeuetai,* John 15:26). The Holy Spirit, as the later church fathers declared, is not a creature; he is not created, and not part of creation.

In John 16:8-11, the Holy Spirit as the Paraclete will "convict" (*elenxei*) the world of sin, righteousness, and judgment. E. F. Scott comments, "Confronted by the holy community in which the divine power is manifested working, the world will be brought to a sense of wickedness and unbelief."[10] This is very close to Paul's thought about preaching in 1 Cor. 14:25. Barrett suggests that in this context, "Paraclete" assumes the meaning of "prosecuting counsel," even if it often means "advocate" or "helper."

In John 20:20-23 the post-resurrection Christ appeared to the apostles and "showed them his hands and his side." He declared, " 'As the Father

---

9. Jürgen Moltmann, *The Spirit of Life: A Universal Affirmation* (London: SCM, 1982), p. 145.

10. E. F. Scott, *The Spirit in the New Testament* (London: Hodder & Stoughton, 1924), p. 201.

has sent me, so I send you.' When he had said this, he breathed on them and said to them, 'Receive the Holy Spirit. If you forgive the sins of any, they are forgiven them; if you retain the sins of any, they are retained.'" In other words, it is Christ himself who bestows the Holy Spirit and the context is the gift of the Spirit for their vocation as apostles. This passage is known often as the Insufflation or the Johannine Pentecost. It is followed by the restoration of Thomas and his confession of Jesus as "My Lord and my God" (20:28). The commission to the apostles is the same "sending" as that of the Father to Jesus Christ. Swete follows Westcott and Godet in seeing the Insufflation as the giving of life through the Spirit, and Pentecost as endowment or empowerment through the Holy Spirit.[11] The two events are complementary. Similarly, they argue, John relates the gift of the Holy Spirit to the resurrection of Jesus; Luke–Acts relates it to the ascension of Jesus.

Gary Burge sums up the message of the Holy Spirit as the defender (*paraklētos*) who will stand with them and lead them into new truths (John 16:8-10, 12-13).[12] He also notes that "the Spirit" is used some twelve times in various places in the gospel, and the Holy Spirit at least three times. In John 7:39, as in 20:22, the Holy Spirit is regarded as given on the basis of the resurrection. Burge concludes, "In summary, the Johannine Christology makes careful use of pneumatology for one of its primary theological categories. For John, there is an intimate unity between Jesus and the Spirit which becomes explicit as Jesus moves towards the hour of glorification. Put another way, the Spirit is the life of Jesus poured out on the cross for the life of the world . . . This promised gift is linked to the hour of glorification (7:38-39; 19:30, 34; 20:22)."[13]

The epistles of John share with the fourth gospel a deep concern for truth, an emphasis on the love of God, and a contrast with the "world," in the sense of its worldliness. The epistles of John share with Paul that an "anointing" by the Holy Spirit is derived from Christ and is a permanent possession of the believer (1 John 2:20, 27). But there is less explicit teaching about the Holy Spirit. Schweizer observes, "The unusual nature of the gifts of the Spirit is not emphasised."[14] All the same, just as in 1 Cor. 12:3, Paul stresses that the Holy Spirit prompts the confession, "Jesus is Lord,"

---

11. Swete, *The Holy Spirit in the New Testament*, p. 167.

12. Burge, "The Gospel of John," p. 105.

13. Burge, "The Gospel of John," pp. 110-11.

14. Eduard Schweizer, *"Pneuma, pneumatikos, pneō, empneō, pnoē, ekpneō, theopneustos*: E. The New Testament,"* in *TDNT*, 6.396-451, here 448.

so 1 John 4:2 urges that the Holy Spirit prompts the confession, "Jesus Christ has come in the flesh [and] is from God." Like Paul, 1 John urges the importance of testing "what is of the Spirit": "Do not believe every spirit, but test the spirits to see whether they are from God" (1 John 4:1).

John Thomas makes a still more explicit connection between 1 John and the fourth gospel, in spite of difficulties about the date and authorship of the Johannine epistles. He takes up the theme of "anointing" in 1 John 2:20: "You have been anointed by the Holy One, and all of you have knowledge." He rightly argues that anointing is "closely associated with the activity of the Holy Spirit," and similarly with the work of the Paraclete in John 14:17, 26.[15] He further suggests the anointing reflects the gift of the Spirit at the baptism of Jesus (John 1:32-33), and that the Greek *chrisma* ("anointing") and *Christos* ("Anointed One") reflect a deliberate word play, where the Holy Spirit witnesses to, and glorifies, Christ. As in both Paul and the fourth gospel, the Holy Spirit is Christ-centered. Further, in the NT *chriō* is nearly always used of anointing Christ (Luke 4:18; Acts 4:27; 10:38; Heb. 1:9); the only exception is 2 Cor. 1:21, where it is used of anointing all Christians at baptism in *Christ* and through *the Spirit* (note also that *1 Clement* 18:1 contains a reference to the anointing of David as king).[16]

The older but still standard book on this subject is that of Swete. He lists as the four relevant passages in 1 John: 3:24; 4:1-6; 4:13; and 5:6-7.[17] We will explore those now.

(1) 1 John 3:24 declares, "All who obey his commandments abide in him, and he abides in them. And by this we know that he abides in us, by the Spirit that he has given (*edōken*) us." This is repeated in 4:13 with minor changes. The Holy Spirit assures us that we permanently abide in him. John Thomas considers this verse, but Swete rightly stresses more clearly the change in lifestyle which the Spirit brings, as part of his assurance or evidence that we abide in God.

(2) Both writers, however, rightly show how readily 1 John 4:1-6 flows from this. Thomas declares that in 4:1-6 "the Spirit receives explicit and extensive treatment."[18] This passage instantly introduces the need to "test the spirits to see whether they are from God; for many false prophets have gone out into the world. By this you know the Spirit of God: every

15. John C. Thomas, "The Johannine Epistles," in Burke and Warrington, eds., *A Biblical Theology of the Holy Spirit*, pp. 250-56, here p. 251.

16. Danker, BDAG, p. 1091.

17. Swete, *The Holy Spirit in the New Testament*, p. 255.

18. Thomas, "The Johannine Epistles," p. 252.

spirit that confesses that Jesus Christ has come in the flesh is from God, and every spirit that does not confess Jesus ... is the spirit of antichrist" (4:1-3). This epistle warns us against false prophecy just as urgently as the serious warnings in Deuteronomy noted above. Moreover, in addition to the ethical conduct of 3:24, here the further criterion of an orthodox belief in the incarnation of Jesus Christ is also added. The "antichrist" is mentioned in the NT only in 1 John, in spite of elaborate theories about the antichrist in the later history of theology.[19] The Spirit is known by the witness that he bears of "worldly" evil opposed to God. Many also argue that "docetic" interpretations of Christ (i.e., a Christ not fully enfleshed) were already abroad.

(3) 1 John 4:13 virtually repeats 3:24, and does not need additional attention here.

(4) 1 John 5:6-9 declares, "The Spirit is the one that testifies, for the Spirit is the truth. There are three that testify: the Spirit and the water and the blood ... this is the testimony of God that he has testified to his Son." The longer text of v. 8, "The Father, the Word, and the Holy Spirit ... are three" is described by Metzger and his UBS Committee as "spurious," since it postdates the Greek church fathers, Syriac, Coptic and Arminian, Ethiopian, and Slavonic.[20] We may also note that, had the longer text been original, Athanasius and Basil would certainly have quoted it as evidence of the Holy Trinity at an earlier date. But the concept of "the Spirit of truth" entirely reflects the fourth gospel, especially John 14:17.

The abiding presence of the Holy Spirit, testing prophecies, and the derived gift of anointing from Jesus Christ, remain three of the many contributions of 1 John to the subject. The witness of the Spirit (alongside possible allusions to water and blood) stresses his relation with the death of Jesus Christ on the cross and purity of life, and his status as the Spirit of truth reflects Qumran and the fourth gospel.

---

19. See Bernard McGinn, *Antichrist: Two Thousand Years of Human Fascination with Evil* (San Francisco: Harper, 1994); and Anthony C. Thiselton, *1 & 2 Thessalonians through the Centuries* (Oxford: Blackwell, 2011), pp. 213-17.

20. Bruce Metzger, *A Textual Commentary on the Greek New Testament,* 2nd ed. (London: United Bible Societies, 1994), pp. 647-49.

CHAPTER 7

The Spirit in the Rest of the New Testament

(1) *The Pastoral Epistles.* In my larger book on the Holy Spirit I had intended to cover the whole NT. But I omitted to allocate a special section to the Pastoral Epistles. Most NT scholars (although not all) regard the Pastorals as non-Pauline in the sense of not being directly dictated by Paul. Hence it has become a convention to consider them separately from Paul. On the other hand, many agree that the writer was probably a disciple of Paul, and that in this sense 1-2 Timothy and Titus are broadly "Pauline." If they were written by a secretary (as a number of epistles were), differences of vocabulary and style are far from decisive. Further, if Paul lived to a relatively old age, he may have seen needs in the churches which related to infrastructure, countering the frequently made objection that the Pastorals evince a more advanced church organization. Hence, as is the case with Ephesians, it is premature to *exclude* the possibility of Pauline authorship. We shall observe the convention of considering them as a separate corpus from Paul, without committing ourselves to accepting the majority view about their authorship.

(i) 1 Timothy 3:16 contains an early Christological creed, which Paul probably quoted. Jesus Christ "was revealed in flesh, vindicated (*edikaiōthē*) in Spirit (*en pneumati,* NRSV "spirit"), seen (*ōphthē*) by angels, proclaimed among Gentiles, believed in throughout the world, taken up (*anelēmphthē*) in glory" (NRSV). The word translated "vindicated" normally means justified and this cannot readily be applied to Christ. *Vindication* refers to his exaltation by God in contrast to his pre-resurrection humiliation and the unbelief of many.

On the basis of Rom. 1:4 ("declared to be Son of God . . . according to the Spirit [NRSV 'spirit'] of holiness") and Rom. 8:11 ("the Spirit of him

who raised Jesus from the dead . . . through his Spirit"), we understand
1 Tim. 3:16 to mean "vindicated by the Holy Spirit" in his post-resurrection
state. "Taken up" may refer to the ascension, and Paul normally prefers
to speak of the resurrection. But there are exceptions. Philippians 2:9-11
hints at ascension (or at least exaltation), and Eph. 4:8 includes "When
he ascended on high . . . he gave gifts to his people." Both of these may be
quotations, as is the creed of 1 Tim. 3:16, but this does not detract from
their significance.

(ii) Titus 3:5-6 asserts that believers are saved "through the water
of rebirth and renewal by the Holy Spirit. This Spirit he poured out on us
richly through Jesus Christ our Saviour." *Rebirth* is less frequently used by
Paul than *new creation* or *raised with Christ,* and it is associated with the Johannine writings. This may be because of its use in the Hellenistic mystery
religions. However, once Paul has made his point, it remains appropriate
for the event of new creation or transfer, while *renewal* by the Holy Spirit
signifies the process of growth, newness and sanctification, and is one of
Paul's favorite words. We have discussed "newness" above. The two terms
follow on from "the water of rebirth," which clearly refers to the event of
baptism. Here the baptized renounce the old life and embrace the new
through this initiatory act of God. It justifies the use of "renewal" in movements today. Baptism is once for all, but as Paul says in his earlier epistles,
"Our inner nature is being renewed day by day" (2 Cor. 4:16).

(iii) 2 Timothy 3:15-16 provides an indirect allusion to the Holy Spirit,
where the English word "inspired" translates the Greek word *theopneustos,
God-breathed.* As Montague comments, "The proper understanding of the
OT writings will help the leader of the church combat false doctrine and
foster fruitful Christian living."[1] This comment fits the context.

(iv) Two passages underline the Spirit's role in prophecy. 1 Timothy
1:18 declares, "I am giving you these instructions, Timothy, my child, in
accordance with prophecies made earlier about you." Later in the same
epistle we read, "The Spirit expressly says that in later times some will
renounce the faith by paying attention to deceitful spirits" (1 Tim. 4:1).
This second passage seems both to affirm the place of genuine prophecy
and to warn us against false prophecy. Prophecy, or claiming to prophesy, is always a sensitive and delicate business. The definition of much
prophecy as "applied teaching" by Hill, Müller, and Gillespie takes us

---

1. George T. Montague, *The Holy Spirit: The Growth of a Biblical Tradition* (Eugene,
OR: Wipf & Stock, 1976), p. 232.

onto much safer ground, but prophecy can sometimes denote more, if it is properly tested.

(v) Three further passages link the Holy Spirit with ordination and the ministry of the Church. 1 Timothy 4:14 commands, "Do not neglect the gift that is in you . . . through prophecy with the laying on of hands by the council of elders." The word for "gift" here is *charisma*. Prayer for the gift of the Holy Spirit accompanied by a corporate laying on of hands has been a key mark of ordination throughout the centuries. In 2 Tim. 1:6 the writer urges his audience to "Rekindle the gift of God that is within you through the laying on of my hands." One of Charles Wesley's hymns repeats this charge in the form of a prayer. Shortly after, 2 Tim. 1:14 has "Guard the good treasure entrusted to you, with the help of the Holy Spirit living in us."

The Pastoral Epistles take up some major themes on the Holy Spirit, which also reflect NT teaching elsewhere, but perhaps more closely relate to ministry, renewal, and later times than other writings.

(2) *Hebrews.* The epistle to the Hebrews is one of the most articulate, powerful, and theologically weighty writings of the New Testament. Differences of emphasis from Paul allow us to safely say that Paul was not its writer. This epistle stresses the ascension of Christ where Paul stresses resurrection; Hebrews emphasizes access to God while Paul emphasizes reconciliation; Hebrews stresses faith in contrast to sight while the present is still unseen, Paul on the other hand portrays faith as trust. One plausible reason for the anonymity of Hebrews is the possibility that it was written by a woman, perhaps Priscilla. If this were the case, some may have doubted the epistle's "apostolicity" and the theological competence of a woman, in spite of the acknowledgment elsewhere of Mary of Magdala and Junia as probable apostles. We cannot move from plausibility to certainty, however.

Westcott argues that "the action of the Holy Spirit falls into the background . . . from the characteristic view which is given of the priestly work of Christ."[2] There are some studies that seek to emphasize the Spirit in Hebrews.[3] The epistle contains four clear references to the Holy Spirit, along-

---

2. B. F. Westcott, *The Epistle to the Hebrews: The Greek Text,* 3rd ed. (New York: Macmillan, 1903), p. 331; similarly Henry B. Swete, *The Holy Spirit in the New Testament* (London: Macmillan, 1921), p. 249.

3. D. M. Allen, "The Forgotten Spirit: A Pentecostal Reading of the Letter to the Hebrews," *JPT* 18 (2009), pp. 51-66; quoted by Alan Hodson, "Hebrews," in Trevor J. Burke and Keith Warrington, eds., *A Biblical Theology of the Holy Spirit* (London: SPCK, 2014), pp. 226-37.

side other references to the human spirit (Heb. 4:12; 12:23); to angels as spirits (1:7, 14); and to other, more ambiguous spirits ("the eternal Spirit," 9:14; "the Father of spirits," 12:9). (Others suggest up to seven references.)

(i) The first allusion occurs in Heb. 2:4, in which "God added his testimony by signs and wonders and various miracles, and by gifts of the Holy Spirit, distributed according to his will." This is a section of practical exhortation in which readers are urged not to "drift" away from their course. It is a nautical metaphor, which suggests a ship slipping away or human lethargy. Drifting drains away faith. But attention to the testimony of God provides an antidote. It also has affinities with 1 Cor. 12:4-11; 2:4-5; and 1 Thess. 1:5, while signs and wonders are promised in Luke–Acts. In Heb. 2:4 "gifts of" is missing in the Greek, where the text reads literally "distributions (or 'apportionments') of the Holy Spirit." What the Spirit confirms is "the message declared . . . through the Lord" (2:2-3).

(ii) The second unambiguous reference occurs in Heb. 6:4, where the writer declares, "It is impossible to restore again to repentance those who have once been enlightened, and have tasted the heavenly gift, and have shared in the Holy Spirit." The basic theme is that readers must not compromise the complete and once-for-all nature of Christ's work by constantly "repeating" where they had begun. Every classic commentator, including F. F. Bruce, Hugh Montefiore, William Lane, Donald Hagner, and Harold Attridge, stresses the intended theme that "going on" or "continuance" is the test of the reality of the reader's faith and commitment. Continued zeal, Attridge and Bruce comment, is the only alternative to apostasy.[4] As Lane remarks, v. 6 argues that such apostasy would be like "crucifying again the Son of God."[5] Without the Holy Spirit, readers could never have come to faith; now humans cannot undo the work of God. If genuine apostasy ever occurs, this signifies that there never was an authentic coming to faith through the Holy Spirit, but only a "psychological" or intellectual apparent conversion.

This controversial passage is not primarily about simply the danger of falling away. It tells us that faith is always moving ahead, or if a Christian takes the logically impossible step of apostasy, appearances must have been deceptive. For the Christian, everything depends on Christ and the Holy Spirit.

---

4. Harold W. Attridge, *The Epistle to the Hebrews* (Philadelphia: Fortress, 1989), p. 166; F. F. Bruce, *The Epistle to the Hebrews* (Grand Rapids: Eerdmans, 1964), p. 112.

5. William L. Lane, *Hebrews 1–8* (Dallas: Word, 1991), p. 142.

(iii) The third unambiguous reference to the Holy Spirit affirms the traditional view that the Holy Spirit inspired Scripture: "As the Holy Spirit says, 'Today, if you hear his voice . . .'" (Heb. 3:7; quoting Ps. 95:7). This introduction is common to many Jewish and Christian sources. The writer repeats this view in 10:15-16, which quotes Jer. 31:33-34. It was to be taken up and endorsed by most of the church fathers, and it is a central theme in the Christian doctrine of the Holy Spirit. There is no contradiction between understanding the Psalms as *both* a word from the Holy Spirit *and* a human word from the Psalmist just as 10:15-16 regards a word of Scripture as spoken *both* by the Spirit *and* by Jeremiah. God addresses us through the Holy Spirit *and* through Scripture.

(iv) The fourth reference is akin to Heb. 6:4-6. Hebrews 10:29 speaks of "those who have spurned the Son of God . . . and outraged the Spirit of grace (*to pneuma tēs charitos enybrisas*)." The verb "outraged" suggests the *hubris,* or overwhelming arrogance, of apostasy, which constitutes an insult to the Holy Spirit.

The writer reminds Christians again of the solemn stakes pressed upon them by pressures to renounce their faith. Some suggest that these pressures are to seek a more secure existence in Judaism. Once God has revealed himself to them, the writer argues, such a relapse would be unthinkable. "The Spirit of grace" has already shown his generosity. Could this be flung back into his face? Never! Some suggest that this passage alludes to Zech. 12:10 (LXX version).

Hebrews may contain other references to the Holy Spirit, but the pertinent passages are more ambiguous. "Through the eternal Spirit" (*dia pneumatos aiōniou*) in Heb. 9:14-15 remains controversial. Swete proposes that it refers neither to the Holy Spirit nor to the spirit of Jesus, but must be understood in a general sense.[6] But Lane and Hodson argue that a reference to the Holy Spirit is an appropriate meaning.[7] The NRSV, REB, NIV, and AV/KJV accept this, translating "the eternal Spirit." Hodson adds one or two more references, including those which repeat other passages.

In conclusion, we should not draw too much from the relative infrequency of references to the Holy Spirit in this major theological and pastoral writing. Just as the centrality of Christ dominates the fourth gospel, so Hebrews writes primarily of the high priesthood of Christ, of access

---

6. Swete, *The Holy Spirit in the New Testament,* p. 252.

7. William L. Lane, *Hebrews 9–13* (Dallas: Word, 1991), p. 240; Hodson, "Hebrews," p. 229.

to God through his finished work, and of the progressive journey of faith towards a future which is, as yet, unseen. What references there are remain illuminating and instructive.

(3) *1 Peter.* Most writers agree that 1 Peter constitutes either a letter or sermon to those who have recently become Christians and may be about to become baptized. Estimates of the date of composition vary from A.D. 63 to the end of the century. It was probably written to churches in northern Asia Minor to encourage them to endure persecution patiently. A number have questioned Peter's authorship of this epistle, especially F. W. Beare. Cranfield gives eight reasons why we might doubt his authorship, but also argues that "this question is not settled," especially if we regard the style and vocabulary as the product of a secretary (such as Silvanus).[8] Additionally, some major scholars, including E. G. Selwyn, J. N. D Kelly, Ernest Best, and John Elliott, understood much or all of the epistle to reflect a very early common tradition, which may have connections with Peter.

1 Peter may include eight references to the Holy Spirit, or at least of the Greek word *pneuma.* Four constitute major ones.

(i) The first reference is to the traditional work of the Holy Spirit in the sanctification of Christians. 1 Peter 1:2 addresses those "chosen and destined by God the Father and sanctified by the Spirit to be obedient to Jesus Christ and to be sprinkled with his blood." The same sanctification phrase in Greek occurs in 2 Thess. 2:13. Since the verse refers to the initial cleansing in the blood of Jesus Christ, *sanctification* probably refers to the *process* of our becoming obedient in our attitudes and actions through the Spirit. This is the traditional meaning of sanctification. Verena Schafroth calls this "consecration," which is not wrong, but too readily suggests event rather than process.[9] The former is conveyed by the blood of the cross, which cleanses the latter by "obedience." She rightly calls 1 Pet. 1:2 one of the richest salutations in the NT, but while saying that the readers are "set apart for a particular task" may be true, it seems to go beyond the evidence.[10]

(ii) 1 Peter 1:11 repeats the traditional theme just noted in Hebrews: "The Spirit of Christ . . . testified in advance to the sufferings destined for Christ." In other words, the Holy Spirit inspired the Scriptural traditions

8. C. E. B. Cranfield, *1 and 2 Peter and Jude* (London: SCM. 1960), p. 16.
9. Verena Schafroth, "1 and 2 Peter," in Burke and Warrington, eds., *A Biblical Theology of the Holy Spirit,* pp. 238-49, here pp. 238-40.
10. Schafroth, "1 and 2 Peter," p. 240.

which spoke of the sufferings of the messiah. The same Spirit "brought you good news by the Holy Spirit sent from heaven — things into which angels long to look" (1:12). Angels can only stare and marvel at the blessings reserved for Christian believers. Schafroth argues correctly that the reference to the sprinkling of blood in Lev. 8:30 is turned "into a sound Christocentric declaration." This reflects the intimate relation between the Spirit and Christ found in Paul and John, and no doubt reflects early common apostolic teaching. Montague comments, "In 1:11 the Spirit of the OT prophets is identified as the Spirit of Christ."[11]

(iii) In 1 Pet. 3:18, "made alive in the Spirit" probably refers to Christ's resurrection by the Holy Spirit (Rom. 1:4; 8:11). Swete, on the other hand, regards it as "the human spirit of the Lord."[12] Best and Kelly disagree. Best asserts, "The contrast is not between two parts in Christ," and Kelly speaks of "heavenly existence, considered as divine Spirit."[13]

Two very controversial verses follow in 1 Pet. 3:19-20, in which Christ "went and made a proclamation to the spirits in prison, who in former times did not obey, when God waited patiently in the days of Noah, during the building of the ark . . ." From the time of Clement of Alexandria this has widely been understood to refer to Christ's descent into hell on Holy Saturday to proclaim the gospel before his resurrection.[14] Many regard "the spirits" as Noah's contemporaries. Some regard them as rebellious angels, but this depends on passages from the Apocrypha and intertestamental Jewish writings.[15] F. W. Beare concludes that the reference to Christ's "descent" scarcely deserves the attention that it has received.[16]

On the other hand Cranfield argues, "The descent into Hades is to be found elsewhere in the NT. It occurs in Acts 2:27, 31; Rom. 10:6-8; Eph. 4:8-10."[17] Acts 2:31 declares, "He was not abandoned to Hades" (quoting Ps. 16:10); Rom. 10:7 asks, "Who will descend into the abyss?" Rendel Harris proposed that "Enoch" was accidentally omitted from the text (1 Enoch 17–36 recounts Enoch's journey to the underworld). Conceivably Christ had preached through Enoch. But people still disagree about whether this

11. Montague, *The Holy Spirit,* p. 313.

12. Swete, *The Holy Spirit in the New Testament,* p. 262.

13. Ernest Best, *1 Peter* (London: Oliphants, 1971), p. 139; and J. N. D. Kelly, *The Epistles of Peter and Jude* (London: Black, 1969), p. 151.

14. Clement, *Miscellanies,* 6.6.44-46.

15. Jubilees 5:6, 1 Enoch 10–16.

16. F. W. Beare, *The First Epistle of Peter* (Oxford: Blackwell, 1961), p. 145.

17. Cranfield, *1 and 2 Peter and Jude,* p. 104.

was a proclamation of grace or of judgment. The passage is not central to Peter's theology of the Holy Spirit.

(iv) 1 Peter 4:14 associates the Spirit with Christ and glory. "The name of Christ . . . [is] the Spirit of glory (NRSV "spirit"), which is the Spirit of God . . . resting on you" (v. 14). The context is that of suffering and endurance. "Resting" (*anapauetai*) comes from Isa. 11:2 (LXX): "The Spirit of God shall rest upon him," which in turn anticipates John 1:32 and Paul. The author explains that principles operating through Christ's death and resurrection apply to believers through the Holy Spirit, who is their permanent gift. It also reflects the blessing of Matt. 5:11-12. Montague correctly sums up the teaching of the epistle: "The pneumatology of 1 Peter is . . . an enrichment of the tradition we have met elsewhere, especially in Paul."[18]

(4) *2 Peter, James, and Jude.* In effect there is only one major reference to the Holy Spirit in each of these short writings.

(i) The major reference in 2 Pet. 1:20-21 is a famous one. "No prophecy of Scripture (NRSV 'scripture') is a matter of one's own interpretation, because no prophecy ever came by human will, but men and women moved by the Holy Spirit spoke from God." The even more famous 2 Tim. 3:16 is parallel: "All Scripture is 'God-breathed (*theopneustos*)' " (NIV). The following verse in 2 Peter shows that the context is not only the Holy Spirit's inspiration of Scripture, but also that "false prophets also arose among the people, just as there will be false teachers among you, who will secretly bring in destructive opinions" (2 Pet. 2:1). False prophets, the writer later adds, "twist [texts] to their own destruction" (2 Pet. 3:16).

The passage in question (1:20-21) is intended to correct an abuse of Scripture by false teachers in the church. As we noted above in the discussion of 1 John, in the NT false prophecy is just as serious and disastrous a phenomenon as it was in Deuteronomy. Careful study of the Scripture through the Holy Spirit of Christ is one antidote to this. Montague comments in the light of 1 Cor. 2:10-16, "Since the prophecies of Scripture were inspired by the Holy Spirit, you need the Holy Spirit to interpret them."[19] We need to add, however, that careful, disciplined study of Scripture as God's Word goes hand in hand with openness to God's Spirit. This is not only "study" of the Scriptures, but *listening* to them in such a way that Scripture shapes us.

18. Montague, *The Holy Spirit*, p. 315.
19. Montague, *The Holy Spirit*, p. 315.

(ii) James 4:5 also offers profound and basic teaching: "The Scripture (NRSV 'scripture') says, 'God yearns jealously for the Spirit that he made to dwell (*katōkisen*) in us.'" We fully endorse Swete's interpretation of this verse. Swete paraphrases: "The Spirit of Christ in us longs after us, but jealously, with a love which resents any counteracting force such as the friendship of the world."[20] This rightly presupposes, or implies, the personhood of the Holy Spirit, and is parallel with "do not grieve the Holy Spirit of God" (Eph. 4:30). Too much friendly preoccupation with the world provokes the Holy Spirit to jealousy in his passionate love for us.

The relative infrequency of references to the Holy Spirit in James may, as Peter Davids suggests, owe something to the place of wisdom in this book. Davids claims that it partly reflects the role of the Spirit in Paul.[21]

(iii) Jude has only one chapter, and many parallels with 2 Peter. A reference to the Holy Spirit occurs in vv. 19-20. Jude speaks of scoffers who indulge their own lusts, commenting that they are "devoid of the Spirit." Jude's "worldly people" claimed to be "spiritual" (*psychikoi*) but were not so at all. The passage is reminiscent of 1 Cor. 3:1-3, and less directly of 1 Cor. 2:14-16. Kelly, probably rightly, argues that these people divide the community by promoting elitism as self-styled "spiritual people."[22] Romans 8:26-27 and 1 Cor. 14:15 similarly speak of the Holy Spirit as the inspirer of prayer.

(5) *Revelation.* There are three notorious barriers to modern readers' understanding and appreciation of this wonderful book. First, the writer is steeped in Old Testament allusions and imagery. It is not surprising that so many fail to understand the book's meaning when it uses constant allusions to Ezekiel, Daniel, and other writings, without spelling passages out or explaining them, because the writer assumes that the readers know their OT in detail. The OT was in effect the Christians' Bible in earliest days. One example of OT allusion concerns the use of "seven." In Daniel "seven" is seldom a numerical unit; neither is it in Revelation. It usually signifies completeness or wholeness.

Second, the author writes as both a prophet and an apocalypticist. In the first century, the convention and images of Jewish apocalyptic would have been well known among Christians. Today most readers have hardly heard of them.

---

20. Swete, *The Holy Spirit in the New Testament*, p. 257.
21. Peter H. Davids, *The Epistle of James: A Commentary on the Greek Text* (Grand Rapids: Eerdmans, 1982), p. 56.
22. Kelly, *The Epistles of Peter and Jude*, p. 284.

Third, Revelation is highly symbolic. As George Caird comments in his commentary, often "to analyse" the book is like trying "to unweave the rainbow."[23] Symbols are chosen for their emotional and evocative power, not for literalist description, as if Revelation were a modern photograph or chronological chart. Do heavenly horses have heavenly stables, which need to be mucked out? Is the Bride of the Lamb really the height and breadth of the New Jerusalem? Do its jewels reflect a monetary value, or are they the jewels of a high-priestly robe?

(i) Our first reference to the Holy Spirit must be interpreted with these three points in mind. Revelation 1:4; 3:1; 4:5; and 5:6 speak of "the seven spirits (of God)." The first passage relates this numerically to the seven churches to whom the author writes (1:4); the others to the seven angels of the Presence in Tobit 12:15. But "seven" is used throughout the book as *a symbol of completeness or perfection.* "Seven" churches probably denotes the Church at large. "Seven spirits" is surely the Holy Spirit in all his complete perfection.[24] It is not numerical, any more than the Holy Trinity is *numerically* "three," as Gregory of Nyssa and Gregory of Nazianzus emphatically point out. The same probably applies to "seven eyes" (Rev. 5:6; Zech. 3:9); seven seals (Rev. 5:1, 5; 8:1); seven stars (Rev. 1:16, 20; 2:1); seven lamps (Rev. 4:5); seven trumpets (Rev. 10:3, 4); seven heads (Rev. 12:3; 13:1; 17:9), and so on.

(ii) The next phrase to consider is "in the Spirit" (Rev. 1:10; 4:2; 17:3; 21:10). Swete describes this as "a state of mental exaltation," but Montague connects it with "prophecy," including committing "the prophecy to writing."[25] Swete also concedes that this heightened state facilitates sights and sounds which remain inaudible to other people. Some reject the view that these four passages allude to the Holy Spirit. Revelation constitutes a prophecy, and yet warns against false prophecy, especially in the case of "Jezebel, who calls herself a prophet . . . beguiling my servants" (2:20). The "beast" of Rev. 13:11-18 performs signs by which it "deceives . . . This calls for wisdom" (13:14, 18). Similar references occur in Rev. 16:13-14; 19:20; and 20:10. The "false prophet" here has affinities with 1 John 4:1-3.

(iii) Revelation 11:11 could be translated: "The breath of life from God

23. George B. Caird, *The Revelation of St. John the Divine* (London: Black, 1966), p. 25.

24. Richard Bauckham, "Scripture and Authority," *Transformation* 15 (1998), pp. 5-11, also takes this view (p. 6).

25. Swete, *The Holy Spirit in the New Testament,* pp. 276-77; Montague, *The Holy Spirit,* p. 323.

entered them" (NRSV). But in the light of Ezek. 37:9 and 37:14, it may well be an allusion to the Spirit of God.

(iv) Revelation 14:13 clearly mentions the Holy Spirit. A voice from heaven is heard and the response to it is: "'Yes,' says the Spirit, 'they will rest from their labors.'" This is a further reference to the Holy Spirit of prophecy, together with Rev. 19:10. Montague sums up the point: "Prophecy occupies a central place in Revelation."[26]

(v) The final explicit reference to the Spirit comes in Rev. 22:17, where "the Spirit and the Bride say, 'Come.'" The Holy Spirit yearns over the life of the Church for completion and triumph, which is the Bride. The Spirit reproduces in the life of the Church *his own longing for the return of Christ*. Woodman interprets this differently. He writes, "The Church and the Spirit join their voices in calling the nations of the world . . . to enter in and drink from the river of life . . . (22:1-2)."[27] Whichever interpretation we follow, here the Holy Spirit, as in Romans 8, longs for God's blessings within the heart and within the community, and joins his longing with ours.

In addition to the above major passages, many allusions and implied allusions occur. *Listening* to the Holy Spirit and obeying him occur in Rev. 2:7: "Let anyone who has an ear listen to what the Spirit is saying to the churches"; this is repeated in Rev. 2:11, 17, 29; 3:6, 13, 22. Implied allusions may occur in the divine seal with which the redeemed are marked (Rev. 7:2-3; 9:4; 13:16; 22:4). This would accord with Eph. 1:13-14; 4:30. Only the Spirit, it can be argued, could provide the ever-new "river of the water of life" (22:1). Once we move from explicit to implied references, references become innumerable. The Spirit bestows on us the post-resurrection life, which is central to understanding the sovereign victory of God in Revelation.

---

26. Montague, *The Holy Spirit*, p. 322.

27. Simon P. Woodman, "The 'Seal' of the Spirit: The Holy Spirit in the Book of Revelation," Johnson T. K. Lim, ed., *Holy Spirit: Unfinished Agenda* (Singapore: Armour, 2015), pp. 75-78, here p. 77.

PART II

Doctrinal Themes

CHAPTER 8

The Holy Spirit and the Trinity: The Spirit's Shared Status with God

(1) *The New Testament.* Many NT scholars regard the doctrine of the Trinity as emerging only in the fourth century with Athanasius and Basil. But in current NT scholarship dissenting voices are emerging both concerning Paul and some of the apostolic fathers. At the time of writing, Wesley Hill has produced *Paul and the Trinity* (2015), and support for its argument comes from Francis Watson, Louis Ayres, Richard Bauckham, Angus Paddison, and others.[1] Hill examines the Pauline epistles, especially 1 Cor. 8:6 and 15:20-28, and Pauline monotheism.

In addition to this, Jürgen Moltmann, Wolfhart Pannenberg, and Eugene Rogers have elaborated a careful approach to the Holy Trinity in terms of NT *narrative* that presupposes or teaches a Trinitarian framework. Moltmann insists, "The New Testament talks about God by proclaiming in narrative the relationship of the Father, the Son and the Spirit."[2] The Father "sends" the Son, the Son obeys the Father, and the Spirit raises the Son (John 3:16; Rom. 8:11).[3] Pannenberg sees the Holy Spirit at work "at every critical point in his [Jesus'] life," and argues that the Spirit "instituted Jesus into his Sonship."[4] He adds, "The fellowship of Jesus as Son with God as Father can obviously be stated only if there is reference to a third as well, the Holy Spirit."[5]

---

1. Wesley Hill, *Paul and the Trinity: Persons, Relations, and the Pauline Letters* (Grand Rapids: Eerdmans, 2015).

2. Jürgen Moltmann, *The Trinity and the Kingdom of God* (London: SCM, 1981), p. 64.

3. Moltmann, *The Trinity,* p. 88.

4. Wolfhart Pannenberg, *Systematic Theology,* 3 vols. (Grand Rapids: Eerdmans, 1991-98), 1.7-10, 36-37, 266.

5. Pannenberg, *Systematic Theology,* 1.267.

Eugene Rogers spells out a number of NT narratives which involve the Father, the Son, and the Spirit as agents. He cites narrative of the resurrection, of the Annunciation, of the baptism of Jesus, of the Transfiguration, and of the Ascension and Pentecost.[6] Probably the clearest of these is the baptism of Jesus (Mark 1:9-11 and parallels, in all four gospels). The *Holy Spirit* "descended like a dove" on Jesus; the *Fath*er said, "You are my Son, the Beloved"; *Jesus* showed obedient solidarity with the people of God. Rogers comments, "The baptism of Jesus is primarily to be understood as an intra-Trinitarian event."[7] God the Father, the Son, and the Holy Spirit all share in the event. John Zizioulas points out that the Holy Spirit takes the initiative in the conception and birth of Jesus, and the Trinity reflect his very nature as a relational being. He writes, "There is, so to say, no Christ until the Spirit is at work."[8]

Without question, from the point of view of preaching and teaching, this *narrative* approach is far easier for a congregation or class to understand than numeral analogies involving shamrocks. As we see in the works of Gregory of Nyssa and Gregory of Nazianzus, numerals or number juggling cannot be applied to the Holy Trinity in any arithmetical sense.

In the same vein Larry Hurtado has shown that the accommodation of Pauline monotheism to include reverence for Christ as a God-like figure has nothing to do with numerals. The "one" God alludes in the first place to the totality of Israel's and Paul's devotion. Paul readily speaks of "one God, the Father, from whom are all things . . . and one Lord, Jesus Christ" (1 Cor. 8:6).[9] Similarly, as we have argued above, the presence of the Holy Spirit signifies the presence and power of God himself. Gordon Fee has made this point clearly.[10]

There are many other telltale hints of all this in the NT. Luke's reference to the performance of the mighty works of Jesus "by the finger of God" (11:20) becomes "by the Spirit of God" in Matthew (12:28). The agent

6. Eugene F. Rogers, *After the Spirit: A Constructive Pneumatology* (London: SCM, 2006), pp. 75-207.

7. Rogers, *After the Spirit,* p. 136.

8. John D. Zizioulas, *Being as Communion* (New York: St. Vladimir's Seminary Press, 1985), p. 127.

9. Larry W. Hurtado, *Lord Jesus Christ: Devotion to Jesus in Earliest Christianity* (Grand Rapids: Eerdmans, 2003), pp. 50-53.

10. Gordon D. Fee, *God's Empowering Presence: The Holy Spirit in the Letters of Paul* (Milton Keynes: Paternoster, 1995 / Peabody, MA: Hendrickson, 1994), throughout.

is primarily Jesus himself, but "finger of God" suggests that this is also God the Father, and "Spirit of God" suggests that it is the Holy Spirit. Matthew and Luke are not concerned with over-sharp distinctions. The phenomena of Pentecost in Acts 2 point not only to the Spirit and Christ, but to OT manifestations of God — for example, in the burning bush (Exod. 3:2), the pillar of fire by night (Exod. 13:21-22), God's speaking out of the fire (Exod. 3:13-15), and God's having a throne of fire (Dan. 7:9-10). Romans 8:11 portrays the shared activity of the Trinity in the resurrection: "If the Spirit of him who raised Jesus from the dead dwells in you, he who raised Christ from the dead will give life to your mortal bodies also through the Spirit that dwells in you."

As we shall see, the fourth-century church fathers made careful exegetical use of 1 Cor. 12:4-6: "The same Spirit . . . the same Lord . . . the same God who activates all of them [gifts] in everyone." In addition to all this, Arthur Wainwright comments on Paul: "These verses are evidence that God, Christ, and the Spirit, were to the forefront of Paul's mind."[11] Origen, Athanasius, and Basil of Caesarea incessantly appeal to biblical texts, especially to 1 Corinthians, as Michael Haykin has conclusively demonstrated.[12]

The significance of this for our shorter book is that, although many readers may be reluctant to spend much time and study on the church fathers, on the subject of the Holy Spirit and his personhood we shall look in greater detail at the fathers of the early Church, more than in other topics. Hints and implications of the Holy Spirit clearly go back to some of the apostolic fathers, to the early apologists, to Clement of Alexandria, to Tertullian, to Origen, and to Novatian. But the main sources for a developed doctrine of the Holy Trinity and the Holy Spirit's shared status with God come from Athanasius, Basil, Hilary, and Ambrose.

(2) *From the Second Century to the Council of Nicaea.* Before we trace historical developments from Clement of Rome, Ignatius, and the *Didachē* to Justin, Irenaeus, Tertullian, and onwards, one brief word of caution should be included. Emil Brunner is one of many who draw a misleading contrast between the Spirit-filled fellowship of the NT and the institutionalization of the Church. Much of his argument comes in *The Misunderstanding of the Church,* but some also appears in two more substantial

---

11. Arthur W. Wainwright, *The Trinity in the New Testament* (London: SPCK, 1962), p. 24.

12. Michael A. G. Haykin, *The Spirit of God: The Exegesis of 1 & 2 Corinthians in the Pneumatomachian Controversy of the Fourth Century* (Leiden: Brill, 1994).

volumes.[13] He writes, "The institutions which we call the Church through a historical process of nearly 2,000 years have built up the shell in which the precious kernel has been contained and preserved."[14] Brunner argues that from the close of the apostolic period, episcopacy and sacramentalism have distorted the Church.[15] His claims are controversial. But even many Protestants regard Ignatius's emphasis on episcopacy as having more to do with the unity of the Church than with obedience to a hierarchy. Nevertheless the point deserves note, even if it serves primarily as a caution about certain developments.

At the beginning of the second century Ignatius (c. 107-12), in a well-known passage, understands God the Father, Jesus Christ, and the Holy Spirit to work together for our salvation. One of his analogies may be crude, but it is also telling. He writes that believers are "made ready for the building of God our Father, carried up to its heights by the engine of Jesus Christ, that is, the cross, and using the rope of the Holy Spirit."[16] Almost as early, Polycarp (d. 155) gives glory to the Holy Spirit, together with the Father and the Son, according to Eusebius.[17] The *Didachē* (c. 90-120) twice speaks of baptism "in the name of the Father, the Son, and the Holy Spirit."[18]

Among the Apologists, Athenagoras (c. 180) states that the Father, the Son, and the Holy Spirit are one "by the unity and power of the Spirit (*henotēti kai dynamei pneumatos*)."[19] God is no more separate from the Holy Spirit than a sun-ray is separate from the sun.[20] Justin (c. 100–c. 165) does not yet write on the coequality of the Holy Trinity, but he speaks of Jesus Christ as "in the second place" to God, and the Holy Spirit "in the third."[21]

Irenaeus (c. 130–c. 200), bishop of Lyons in 180, develops the traditions from both the Eastern and Western Churches. He regards Christ

13. Emil Brunner, *The Misunderstanding of the Church* (London: Lutterworth, repr. 2002); idem, *Truth as Encounter* (Philadelphia: Westminster, 1964); and his *Dogmatics,* vol. 3: *The Christian Doctrine of the Church, Faith and Consummation* (London: Lutterworth, 1962), pp. 3-133.

14. Brunner, *The Misunderstanding of the Church,* p. 116.

15. Brunner, *The Misunderstanding of the Church,* pp. 77-78.

16. Ignatius, *To the Ephesians,* 9:1 (in Lake, *Apostolic Fathers,* 1.183).

17. Eusebius, *Church History,* 5:15.

18. *Didachē,* 7:1-3 (in Lake, *Apostolic Fathers,* 1.319-21).

19. Athenagoras, *Embassy,* 10:3.

20. Athenagoras, *Embassy,* 10:3, 12.

21. Justin, *First Apology,* 13 (*ANF,* 1.166-67).

and the Holy Spirit as "of the same order of being as God."[22] He sees the Son and the Spirit as "the two hands of God."[23] He continues, "The Word, namely the Son, was always with the Father . . . Wisdom also, which is the Spirit, was present with him and anterior to all creation."[24] Clement of Alexandria (c. 150–c. 215) claimed that even Plato's "order of beings" in the *Timaeus* really understood "nothing else than the Trinity to be meant, for the Spirit is the third (in order) and the Son the second."[25] Tertullian (c. 160-220) expounds the Trinity in his work *Against Praxeas.* He appeals to John 14:16, 20, and 16:14. [26] He argues, "Neither the Son nor the Holy Spirit is separable from the Father in the way in which emanation in Valentinus would be."[27] He adds, "I believe the Spirit to proceed from no other source than from the Father through the Son." [28]

Origen of Alexandria (c. 185–c. 254) states that the Holy Spirit works "with the cooperation of the entire Trinity," and "it is impossible to become partakers of the Father or the Son without the Holy Spirit." [29] He declares that baptism remains "not complete, except by the authority of the most excellent Trinity of them all."[30] The Holy Spirit is neither "made" (*factura*) nor "created" (*creatura*).[31] This basic principle would be emphasized in more detail by Athanasius and Basil. Even though Origen also says that the Son and the Spirit are inferior to the Father, this comment is "economical," i.e., in terms of their work in the world, rather than ontological.

Hippolytus (c. 170–c. 236) also asserts that there is one God, yet the Holy Spirit and Christ remain distinct persons. He appeals in this connection to Rom. 8:11, where Paul declares, "He shall question your mortal body by the Holy Spirit, who dwells in you."[32] His rival Novatian (perhaps c. 210–c. 280) produced his work *On the Trinity,* which some regard as a bridge between Tertullian and Augustine. Most of this treatise defends the deity of Jesus Christ, but chapter 29 also concerns the Holy Spirit, who

22. Irenaeus, *Against Heresies,* 1.12.7 (*ANF,* 1.372).
23. Irenaeus, *Against Heresies,* 4.20.1 (*ANF,* 1.487).
24. Irenaeus, *Against Heresies,* 4.20.3 (*ANF,* 1.488).
25. Clement, *Miscellanies,* 5.14 (*ANF,* 2.468).
26. Tertullian, *Against Praxeas,* 25 (*ANF,* 3.621).
27. Tertullian, *Against Praxeas,* 8 (*ANF,* 3.603).
28. Tertullian, *Against Praxeas,* 4 (*ANF,* 3.599).
29. Origen, *On First Principles,* 1.3 (*ANF,* 4.253).
30. Origen, *On First Principles,* 1.3 (*ANF,* 4.252).
31. Origen, *On First Principles,* 1.3 (*ANF,* 4.252).
32. Hippolytus, *Against Noetus,* 2.4 (*ANF,* 5.225).

anointed the Messiah, while chapter 30 includes references to "the Father, the Son and the Holy Spirit" as the Church's rule of faith.[33]

(3) *Athanasius and Basil.* In the history of works on the Holy Spirit, the post-Nicene fourth century represents a high point in elaborating the *person* of Spirit and the Trinity. In the medieval, Reformation, and post-Reformation periods more attention is paid to the Spirit's *work,* in revelation, sanctification, spiritual gifts, and other aspects.

Athanasius of Alexandria (c. 296-373) opposed not only Arianism, which denied the eternal divinity of Christ, but also the *Tropici* or *Pneumatomachi,* who denied the eternal divinity of the Holy Spirit. Again and again Athanasius insists that the Holy Spirit is not a creature (*ktisma*). To call him such is "blasphemy against the Holy Triad."[34] When in Rom. 8:16 Paul writes of the "Spirit bearing witness with our spirit," "Spirit" does not mean *wind:* the wind is a created thing; the Spirit is not.[35] "If He were a created thing," he repeats, "He would not be ranked with the Triad. For the whole Triad is one God."[36] The equivalent today to the Tropici would be to call the Holy Spirit "it," as if he were a "thing," or part of God's creation.

Athanasius continues with the assertion that the Father and the Spirit cannot be separated. This is clear from the teaching of Jesus and from Pauline and apostolic preaching.[37] Commenting on the Council of Nicea, he affirms: "Our faith is in the Father, Son, and Holy Spirit."[38] The Spirit is "indivisible from the Son,"[39] as "the grace" of 2 Cor. 13:13 indicates.

Basil of Caesarea (c. 329-79) continues and builds on the work of Athanasius. In his treatise *On the Holy Spirit* he insists, following Didymus, that the Holy Spirit is coequal and coessential with God. He was a learned student of the Bible as well as Nicene theology. The Spirit is "of the same nature" or "same being" (*homoousios*) as God, just as Christ is. He recalls that he urged the churches to give glory in coequal measure to God the Father "with the Son, together with the Holy Spirit."[40] Like Athanasius, he attacks the *Pneumatomachi* regarding their contention that "the Spirit is

33. Novatian, *Treatise concerning the Trinity,* 30:1 (*ANF,* 5.641).

34. Athanasius, *First Epistle to Serapion,* 1:10, 16 (Eng. C. R. B. Shapland, *The Letters of St. Athanasius concerning the Holy Spirit* [London: Epworth, 1951], p. 30).

35. Athanasius, *First Epistle to Serapion,* 1:7-9 (Shapland, *Letters,* pp. 77-79).

36. Athanasius, *First Epistle to Serapion,* 1:17 (Shapland, *Letters,* p. 103).

37. Athanasius, *First Epistle to Serapion,* 1:28-31 (Shapland, *Letters,* pp. 121-24).

38. Athanasius, *First Epistle to Serapion,* 2:6 (Shapland, *Letters,* p. 160).

39. Athanasius, *First Epistle to Serapion,* 3:5 (Shapland, *Letters,* p. 181).

40. Basil, *On the Holy Spirit,* 1:3 (*NPNF,* ser. 2, 8.3).

not to be ranked alongside the Son and the Father."[41] In *On the Holy Spirit* chapters 2–8 he examines a number of relevant biblical passages.

When Scripture uses "through whom," Basil continues, this applies to Jesus Christ and the Holy Spirit alike.[42] Paul frequently associates together the Father, the Son, and the Holy Spirit, as working together for the same purpose.[43] Chapters 17–22 return to the theme of the coequality, deity, and glorification of the Holy Spirit. The Trinitarian name must be used in baptism, he stresses, and "according to the co-ordination of words delivered in baptism, the relation of the Spirit to the Son is the same as that of the Son to the Father. And if the Spirit is co-ordinate with the Son, and the Son with the Father, it is obvious that the Spirit is also co-ordinate with the Father."[44] Basil then adds, "The Holy Spirit . . . [is] conjoined . . . to the one Father through the one Son . . . completing the adorable and blessed Trinity."[45] Basil explores many other aspects of the Holy Spirit's person and work, but his utter belief in the Holy Trinity is abundantly clear.

(4) *Gregory of Nyssa and Gregory of Nazianzus.* The first of these two figures, Gregory of Nyssa (c. 330-95), was Basil's younger brother. At Basil's urging, he became bishop of Nyssa, much against his will. Both Gregory of Nyssa and Gregory of Nazianzus disentangled any supposed numerical significance of "three," as if the Holy Trinity were like a society of "three" human beings. This emerges in Gregory of Nyssa's six-page treatise *On "Not Three Gods"* (with no numbered sections), as well as in *On the Trinity*. There is no evidence at all, Gregory insists, that the Father "does anything by himself," as if he were one among three; similarly, it is false to assert that "the Son does not work conjointly," but every operation of God "has its origin in the Father, and proceeds through the Son, and is perfected in the Holy Spirit."[46] Moreover, "the Deity is spoken of in the singular as one God and one Godhead, even though the Three Persons are not separated . . ."[47]

Gregory of Nazianzus (c. 330-90), Basil's friend, makes the issue about the non-numerical nature of "three" of the Trinity still clearer. He finds "a swarm of biblical texts" which imply the deity of the Spirit. In contrast to some who had accorded different rank to the Father, the

---

41. Basil, *On the Holy Spirit,* 6:13 (*NPNF,* ser. 2, 8.8).
42. Basil, *On the Holy Spirit,* 5:10 (*NPNF,* ser. 2, 8.7).
43. Basil, *On the Holy Spirit,* 13:29 (*NPNF,* ser. 2, 8.18-19).
44. Basil, *On the Holy Spirit,* 17:43 (*NPNF,* ser. 2, 8.27).
45. Basil, *On the Holy Spirit,* 18:45 (*NPNF,* ser. 2, 8.28).
46. Gregory of Nyssa, *On "Not Three Gods"* (*NPNF,* ser. 2, 5.334).
47. Gregory of Nyssa, *On "Not Three Gods"* (*NPNF,* ser. 2, 5.334).

Son, and the Spirit, Gregory insists that each is of "co-equal honour."[48] The Holy Spirit is "most certainly God . . . He is consubstantial . . . He is God."[49] But the Trinity is "not Three Gods."[50] Gregory explores various analogies. We can speak of "three Peters," or three fountains, or three rivers. But this is because they are contingent *creatures*.[51] One could even speak of three angels. Today, he might say the same about analogies with shamrock, a three-leaf clover, and the rest. It is unhelpful to "count" the manifestations of God, as if to speak "of three gods."[52] For these are not "creatures."

Gregory is brilliant at what today we call logical or linguistic analysis. If we conceive of "two sons," he argues, they must either be twins, or one "older" than the other.[53] Most of all, he reflects, to speak of "three men" or "three gods" would be quite different from trying to apply "three" to the Holy Trinity. Thus "Peter, James and John" may be "three" because they are "not consubstantial" (or one in Being); even "Three Peters" or "Three Johns" are different from the Father, the Son, and the Spirit, *for in this latter case "three" cannot be numerical, as if they were independent "things"* (my italics).[54] Gregory has identified a key issue, which theologians, teachers, and preachers would do well to observe carefully today, especially when they try to weave self-created analogies rather than following biblical narrative about the unique states of the Holy Trinity.

(5) *The Post-Nicene Fathers in the Western Church, especially Hilary, Ambrose, and Augustine.* Athanasius and the Eastern Church, as well as Tertullian and Origen, profoundly influenced Hilary of Poitiers (c. 312-67/68). He produced twelve books *On the Trinity* (362), arguing that the Father and the Son are "one" (*unus*), and "no difference is revealed to serve them."[55] We confess one God, in whom the Holy Spirit "is joined with the Father and the Son" (Gal. 4:6; 1 Cor. 2:12; Rom. 8:9).[56] He discusses 1 Cor. 12:4-9, in which "all Persons of the Trinity are involved." The Holy Spirit is emphatically *not* a "creature, seeing that he proceeds from

---

48. Gregory of Nyssa, *On "Not Three Gods"* (*NPNF,* ser. 2, 7.322).

49. Gregory of Nyssa, *On "Not Three Gods"* (*NPNF,* ser. 2, 7.321).

50. Gregory of Nyssa, *On "Not Three Gods"* (*NPNF,* ser. 2, 7.322).

51. Gregory of Nyssa, *On "Not Three Gods"* (*NPNF,* ser. 2, 7.328).

52. Gregory of Nyssa, *On "Not Three Gods"* (*NPNF,* ser. 2, 7.323).

53. Gregory of Nyssa, *On "Not Three Gods"* (*NPNF,* ser. 2, 7.320).

54. Gregory of Nyssa, *On "Not Three Gods"* (*NPNF,* ser. 2, 7.323).

55. Hilary, *On the Trinity,* 7.2 (*NPNF,* ser. 2, 9.118).

56. Hilary, *On the Trinity,* 7.2 (*NPNF,* ser. 2, 9.118).

You [God]."[57] The unity and diversity of the Church reflect the unity and diversity of God.

Ambrose of Milan (c. 339-97) was elected bishop of Milan by popular acclamation on the death of his predecessor in 374. He insists, "The Holy Spirit is not among, but above, all things (*non inter omnia, sed super omnia, spiritus sanctus est*)."[58] Like Athanasius and Basil, Ambrose constantly asserts that the Holy Spirit is not a creature, not a thing, not an "it." He follows in insisting that the Holy Spirit is to be glorified, along with the Father and the Son. He carefully expounds 1 Cor. 12:4-7, arguing that "the same God" prohibits the "severing of the Trinity."[59] In all acts God the Father, the Son, and the Holy Spirit work *together* and are *inseparable*.

Today this profound truth is regularly neglected, as when worshipers select a person of the Trinity for their prayer, even if after long perplexity. It can never be wrong to address God as Father, as Jesus did. Ambrose repeats, "The Holy Spirit is of one will and operation with God the Father."[60] In passing, he observes, "The whole of the divine gifts cannot exist in each . . . man."[61]

Augustine of Hippo (354-430) was the last of the great church fathers of the West, unless we include Gregory of Rome. But Gregory's world was of a different, more medieval kind, which was dominated by the Church. The most distinctive feature which is most widely known is Augustine's conception of the Holy Spirit as the bond of mutual love between the Father and the Son. The advantage of this view is no longer to define the Holy Spirit only in relation to our world of human beings, as if what he does for *us* is the sum of his nature. In his work *On the Trinity*, Augustine writes that the Father, the Son, and the Spirit "are God, one alone (*deus unus, solus*) . . . That [their] communion is consubstantial and co-eternal . . . but [the Spirit] is more aptly called love (*caritas*) . . . God is love."[62]

Perhaps the two church fathers who most influenced Augustine were Gregory of Nazianzus and Ambrose, whose preaching he heard. He had reservations about speaking of "three persons," most of all in any numerical sense. But he regards the Father, Son, and Spirit as "memory, understanding and will, not three 'lives', but 'one life'; not three minds, but one mind

57. Hilary, *On the Trinity*, 17.55 (*NPNF*, ser. 2, 9.233).
58. Ambrose, *On the Holy Spirit*, 1.1.19 (*NPNF*, ser. 2, 10.96).
59. Ambrose, *On the Holy Spirit*, 2.12.138 (*NPNF*, ser. 2, 10.132).
60. Ambrose, *On the Holy Spirit*, 2.12.142 (*NPNF*, ser. 2, 10.133).
61. Ambrose, *On the Holy Spirit*, 2.12.150 (*NPNF*, ser. 2, 10.134).
62. Augustine, *On the Trinity*, 6.5.7 (*NPNF*, ser. 1, 3.100).

. . . One mind and one essence [being]" (*una essentia*).[63] In modern times Karl Barth would experience the same hesitancy about "three persons." Nevertheless, God is still relational. Augustine writes, "The Holy Spirit according to the Scriptures is neither of the Father alone, nor of the Son alone, but of both, and so intimates to us a mutual love."[64] Augustine's theology of the Holy Spirit and the Trinity set the tone for virtually the whole of the medieval Western Church as well as for the Reformation and post-Reformation Church.

(6) *Thomas Aquinas* (c. 1225-74) expounds his theology of the Trinity in the first part of his *Summa Theologiae,* qu. 27-43. Like Augustine, he insists on "the double procession" of the Holy Spirit, i.e., he proceeds from the Father and the Son, and is emphatically not "made" or "created," as if he were a "thing." Thomas concludes, "The Holy Spirit is from the Father and the Son, not made, not begotten, but proceeding."[65] Aquinas also adds the second of Augustine's concerns: "The name 'Love of God' . . . if taken personally . . . is the proper name of the Holy Spirit, as Word is the proper name of the Son."[66] Like Augustine, he also says many things about the work of the Holy Spirit, which come under other headings than the Trinity.

After Aquinas, other Western medieval writers, such as Catherine of Siena (1347-80), follow Augustine in the "double procession." She affirms the Spirit's procession from the Father and the Son.[67] Julian of Norwich (1342-1416) follows similarly: The Father, the Son, and the Spirit are inseparable: "Where Jesus appears, the blessed Trinity is understood."[68] In the Reformation era Martin Luther (1483-1546) follows the orthodox Augustinian view, although he stresses the Spirit's work in sanctification more strongly. John Calvin (1509-64) and the other "magisterial" Reformers follow the same path. The post-Reformation writers add little of substance on this subject, although Owen has very helpful insights into sanctification and other matters. Trinitarian orthodoxy is presupposed in John Owen (1616-83), Jeremy Taylor (1613-67), Philipp Spener (1635-1705), John Wesley (1703-91), and Jonathan Edwards (1703-58).

---

63. Augustine, *On the Trinity,* 10.11.18 (*NPNF,* ser. 1, 3.142).

64. Augustine, *On the Trinity,* 15.17.1 (*NPNF,* ser. 1, 3.215).

65. Aquinas, *Summa Theologiae,* 60 vols. (London: Eyre & Spottiswoode / New York: McGraw-Hill, 1964-81), 1, qu. 36, art. 2, reply.

66. Aquinas, *Summa Theologiae,* 1, qu. 37, art. 1, reply.

67. Catherine, *Dialogue* (London: Kegan Paul, Trench, & Trubner, 1907) §78.

68. Julian, *Revelations of Divine Love* (Longer text; London: Penguin, 1968) 4 §2.

(7) The next genuinely new stage of thought came with Georg W. F. Hegel (1770-1851). Hegel was more a philosopher or philosophical theologian than a theologian in the strict sense. He produced his *Phenomenology of Spirit* (*Geist*) in 1807. In this work and in his *Science of Logic* (1812-16) he postulated a ladder of "speculative dialectic of identity and difference," in which a "higher" stage involves a separation (or negation), mediation, and synthesis. When it is applied to the world, each finite reality raises itself (*erheben*) and "sublates" (*aufheben*) itself into something higher.

Hegel applied this not only to the world and to logic, but to the being of God. God the Father, he speculates, is Absolute Spirit. The incarnation becomes a negation of this, especially the death of Christ. God the Son expresses the antithesis of Absolute Spirit by becoming earthly, finite, and subject to death. This manifestation permits a *differentiation* in God, in which the Absolute becomes relative to time and location. However, Calvary and the Holy Spirit are, in effect, the death of death. Hegel carries the process forward, as the Spirit raises Christ and is poured out on the people of God. God once again reigns as Spirit. He is God's crowning revelation.

Hegel expounds this more fully in vol. 3 of his *Lectures on the Philosophy of Religion*. God was "the absolute, the eternal Idea . . . in and for itself, God in his eternity before the creations of the World."[69] But God creates "otherness" or "other-Being."[70] The Divine "unfolds itself in . . . three forms . . . in the process of self-differentiation."[71] He makes a very practical polemical application of this. He writes, "It is possible also to occupy a standpoint at which we do not get beyond the Son. . . . This is the case in Catholicism."[72] In Hegel's view the Roman Catholic Church absolutizes the crucified Christ in a *static crucifix,* bracketing out the third triumphant stage. It omits the Spirit and a truly "spiritual" community, retaining an "outward" formal religion in place of an inner one.[73] It stifles subjectivity in fixed institutionalism and dogma.

In one respect Hegel has placed the Holy Trinity at the center of his system. Theologically it involves the living, spiritual Christ. In another respect Hegel risks making the Holy Trinity a tool of his speculative, dynamic logic,

69. Georg W. F. Hegel, *Lectures on the Philosophy of Religion,* 3 vols. (London: Kegan Paul, Trench, & Trubner, 1895) 3.1.

70. Hegel, *Philosophy of Religion,* 3.1.

71. Hegel, *Philosophy of Religion,* 3.2-3.

72. Hegel, *Philosophy of Religion,* 3.103.

73. Hegel, *Philosophy of Religion,* 3.104. For a basic introduction to Hegel's thought, see P. C. Hodgson, *Hegel and Christian Theology* (Oxford: Oxford University Press, 2008).

and also of his philosophy of history. Hegel had once entered the University of Tübingen as a Lutheran, but later became disillusioned with the scholastic Lutheranism of his time. He leaned more toward Kant and Romanticism. Nevertheless, there are important fundamental elements in Hegel. In contemporary Catholicism, Hans Küng draws attention to this in his brilliant book *The Incarnation of God;* in the Lutheran tradition Wolfhart Pannenberg explores the thought of Hegel, especially about history and revelation, in numerous volumes; and in the Reformed Tradition, Jürgen Moltmann examines Hegel especially in his work on history and the Trinity.[74] There are even affinities between Hegel and John Zizioulas in the Greek Orthodox tradition. From being deeply unfashionable in the 1950s and early 1960s, Hegel's thought has once again become more widely and carefully appreciated.

Hegel's contemporary, Friedrich Schleiermacher, argued that the Holy Trinity constituted the climax of his *The Christian Faith,* but to allocate some dozen pages out of 750 to the Trinity hardly makes such a claim convincing.[75] The doctrine is far too man-centered, seeing the Trinity as somehow reflecting or grounding a communal doctrine of the Church.

(8) The *nineteenth century as a whole* had tended to represent several points of view, but mainly two. Liberal scholarship tended to regard the Trinity as a mere ecclesial doctrine of secondary importance. More conservative writers such as Charles Hodge, George Smeaton, Abraham Kuyper, and H. B. Swete tended to repeat the orthodox view of Augustine and Aquinas. The next creative step forward came with Karl Barth (1896-1968), well known for his *Commentary on Romans* (1919 and 1922) and his fourteen-volume (in English) *Church Dogmatics.* He showed his critique of classical literalism when he wrote, "It is not right human thoughts about God which form the content of the Bible, but *right divine thoughts about man.*"[76] Paul, Barth declared, stresses "the Wholly-Otherness of God."[77]

---

74. Hans Küng, *The Incarnation of God: An Introduction to Hegel's Theological Thought* (Edinburgh: T&T Clark, 1987); Wolfhart Pannenberg, "The Significance of Christianity in the Philosophy of Hegel," in his *Basic Questions in Theology,* vol. 3 (London: SCM, 1973), pp. 144-77; Jürgen Moltmann, *Theology of Hope* (London: SCM, 1967), pp. 48-50, 167-72; idem, *The Crucified God* (London: SCM, 1974), pp. 33-37, 253-56.

75. Friedrich Schleiermacher, *The Christian Faith* (Edinburgh: T&T Clark, 1989), pp. 738-51.

76. Karl Barth, *The Word of God and the Word of Man* (London: Hodder and Stoughton, 1928), p. 43.

77. Karl Barth, *The Epistle to the Romans* (Oxford: Oxford University Press, 1933), p. 386.

Theology, he added, is not much *about,* but *from* God and *from* the Holy Spirit.

In harmony with the Western Church, Barth understands the Spirit as "the Spirit of the Father and the Son."[78] Following Augustine, he regards the Holy Spirit as "the fellowship or act of communion of the Father and the Son."[79] The Holy Spirit is God, and "outside us" remains undivided.[80] Barth is less concerned with the *phenomena* of the Spirit, but "with their *whence?* and *whither?* To what do they point?"[81] Barth writes very much more on the Holy Spirit, but on the Trinity he emphasizes, like Augustine, the *oneness* of God. He thus prefers to speak of God's *"modes of being"* rather than of his being "three persons," for reasons which we noted under Gregory of Nazianzus. Barth also shows reluctance to speak of "persons" rather than "modes of existence," not least because of a popular tendency to construct anthropomorphic or human-like language about the Holy Trinity, especially the so-called social Trinity model, which may owe something to fashionable trends in sociology or politics.

(9) Later in the *twentieth century and through to the twenty-first,* Yves Congar (1904-95), Jürgen Moltmann (b. 1926), John Zizioulas (b. 1931), and Wolfhart Pannenberg (1928-2014) have all contributed insights on the Holy Trinity. Congar's work on the Holy Spirit is more closely related to the balance between institutional and charismatic than to the doctrine of the Trinity as such. Yet he does comment on the divergence between the Eastern and Western Churches regarding whether the Spirit proceeds from the Father (the Eastern tradition) or from the Father and the Son (the Western tradition). He regards the two as complementary: the East is more reliant on symbols, he says; the West is more analytical.[82] Probably most contemporary theologians can see merit in both proposals. As a Catholic, Congar argues that the Eastern Church was too heavily influenced by Photius of Constantinople (c. 810-90), who made his view polemically an article of faith. He is not alone in arguing this point. The Eastern Orthodox Andrew Andreopoulos also argues that Photius brought a political dimension to the issue.

Moltmann is one of the most widely read twenty-first century theo-

---

78. Karl Barth, *Church Dogmatics,* 14 vols. (Edinburgh: T&T Clark, 1957-75), 1.479.

79. Barth, *Church Dogmatics,* 1.469-70.

80. Barth, *Church Dogmatics,* 1.442.

81. Karl Barth, *The Resurrection of the Dead* (London: Hodder & Stoughton, 1933), p. 80.

82. Yves Congar, *I Believe in the Holy Spirit: Lord and Giver of Life,* 3 vols. (New York: Seabury, 1983) 3.8.

logians. Like Congar, he insists that "revelation" and "experience" are not competing alternatives. Unlike Congar, he insists, "The Holy Spirit has a wholly unique personhood," and like Zizioulas he declares that the Spirit is always also "a Being-in-relationship."[83] He expounded the Trinitarian communion of the Holy Spirit with the Father and the Son, especially in *The Trinity and the Kingdom of God.*[84] Nevertheless, as we saw when we explored the NT in Part I, his most distinctive contribution (with Pannenberg and Rogers) becomes clear when he comments: The NT talks about God "by *proclaiming in narrative* the relationships of the Father, the Son, and the Spirit."[85] We illustrated this point from various gospel narratives, such as those featuring the baptism of Jesus and his messianic vocation. Moltmann also expresses concern about the Western *filioque* ("and the Son") clause of Western creeds.[86] The Father breathes out his Word in the eternal Spirit. Indeed he explicitly states that "remodeling" the Holy Trinity, which is needed, would be possible "if we once again remove the *filioque* from the Western creeds leaving it that the Spirit proceeds from the Father alone."[87] This, he says, is because "the mutual relationship between pneumatology and Christology must be viewed as a fundamental principle of Christian theology."[88] The three persons of the Trinity, he argues, are coequal in honor and equally to be glorified. On the other hand, many have maintained the view of the Latin Church. Again, most see the value of both approaches. At the recent institution of Justin Welby as Archbishop of Canterbury, interestingly, the Eastern version of the creed was used, not least as a sign of reconciliation.

As we noted earlier, John Zizioulas emphasizes the role of the Holy Spirit so greatly that he declares, "There is, so to say, *no Church until the Spirit is at work . . . [He] constitutes his very identity as Christ,* either at his baptism (Mark) or at his biological conception (Matthew and Luke)."[89] Zizioulas remains one of the most influential theologians of the Greek Orthodox Church, and has been Metropolitan (Archbishop) of Pergamon,

83. Jürgen Moltmann, *The Spirit of Life: A Universal Affirmation* (London: SCM, 1992), pp. 12, 14.

84. Jürgen Moltmann, *The Trinity and the Kingdom of God: The Doctrine of God* (London: SCM, 1981), esp. pp. 97-190.

85. Moltmann, *The Trinity and the Kingdom,* p. 64 (my italic).

86. Moltmann, *The Spirit of Life,* pp. 71-73.

87. Moltmann, *The Spirit of Life,* p. 71.

88. Moltmann, *The Spirit of Life,* p. 72. This quotation comes from L. Vischer.

89. Zizioulas, *Being as Communion,* pp. 127-28 (his italics).

and professor at Glasgow, King's College, London, and Thessalonica. He has criticized Vatican II for not allowing "pneumatology" to play a more adequate role in the deliberations.

Wolfhart Pannenberg takes a more traditional view of the Holy Trinity than Moltmann or Zizioulas, although, like Moltmann and Rogers, he commends a "narrative" approach to the Trinity in the NT. He writes, "The fellowship of Jesus as Son of God with the Father can obviously be stated only if this is a reference to a third as well, the Holy Spirit."[90] Like Zizioulas, he calls the word "Father" "a relational term."[91] Thus *within the NT itself,* he urges, "A distinction emerges in the essence of God himself" which "is the beginning point for the doctrine of the Trinity systematically as well as historically."[92] Such a comment directly alludes to Hegel's notion of God's "self-differentiation." This term is used by Pannenberg.[93]

Pannenberg draws further on biblical material. He argues that *creation* was a Trinitarian event. He writes, "The Spirit is at work already in creation as God's mighty breath, the origin of all movement and life."[94] We must not restrict the Spirit simply to "supernatural" gifts; the Spirit is the Creator of all life, not least in what often appear as natural occurrences. On the narratives of the Gospels, he observes, "Only to the degree that the Son is manifested in creaturely life does the work of the Spirit take the form of gift."[95] "Father," however, is no arbitrary term; it denotes the one who provides, cares, plans, and purposes. As a final note on twenty-first-century developments we may observe that the Pentecostal movement, which has traditionally tended to isolate and focus on the Holy Spirit, has found a new impetus to attend to Trinitarian theology. In particular Amos Yong brings to bear an added experience of Eastern Orthodoxy, which can be seen in his book *Spirit – Word – Community.*[96] Similarly Veli-Matti Kärkkäinen draws on the Eastern fathers in several books, including *The Trinity: Global Perspectives* and *The Holy Spirit: The Sources of Christian Theology.*[97]

---

90. Pannenberg, *Systematic Theology,* 1.267.

91. Pannenberg, *Systematic Theology,* 1.173.

92. Wolfhart Pannenberg, *Jesus: God and Man* (London: SCM, 1968).

93. Pannenberg, *Systematic Theology,* 1.269, 273.

94. Pannenberg, *Systematic Theology,* 3.1.

95. Pannenberg, *Systematic Theology,* 3.9.

96. Amos Yong, *Spirit–Word–Community: Theological Hermeneutics in a Trinitarian Perspective* (Burlington, VT: Ashgate, 2002).

97. Veli-Matti Kärkkäinen, ed., *Holy Spirit and Salvation: The Sources of Christian Theology* (Louisville: Westminster/John Knox, 2010).

CHAPTER 9

The Holy Spirit and Jesus Christ

In the New Testament the Holy Spirit is sometimes called "the Spirit of Jesus," such as when the Holy Spirit forbade Paul and Silas to speak in Asia, but "the Spirit of Jesus" led them to Troas and ultimately to Greece (Acts 16:7). He is at other times called "the Spirit of Christ," such as when Paul declares: "Anyone who does not have the Spirit of Christ does not belong to him" (Rom. 8:9), also when Peter speaks about "the Spirit of Christ" indicating Christ's sufferings (1 Pet. 1:11). He is, third, called "the Spirit of Jesus Christ" when Paul speaks of "your prayers and the help of the Spirit of Jesus Christ" (Phil. 1:19).

In theological terms, the *anointing of Jesus by the Holy Spirit* for his messianic work is a high point. In the nineteenth century the Scottish writer George Smeaton noted this. He declared, "For all his offices, the Lord Jesus Christ received *the unction of the Spirit. . . .* The Spirit interposes his power . . . to execute the will of the Son."[1] He devotes twenty pages to this subject.[2] All four gospels recount the baptism of Jesus, at which "he saw . . . the Spirit descending like a dove on him" (Mark 1:10, with parallels in Matt. 3:16; Luke 3:21-22; John 1:32-33). It constitutes one of the six clear references to the Holy Spirit in Mark.

Although a number of NT scholars in modern times have doubted the historical importance of the virgin birth, the phenomenon was significant for Matthew, Luke, and for early Christian writers from at least the time of Justin Martyr onward. Luke 1:35 asserts, "The Holy Spirit will come upon

---

1. George Smeaton, *The Doctrine of the Holy Spirit* (London: Banner of Truth, 1958), pp. 118, 120 (his italics).

2. Smeaton, *The Doctrine of the Holy Spirit,* pp. 116-36.

you . . . the child to be born will be holy; he will be called Son of God." Matthew relates, "the child conceived in her [Mary] is from the Holy Spirit" (Matt. 1:20). Even scholars who doubt the agency of the Holy Spirit in genetic or biological terms stress his role in inaugurating a new stage in salvation history through the birth of Jesus Christ. Joel Green, for example, sees it as stressing "the initiative and powerful work of God," and adds, "the Holy Spirit is identified with God's power."[3] Many writers have defended the historicity of the event, although not usually in biological terms.[4]

Justin (c. 100–c. 165) states, "This [Spirit] came upon the Virgin and overshadowed her, made her pregnant . . . by an act of power," alluding to Luke 1:35.[5] We earlier qualified our reference to Justin by "at least," for there are hints of the virgin birth in Ignatius (c. 34–c. 108). Ignatius speaks of "the virginity of Mary" and of God's being "manifest as man for the newness of eternal life . . . prepared by God from the beginning."[6] He had earlier written, "Our God, Jesus the Christ, was conceived of Mary (Greek, *ekyophorēthē hypo Marias*) . . . as of the Holy Spirit."[7] He writes to the Smyrnaeans about Christ "in flesh and spirit (*sarki te kai pneumati*) . . . God's Son by the will and power of God, truly born of a virgin."[8]

Many of the church fathers quote an account of the *baptism of Jesus and his anointing* by the Holy Spirit. To return to the NT, the Gospel of John expresses an intimate relation between the Holy Spirit and Christ in the Paraclete discourses. The Paraclete is virtually "Christ's second self" or his deputy. In John 14:18 Jesus says, "I will not leave you orphaned; I am coming to you." And this presence and coming turns out to be "the Advocate, the Holy Spirit, whom the Father will send in my name" (14:26). In 15:26, "the Advocate comes, whom I will send to you from the Father, the Spirit of truth . . . he will testify on my behalf." The theme is repeated in the following chapter: "If I do not go away, the Advocate will not come to you; but if I go, I will send him to you" (16:7). Jesus continues, "I still have many things to say to you . . . When the Spirit of truth comes, he will

3. Joel Green, *The Gospel of Luke* (Grand Rapids: Eerdmans, 1997), pp. 89, 90.
4. J. Gresham Machen, *The Virgin Birth of Christ* (Cambridge: James Clarke, 1930); C. E. B. Cranfield, "Some Reflections on the Subject of the Virgin Birth," *SJT* 41 (1988), pp. 177-89; and in relation to modern science, R. J. Berry, "The Virgin Birth of Christ," *Science and Christian Belief* 8 (1996), pp. 101-10.
5. Justin, *First Apology,* 33 (my translation; cf. *ANF*, 1.174), which includes Greek *pneuma*.
6. Ignatius, *To the Ephesians,* 19:1-2 (in Lake, *Apostolic Fathers*, 1.192-93).
7. Ignatius, *To the Ephesians,* 18:2 (in Lake, *Apostolic Fathers*, 1.190-93).
8. Ignatius, *To the Smyrnaeans,* 1:1 (in Lake, *Apostolic Fathers*, 1.252-53).

guide you into all truth; for he will not speak on his own (Greek, *ou gar lalēsei aph' heautou*), but will speak whatever he hears. . . . He will glorify me . . . he will take what is mine and declare it to you" (16:12-15).

Nothing could more clearly express the intimate relationship of the Spirit to Christ. The Paraclete, Advocate, or Spirit of truth will not speak on his own authority or in his own name, but will speak as Jesus himself would speak to his people. The Paraclete will glorify Christ. God will send him through Christ, to witness to the deeds and teaching of Christ. Swete comments, "The Spirit in his working was found to be in effect the equivalent of Jesus Christ."[9]

In Paul, the Spirit of God's Son is the perfect expression of Christ and believers sharing filial obedience to the Father. Christian believers share by adoption the attitude to God the Father as "Abba," which Jesus by nature and believers by adoption express (Rom. 8:15-16; Gal. 4:6-7). The Holy Spirit witnesses to this relationship. In John 20:22, Jesus Christ breathes directly upon the apostles, saying, "Receive the Holy Spirit."[10] Origen, among others, cites this "Johannine Pentecost" as well as the descent of the Spirit at the baptism of Jesus. He also quotes 1 Cor. 12:3, "No one can say 'Jesus is Lord' except by the Holy Spirit."

Among the post-Nicene Fathers, Ambrose of Milan (c. 339-97) emphasizes the Holy Spirit's anointing of Christ in book 3 of his work *On the Holy Spirit* and in his *Exposition of the Christian Faith*. He calls attention to the witness of Jesus[11] and declares, "Where the Spirit is, there also is Christ." He also quotes Isa. 61:1 and Luke 4:18: "The Spirit of the Lord is upon me . . . he has anointed me to bring good news to the poor."[12] Ambrose declares, "The Holy Spirit . . . is not separated from the Father, nor separated from the Son."[13] He adds, "We certainly cannot proclaim him [the Lord Jesus] without the Spirit."[14] Finally, he recognizes "the oneness of the majesty . . . of the Father, the Son, and the Holy Spirit."[15]

---

9. Henry B. Swete, *The Holy Spirit in the New Testament* (London: Macmillan, 1921), p. 301.

10. Origen, *On First Principles*, 1.3.2 (*ANF*, 4.242); similarly in *Against Celsus*, 51 (*ANF*, 4.632).

11. Ambrose, *Exposition of the Christian Faith*, 3.9.79 (*NPNF*, ser. 2, 10.234).

12. Ambrose, *Exposition of the Christian Faith*, 3.9.79 (*NPNF*, ser. 2, 10.234); and idem, *On the Holy Spirit*, 1.9.101 (*NPNF*, ser. 2, 10.107).

13. Ambrose, *On the Holy Spirit*, 1.11.120 (*NPNF*, ser. 2, 10.109).

14. Ambrose, *On the Holy Spirit*, 1.11.124 (*NPNF*, ser. 2, 10.109).

15. Ambrose, *On the Holy Spirit*, 3.22.165 (*NPNF*, ser. 2, 10.158).

Augustine, the medieval West, and the Reformers perpetuated the Latin or Western addition to the creed, namely "proceeds from the Father *and the Son.*" Augustine declares, "The Holy Spirit, according to the Scriptures, is neither of the Father alone, nor of the Son alone, but of both."[16] He insists, "The Holy Spirit proceeds from the Son also."[17] The Fathers of the Eastern Church, however, retained the traditional form, "proceeds from the Father," and Photius of Constantinople (c. 810–c. 895), a prolific writer of the Byzantine renaissance, provided numerous reasons for rejecting the Western formulation, supported by a polemical political agenda. Today, as we noted, many theologians believe that each formulation conveys valid insights. Moltmann supports the Eastern formulation, and at his installation the Archbishop of Canterbury, Justin Welby, we noted, used this form for both ecumenical and theological reasons.

We have also noted that the Greek Orthodox theologian John Zizioulas claimed that the relationship of the Spirit to Christ was such that "there is, so to say, *no Christ until the Spirit is at work* . . . as the one who constitutes his very identity as Christ."[18] The Russian Orthodox theologian Vladimir Lossky (1903-58) maintains the Eastern views, but he considers the Eastern reaction to Western formulations (e.g., by Photius) to be often exaggerated. He regards the Holy Spirit as facilitating divine participation in the evolving fruitfulness of the world.[19]

Among contemporary theologians who emphasize the Holy Spirit's relation to Jesus Christ we must note the work of Michael Welker (b. 1947) of Tübingen, Münster, and Heidelberg. He devotes nearly fifty pages of *God the Spirit* to this subject.[20] His background includes an interest in process thought and postmodern pluralism, which some may consider not the best part of his work. But in his chapter on Jesus Christ and the concrete presence of the Spirit, he renews and reinvigorates the material of the first three gospels on the Holy Spirit in the pre-resurrection life of Jesus, as

16. Augustine, *On the Trinity,* 15.17.1 (*NPNF,* ser. 1, 3.215).

17. Augustine, *On the Trinity,* 15.17.29 (*NPNF,* ser. 1, 3.216).

18. John D. Zizioulas, *Being as Communion* (New York: St. Vladimir's Seminary Press, 1997), pp. 127-28 (his italics).

19. Vladimir Lossky, *The Mystical Theology of the Eastern Church* (Cambridge: James Clarke, 1957).

20. Michael Welker, *God the Spirit* (Minneapolis: Fortress, 1994), pp. 183-227; cf. idem, *The Work of the Spirit* (Grand Rapids: Eerdmans, 2006).

Pannenberg also does. He repeatedly stresses that "the Holy Spirit is the power that *publicly* installs the Christ."[21]

Predictably, Welker draws attention to the role of the Holy Spirit in the birth and baptism of Jesus, but also rightly stresses the importance of the temptations of Jesus in the wilderness, together with healings, exorcisms, and OT messianic promises.[22] The Spirit "drove" (Mark) or "led" (Matthew) Jesus to be tested for the messianic vocation. This, we may comment, was not only to prove the goals for which he would work, but also his obedience to God's *way* of achieving them. Like Pannenberg, Welker stresses the significance of Jewish expectation. The "open heaven" (Mark 1:10-11; Matt. 3:16-17; Luke 3:21-22) is a sign of salvation, while the baptism and much else is Jesus' "self-abasement in solidarity with sinful human beings."[23] Again, Welker underlines the "public sphere" of the work of Jesus, empowered by the Spirit. Part of his work is "mercy on the sick and the weak, righteousness for Israel and for the Gentiles."[24] Nevertheless, "Jesus does not want to act in such a way that his messianic identity is made known only in the light of healings he has performed."[25] In John, "through the Paraclete, Jesus and Jesus' words are made present in *many* experimental contexts."[26] In the person of Christ, Welker concludes, the Holy Spirit is both universalized and made concrete, overcoming powerlessness both in general and in concrete situations.

Finally, the contemporary Pentecostal theologian, Kärkkäinen, has provided a masterly panorama of writers on the Holy Spirit from all traditions and all times, up to today. He selects the Puritan theologian Richard Sibbes as one example among many who emphasize the relationship between the Holy Spirit and Christ. Sibbes wrote, "He [Christ] received the Spirit without measure (John 3:34), that is in abundance." He declared, "We have not the Holy Ghost immediately from God, but have him as sanctifying Christ first, and then us, and whatsoever the Holy Ghost doth in us, he does the same in Christ first, and he doth in us because [we are] in Christ. . . . The Holy Ghost fetcheth all from Christ. . . . [He] works in us as in Christ."[27]

21. Welker, *God the Spirit*, p. 185 (italics his).
22. Welker, *God the Spirit*, pp. 186-87.
23. Welker, *God the Spirit*, p. 190.
24. Welker, *God the Spirit*, p. 192.
25. Welker, *God the Spirit*, p. 207.
26. Welker, *God the Spirit*, p. 223 (his italics).
27. Cited in Veli-Matti Kärkkäinen, ed., *Holy Spirit and Salvation: The Sources of Christian Theology* (Louisville: Westminster/John Knox, 2010), p. 194, from Richard Sibbes, *Work of Richard Sibbes* (Edinburgh: Banner of Truth, 1973), pp. 17-19.

CHAPTER 10

The Holy Spirit and the Church

To relate the Holy Spirit to the Church verges on a tautology. Without the Holy Spirit, the Church could not exist. In the NT the Spirit is given to individuals only for the benefit of the Church: "To each is given the manifestation of the Spirit for the common good" (1 Cor. 12:7). Virtually every book of the NT makes this clear. But if we must select starting points, we may select a passage from Acts, a passage from Paul, and a passage from John.

(1) In the Great Commission, Jesus tells the apostles, "You will receive power when the Holy Spirit has come upon you; and you will be my witnesses in Jerusalem, in all Judea and Samaria, and to the ends of the earth" (Acts 1:8). Jesus then ascended to his Father, and the Great Commission began to be fulfilled on the day of Pentecost, when the apostles "were all together in one place. . . . All of them were filled with the Holy Spirit. . ." (Acts 2:1, 4). That Pentecost was literally the birthday of the Church, owing to the outpouring of the Holy Spirit. Later passages in Acts corroborate this.

(2) In Paul, among many passages which underline this point, his use of the phrase "the communion (NRSV; alternatively 'fellowship,' 'sharing in'; Greek *koinōnia*) of the Holy Spirit" occurs not only in the well-known "grace" of 2 Corinthians (13:13), but also in Phil. 2:1, where he writes of the "sharing (*koinōnia*) in the Spirit." Thornton spends some half-dozen pages discussing whether the genitive "of the Spirit" is subjective or objective. If it is the former, it means "the fellowship imparted by the Holy Spirit"; if the latter, it denotes "participation [or 'sharing'] in the Holy Spirit."[1] There

---

1. Lionel S. Thornton, *The Common Life in the Body of Christ*, 3rd ed. (London: Dacre, 1950), p. 69.

are good reasons for accepting either, he argues, but a stronger case can be made for the latter, regarding the Holy Spirit as the One in whom we all participate or share.[2] The Holy Spirit is the common possession that all Christians (who make up the true Church) share together. This marks the fulfilment of the OT scriptures, that in the last days "I will pour out my Spirit upon all flesh" (Acts 2:17; Joel 2:28). "On all flesh," especially in Luke–Acts, usually means "on all kinds of people." For Paul obviously the Spirit is shared. The Greek *koinōnos* may even denote "shareholders."

(3) In John 14–16, Jesus promises the Paraclete, or Holy Spirit, to "you"; all (at least five) of the Greek words for the second person are plural (*hymin* and *hymas*). Swete comments, "Jesus spoke of the Spirit as to be given to His disciples collectively. . . . The Spirit was representative of the whole Church. . . . The Spirit was the corporate possession of the Body of Christ."[3] This harmonizes with the Johannine concept of the Church as a single vine, flock, or people (John 15:1-11; 10:11-18; 17:6-24). 1 Peter speaks of the Church as a temple (1 Pet. 2:5), and Ephesians speaks of it as Christ's body (Eph. 1:22-23).

(4) As we have noted, many other NT passages point in the same direction. Hebrews 6:4 discusses those who "have shared in the Holy Spirit (*metochous . . . pneumatos hagiou*)," although it uses a different Greek word from the *koinōnia* group. But *metochos* is the regular word for "sharing in," "participating in," and may occasionally even mean "business partner."[4] The other NT writings contain many helpful themes on this subject. Paul, again, calls the local congregation the "sanctuary," "shrine," or "temple" (*naos*) of the Holy Spirit (1 Cor. 3:16). He gives a stern warning about the need for great care about how anyone seeks to build upon it (3:10-16), and especially its holiness (3:17), for it is of the Holy Spirit.

(5) Paul also refers to admission to the Church when he writes, "In the one Spirit we were all baptized into one body" (1 Cor. 12:13). In Col. 2:19 Paul speaks of "the whole body" needing to grow and be nourished. If Ephesians is broadly Pauline (i.e., written either by Paul or a Pauline disciple), we learn much more about the Holy Spirit and the Church in the Pauline corpus. The church has access to God through the Spirit and is "built upon the foundation of the apostles and prophets" (Eph. 2:20).

---

2. Thornton, *Common Life,* pp. 69-77.

3. Henry B. Swete, *The Holy Spirit in the New Testament* (London: Macmillan, 1921), pp. 306, 307, and 308.

4. Danker, BDAG, p. 643.

Paul urges the Church "to maintain the unity of the Spirit," just as "there is one body and one Spirit" (Eph. 4:3-4). Believers have "one Lord, one faith, one baptism" (Eph. 4:5). The body is growing "in building itself up in love" (4:16). We shall later note how differing gifts serve "to equip the saints for the work of ministry" (4:12; cf. vv. 7-13). Paul regularly addresses the church as "holy ones" (*hagioi;* NRSV "saints"), e.g., in Rom. 1:7; 1 Cor. 1:2; 2 Cor. 1:1.

(6) In Acts, as we noted above, the Holy Spirit is the driving force of its missionary growth, expansion, and outreach. Yet the early Christians "devoted themselves to the apostles' teaching and fellowship (*koinōnia*), to the breaking of bread and the prayers" (Acts 2:42). In Acts 8:15-17 Peter and John prayed for the Samaritans "that they might receive the Holy Spirit," then the disciples "laid their hands on them, and they received the Holy Spirit." This "Samaritan Pentecost" stood in full continuity and communion with the chief Jerusalem apostles. The Council of Jerusalem ensured further that the theology and practice of the Church was one and universal, signified by the giving of the Holy Spirit (Acts 15:8). Notably, in Acts 10:44 the Holy Spirit fell on the Gentiles without the laying on of hands, presumably because Peter was already present and involved. However, in Acts 19:6-7 Paul did lay hands on the disciples of John the Baptist, to regularize an unusual situation, and "the Holy Spirit came upon them."

(7) As we suggested above, gifts of the Holy Spirit to individuals were for the benefit of the whole Church in the NT. Thus the *charismata* ("gifts") listed in 1 Cor. 12:4-11, and more broadly throughout 1 Cor. 12–14, were given by the Holy Spirit "for the common good" (12:7). In addition to gifts of wisdom, teaching, preaching or prophecy, and kinds of healings, the Spirit gave administrative gifts (e.g., 12:28). Elmer Towns observes, "Organization, administration, building infrastructure, marketing and advertisement" are as necessary as "prayer, renewal, worship, soul-winning."[5] Ephesians 4:11-13 takes up the theme. The gifts of the exalted, victorious Christ are to enable the Church, through the Spirit and its ministers, to reach "maturity, to the measure of the full stature of Christ" (4:13). Romans 12:4-8 exactly repeats the theology of 1 Corinthians 12: "We have gifts that differ" (12:6). But each gift of preaching or prophecy, of ministry, of exhortation, and of giving, is for the benefit of the whole Church (12:7-8).

5. Elmer Towns, "The Holy Spirit and Church Growth," in Johnson T. K. Lim, ed., *Holy Spirit: Unfinished Agenda* (Singapore: Armour, 2015), pp. 175-79, here p. 175.

(8) Attention to infrastructure and ministry might well be expected in the Pastoral Epistles. A reference to the Holy Spirit occurs in 2 Tim. 1:14, where he assists in guarding "the good treasure entrusted to you." The treasure probably refers to the "sound teaching" (*hygiainontōn logōn,* lit. "health-giving speech") of v. 13. But the Holy Spirit helps or guarantees authentic transmission of teaching in the Church. Titus 3:5 refers only to rebirth and renewal by the Holy Spirit. But the passage on the office of a bishop or elder (*episkopē,* lit. "oversight") in 1 Tim. 3:1-7, and of a deacon in vv. 8-13, lists qualities of dispositions which are usually associated with the Holy Spirit. These qualities include being skilled in teaching, hospitable, peace-loving, not eager for money, and a good manager (vv. 2-5). Titus 1:6-9 has a comparable list of qualities, which includes self-control and humility, and gifts not unlike the fruit of the Spirit in Gal. 5:22-23. After their earlier concern about the gospel *message,* it is not irrational to suppose that the apostles may have turned to the *infrastructure* of the Church at a later stage, when the essentials of the gospel had become clear.

(9) These latest writings of the NT naturally blend into the concerns of the apostolic fathers or sub-apostolic writings. *1 Clement* (c. 96) literally echoes the Pastorals: "They appointed their first converts, testing them by the Spirit (*dokimasantes tō pneumati)* to be bishops (*episkopous*) and deacons (*diakonous)* of the future believers."[6] This was "no new method," for the Church had set apart (probably ordained) bishops and deacons "for many years."[7] As is well known, Ignatius (c. 35-108) argues in his epistle to the Ephesians, "You should live in harmony with the will of the bishop (*episkopos*). For your justly famous presbytery . . . is attuned to the bishop as the strings of a harp."[8] Later he encourages the readers to "obey the bishop and the presbytery with an undistorted mind, breaking our bread."[9] This exhortation is not peculiar to the situation at Ephesus. Ignatius writes to the Trallians, "You are in subjection to the bishop as to Jesus Christ . . . living . . . after Christ."[10] More generally Ignatius urges, "If any one follow a maker of schism, he does not inherit the kingdom of God."[11] Throughout his authentic letters he utters fragments of orthodox creeds, urging doctoral unity and purity as well as purity and unity of practice. As Ignatius

---

6. *1 Clement* 42:4 (in Lake, *Apostolic Fathers,* 1.80-81).

7. *1 Clement* 42:5 (in Lake, *Apostolic Fathers,* 1.80-81).

8. Ignatius, *To the Ephesians,* 4:1 (in Lake, *Apostolic Fathers,* 1.176-77).

9. Ignatius, *To the Ephesians,* 4:1 (in Lake, *Apostolic Fathers,* 1.194-95).

10. Ignatius, *To the Trallians,* 2:1 (in Lake, *Apostolic Fathers,* 1.212-13).

11. Ignatius, *To the Philadelphians,* 3:3 (in Lake, *Apostolic Fathers,* 1.242-43).

approaches certain martyrdom in Rome, church order remains paramount in his mind. This is elsewhere called "the unity of the Spirit" (Eph. 4:3). Some stress that his concern about the authority of the bishop and the presbyters is less about authority as such than about the doctrinal purity of the Church, which would follow from this. We noted above that Ignatius also has other concerns about the Spirit and salvation, not only about institutional church order.

The *Didachē* (c. 100) also has material about the Spirit. It also teaches new converts about "the two Ways," of life and death, with reference to the Ten Commandments and other moral qualities of life (chs. 1–6). It introduces baptism in the threefold name (7:1-4) and the Eucharist (9:1-5), including the prayer, "As the broken bread was scattered on the mountains but was brought together . . . so let the Church be gathered together from the ends of the earth into Thy kingdom" (9:4). But then there follow tests for false and true prophecy (11:3–12:5). The *Didachē* also enjoins, "Appoint therefore for yourselves bishops and deacons worthy of the Lord, meek men, and not lovers of money, truthful and approved."[12] Earlier the *Didachē* expressed its concern for the unity of the Spirit: "Thou shalt not devise a schism but shall reconcile those that strive."[13]

(10) Irenaeus (c. 130–c. 200) became bishop of Lyons in 180. He stresses the importance of public (as opposed to private) tradition to maintain doctrinal and practical continuity in the Church. This transmission for the faith is a key factor for the identity of the Church.[14] It stands in contrast to the anarchy which would follow private revelations among the Gnostics. Irenaeus argues, "The preaching of the Church is everywhere consistent, and continues to be on an even course, and receives testimony from the prophets (or preachers), the apostles, and all the disciples . . . by the Spirit of God."[15]

Tertullian of Carthage (c. 150–c. 220) differs in his pre-Montanist period from after his "conversion" to Montanism. In his post-Montanist period he stresses the immediacy of the Holy Spirit, and even ecstatic prophecy. In his pre-Montanist period he repeats Irenaeus's emphasis on the "rule of faith" and the unity of the Holy Spirit. He later tended toward

---

12. *Didachē*, 15:1 (in Lake, *Apostolic Fathers*, 1.330-31).
13. *Didachē*, 4:3 (in Lake, *Apostolic Fathers*, 1.314-15).
14. Irenaeus, *Against Heresies*, 1.10.1 (*ANF*, 1.330).
15. Irenaeus, *Against Heresies*, 3.23.1 (*ANF*, 1.458).

asceticism and the notion of a "pure" church, in anticipation of the later Donatists. He speaks of Christians "shut up in prisons for nothing but fidelity to the cause of God's Church."[16] On the growth of the Church he comments, "The oftener we are mown down by you, the more in number we grow."[17] Tertullian also links the Holy Spirit with baptism in the Church. He states, "In the waters [of baptism] we obtain the Holy Spirit. . . . After this . . . a hand is laid upon us, invoking and inviting the Holy Spirit through benediction."[18] He thus connects the work of the Spirit with church order, worship, and a sacrament.

We need not pursue our argument in detail in the later fathers. As Simon Chan points out, the eucharistic prayer in Hippolytus (c. 170–c. 236) has "in your holy Church" (*in sancta Ecclesia tua*) in parallel with "in the unity of the Holy Spirit" (*in unitate Spiritus Sancti*) in the Roman rite.[19] Hippolytus regards the Holy Spirit as a guardian of church order. He writes, "The Holy Spirit [was] bequeathed to the Church whom the Apostles received [and] have transmitted to those who have rightly believed."[20] He lays down criteria for the appointment of a bishop and presbyter. Cyprian (c. 258) goes even further, regarding the Church as held together by the episcopate, and relating the Holy Spirit also to baptismal rites within the Church.[21] After Nicea, as Simon Chan, Kärkkäinen, and others point out, both the Western and especially the Eastern fathers stress the relation between the Holy Spirit and the Church. This is stressed also in Eastern Orthodoxy today.

In the Western Church, Augustine (354-430) declares, "Whoso is not of this Church does not now receive the Holy Spirit."[22] In the Eastern Church, Cyril of Jerusalem (c. 315-87) expounds the work of the Holy Spirit in the context of baptism and the Eucharist. He agrees with Paul the Apostle that "Receiving the Holy Spirit is synonymous with being a Christian" (cf. Rom. 8:9).[23] But baptism is also "the antitype of the Holy Spirit."[24] John Chrysostom (c. 347-407) regards the gifts of the Spirit in

---

16. Tertullian, *Apology*, 39 (*ANF*, 3.46).

17. Tertullian, *Apology*, 50 (*ANF*, 3.55).

18. Tertullian, *On Baptism*, 6 and 8 (*ANF*, 3.672).

19. Simon Chan, *Pentecostal Ecclesiology* (Blandford Forum, UK: Deo, 2011), p. 24.

20. Hippolytus, *Refutation of All Heresies*, Preface 5 (*ANF*, 5.10).

21. Cyprian, *On the Unity of the Church* (*ANF*, 5.421-29).

22. Augustine, *On the Gospel of John*, Tractate 32:7 (*NPNF*, ser. 1, 7.195).

23. Cyril of Jerusalem, *Catechetical Lectures*, 17:5 (*NPNF*, ser. 1, 7.125).

24. Cyril of Jerusalem, *Mystagogic Lectures*, 3:1 (*NPNF*, ser. 1, 7.149).

1 Cor. 12:4-27 as given *for the Church,* and thought that "tongues" have ceased only because the Church has become well-established.[25]

(11) From Gregory the Great (c. 540-604) to Luther in the West, and from John Cassian (c. 360–c. 435) to the beginning of the modern era in the East, "Christendom" was virtually identical with the formal boundaries of the mainline church. Dionysius discusses the sacraments and orders of clergy in his *Ecclesiastical Hierarchy.* Gregory of Rome focuses on pastoral care and administration in his *Book of Pastoral Rule,* or *On Pastoral Care.* Bede (c. 673-735) and Alcuin (c. 735-804) follow Augustine, including his work in *The City of God.* Alcuin writes, "All baptized people . . . receive the Holy Spirit from the Bishop by the imposition of hands."[26] Photius of Constantinople (c. 810–c. 890) defends the Eastern procession of the Holy Spirit from God the Father alone. Anselm (c. 1033-1109) closely follows Augustine on the Spirit.

Bernard of Clairvaux (1090-1153) mainly addresses Christians in the Church, urging "greater fervour and increased faithfulness in seeking the Spirit."[27] Hildegard of Bingen (1098-1179) attacks overly lax clergy and urges obedience to monastic rules. Her visions use much biblical and ecclesial imagery and pictures.[28] She also defends the Holy Spirit's relation to the Church by opposing the dualism and sectarianism of the Cathars, who were condemned at the Fourth Lateran Council of 1215. Bonaventura (1221-74), like many medieval mystics, speaks of "the soul's ascent to God. . . . This universe is a ladder whereby we may ascend to God," while the major Reformers believe that it is more true to the gospel to stress the *downward* movement of God, Christ, the Spirit, and grace, to rescue humankind.[29] Thomas Aquinas (c. 1225-74) again closely follows Augustine, although he did not live to complete the *Summa Theologiae.*

(12) Martin Luther (1483-1546), as we have argued, was closer in *some* doctrines to the Catholic Church than to the "radical Reformers." The so-called Finnish interpretation of Luther stresses his high regard for the Church. Simon Chan, Veli-Matti Kärkkäinen, and David Yeago have recently called attention to this.[30] Luther regards the Church as a

---

25. John Chrysostom, *Homilies on 1 Corinthians,* 19:1 and 32:3-4 (*NPNF,* ser. 1, 7.168, 186-87).

26. Alcuin, *Letters,* 80.

27. Bernard of Clairvaux, *Sermon on the Lord's Ascension.*

28. Hildegard of Bingen, *Scivias* (Mahwah, NJ: Paulist, 1990), 2:2; 3:9.

29. Bonaventura, *Itinerary* 1:20 (in Perry, ed., *Late Mediaeval Mysticism,* p. 132).

30. Chan, *Pentecostal Ecclesiology,* pp. 44-49; Veli-Matti Kärkkäinen, ed., *Holy Spirit*

concrete, worshiping community called by God to be a holy community. Its "core practices" are the preached word, baptism, the Lord's Supper, church discipline, church offices, worship, and bearing the cross.[31] It is this Church whereby the Holy Spirit effects in us life and sanctification in Christ.[32] This is how "the Holy Spirit fashions a holy people in the world."[33] Further, as Chan points out, the ordained minister is not so much a representative of the people, but "that organ through which and in which the Church is speaking and acting."[34] Kärkkäinen comments, "The sanctifying work of the Spirit is . . . the way to connect the Spirit to salvation and the church."[35] Luther himself declares, "The Holy Spirit sanctifies through . . . [leading] you into the holy, catholic church and places you in the bosom of the church."[36]

John Calvin (1509-64) devotes almost all of book 4 of the *Institutes* to the subject of the Church. Chapters 1 and 2 discuss the true and false church. Chapter 3 examines the ministry; chapters 4 and 5 consider the governance of the Church. But the work of the Holy Spirit is clearest on the sacraments in chapter 14. Calvin declares, "The sacraments duly perform their office only when accompanied by the Spirit, the internal Master, whose energy alone penetrates the heart, stirs up the affections, and procures access for the sacraments into our soul. . . . This ministry, without the agency of the Spirit, is empty and frivolous."[37] The Church is also the setting for the preaching of the Word of God, which is made effective by the Holy Spirit.

Also in the sixteenth century, Richard Hooker (1554-1600) considered the Holy Spirit and the Church with special reference to baptism and confirmation. He constantly appeals to Scripture, the tradition of the church fathers, and reason, and applies this to baptism and confirmation

---

and Salvation: The Sources of Christian Theology (Louisville: Westminster/John Knox, 2010), pp. 155-62, and 325-26; David S. Yeago, "'A Christian, Holy People': Martin Luther on Salvation and the Church," *Modern Theology* 13 (1997), pp. 101-20.

31. Martin Luther, "On the Councils and the Church," in *Luther's Works,* 55 vols. (St. Louis and Philadelphia: Concordia and Fortress, 1955-86), 41.148-66 .

32. Luther, "On the Councils and the Church," p. 166.

33. Luther, *Luther's Works,* 41.110.

34. Luther, *Luther's Works,* 41.112; Chan, *Pentecostal Ecclesiology,* p. 46.

35. Kärkkäinen, ed., *Holy Spirit and Salvation,* p. 155; R. Hütter, *Suffering Divine Things* (Grand Rapids: Eerdmans, 2010), and idem, "The Church as Public Dogma, Practice, and the Holy Spirit," *Pro Ecclesia* 3 (1994), pp. 334-61.

36. Luther, "The Sermons on Catechism," in *Luther's Works* (St Louis: Concordia, 1959), 51.166.

37. Calvin, *Institutes of the Christian Religion,* IV.14.9 (in Beveridge, ed., 2.497).

in his *Laws of Ecclesiastical Polity,* book 5.[38] Confirmation, or the imposition of hands, he says, is to "confirm and perfect that which the grace of the same Spirit had already begun at baptism."[39] This does not include "miraculous gifts," since, as Augustine taught, these did not last, "lest man should wax cold with the commonness of that strangeness [which] at the first inflamed them."[40] He appeals to Tertullian and Cyprian for the laying on of hands *after* baptism, but also insists that "the bishop's confirmation after . . . baptism" is not "needful for the *obtaining* of the Holy Ghost," as Jerome confirms.[41] Hooker's theology remained influential from the Elizabethan settlement onwards.

In modern times Karl Barth (1896-1968) links the Holy Spirit most closely to the Word of God, but for Barth the normal context of this remains the Church. He writes, "The Holy Spirit continually makes us *listen* to the Word of the Creator."[42] He declares, "The Holy Spirit . . . cannot be separated from the Word."[43] Eduard Schweizer (1915-2006) insists that in Acts the Holy Spirit is often identified with visible phenomena, which include the life and actions of the Church. This is also a regular theme in James D. G. Dunn (b. 1939), who meticulously examines the relation of the Holy Spirit to baptism and to the Church. Typically Dunn asserts "Pentecost inaugurated the age of the Church."[44] From the standpoint of the Pentecostal community, Simon Chan provides an excellent case for treating the relation between the Holy Spirit and ecclesiology in his book *Pentecostal Ecclesiology.* Citing Vandervelde, he repeats the basic point that "you" is regularly plural in Paul when he speaks of the Spirit (as we have noted) while "temple" is singular, thereby "stressing the corporate, communal life of the church."[45] He argues that the Eastern Orthodox

---

38. Richard Hooker, *Treatise of the Laws of Ecclesiastical Polity,* 7th ed., 3 vols. (Oxford: Clarendon, 1888) 1.337-48, bk. 5 ch. 66.

39. Hooker, *Laws,* 1.337, bk. 5 ch. 66.

40. Hooker, *Laws,* 1.339, bk. 5 ch. 66; Augustine, *On True Religion,* 25.

41. Hooker, *Laws,* 1.343, bk. 5 ch. 66 (my italics).

42. Karl Barth, *The Holy Spirit and the Christian Life* (Louisville: Westminster/John Knox, 1993), p. 9 (italics his).

43. Karl Barth, *Church Dogmatics,* 14 vols. (Edinburgh: T&T Clark, 1957-75), 1.150 (1:1, sect. 5).

44. James D. G. Dunn, *Baptism in the Holy Spirit* (London: SCM, 1970), p. 49; also *Jesus and the Spirit: A Study of the Religious and Charismatic Experience of Jesus and the First Christians as Reflected in the New Testament* (London: SCM, 1975).

45. Chan, *Pentecostal Ecclesiology,* p. 39; George Vandervelde, "The Challenge of Evangelical Ecclesiology," *Evangelical Review of Theology* 27 (2003), pp. 4-26, here 19.

Church, as exemplified by Zizioulas, takes account of the divine nature of the Church, and also the importance of solidarity or *sobornost,* relationality or community. As Edmund Rybarczyk observes, both the Eastern Orthodox and Pentecostals make much of *participation,* which was exactly the starting point of this chapter.[46] Chan also makes illuminating comments on Luther and Congar, and Thornton regularly uses this term.

Jürgen Moltmann (b. 1926), however, deserves pride of place in twentieth-century theology in light of his *The Spirit and the Church.* In *The Church in the Power of the Spirit* he argues that the Spirit *participates in the Trinitarian history of God* and also constantly moves the Church towards the goal of history. The Holy Spirit *empowers* the Church for mission, and does not exist in and for itself.[47] In his later book *The Spirit of Life,* like Zizioulas, he declares, "Personhood is always being-in-relationship. . . . The Spirit has a wholly unique personhood."[48] The Spirit leads us to seek "sociably" and makes possible the creation of a community. Tellingly, he asserts that the Spirit means "opening ourselves for one another, giving one another a share in ourselves."[49] The Spirit *frees us from "ego-mania."*[50] The Holy Spirit no longer allows us "the autonomous right of disposal over oneself and one's property," but plumbs the depth of "the hitherto unexplored power of God," which is life-giving "through love."[51] All this, including much material in his other books, reaches a pinnacle in expounding the theological and practical meaning of "the Holy Spirit and the Church."

The only other major theologian of the twentieth and twenty-first centuries who comes near to this pinnacle, at least among Protestant theologians, is Wolfhart Pannenberg, in the section of his *Systematic Theology* entitled "The Outpouring of the Spirit and the Church."[52] The Spirit, he declares, "aims at the building up of the fellowship of believers."[53] The Holy

---

46. Edmund J. Rybarczyk, *Beyond Salvation and Classical Pentecostalism on Becoming Like Christ* (Carlisle: Paternoster, 2004), pp. 8, 13.

47. Jürgen Moltmann, *The Church in the Power of the Spirit* (London: SCM, 1975), p. xv.

48. Jürgen Moltmann, *The Spirit of Life: A Universal Affirmation* (London: SCM, 1992).

49. Moltmann, *The Spirit of Life,* p. 217.

50. Moltmann, *The Spirit of Life,* p. 251 (my italics).

51. Moltmann, *The Spirit of Life,* p. 118.

52. Pannenberg, *Systematic Theology,* 3 vols. (Edinburgh: T&T Clark / Grand Rapids: Eerdmans, 1994), 3.12-27.

53. Pannenberg, *Systematic Theology,* 3.12.

Spirit belongs to all covenant people. He regards Pentecost as "above all a theological statement about the relation between the church and the Spirit."[54] Within this framework, he observes, "The only criterion of authentic spirituality is the relation to [one's] confession of Christ" (1 Cor. 12:3).[55] One reason for the relative slowness of some to focus on this subject is that until more recent times, "the doctrine of the church was not an independent theme" in dogmatic theology. Over the centuries, it was often a mere appendix to issues about the sacraments.[56]

54. Pannenberg, *Systematic Theology,* 3.15.
55. Pannenberg, *Systematic Theology,* 3.18.
56. Pannenberg, *Systematic Theology,* 3.21.

CHAPTER 11

The Holy Spirit, Revelation, and Inspiration

Revelation and inspiration are intimately connected and both are operations of the Holy Spirit. But their technical meaning differs. Revelation constitutes a free, sovereign act of God whereby he takes the initiative in making himself known. It is God's chosen self-disclosure of himself and his ways. It is a *divine act of communication,* in contrast to a merely human act of discovery. It presupposes that God's ways are hidden until he has revealed himself. Revelation is therefore a profound act of love which initiates the possibility of communication and love between God and humankind.

Inspiration is different. Whereas revelation is God's gracious self-disclosure, inspiration guarantees the *preservation* of revelation in some permanent and *authoritative* form. In Christian thought, inspired Scripture assumes a primary place among mechanisms or agents for preserving revelation. This distinction is adopted by James Orr, among many others. Orr comments, "The denial of the Holy Spirit in the community of God's people may fitly be described as the *primal heresy.*"[1]

Karl Barth devoted many pages to the discussion of revelation and the Word of God, as the first subject of his *Church Dogmatics.* He asks, "Does Christian utterance derive from God? Does it lead to Him? Is it conformable to Him?"[2] The Word of God, he says, comes to us as his *gift* and *address,* and as his *act.* This Word comes in a threefold form: the Word preached, the Word written, and the Word revealed; these three correspond respectively to the word in the Church, the word of Scripture, and

---

1. James Orr, *Revelation and Inspiration* (London: Duckworth, 1909), p. 156 (his italics).
2. Karl Barth, *Church Dogmatics,* 14 vols. (Edinburgh: T&T Clark, 1957-75), 1.4 (1:1).

the Word that is Christ.[3] This last, the Word of God, namely Christ himself, is the primary focus of revelation; then revelation comes through Scripture; the third form of revelation comes through the Church. Barth also acknowledges that the Holy Spirit may choose to use other vehicles of revelation besides the Bible, even "a flute concerto or a blossoming shrub": God "speaks," he declares, "where and when he chooses."[4]

I find it difficult to understand why some writers have denied that revelation has any place in Christian theism.[5] The Hebrew *g-l-h,* "reveal" or "uncover" (or sometimes "go away" or "send") occurs some 180 times in the OT, while the Greek *apokalyptō* ("reveal") and *apokalypsis* ("revelation") occur some 35 times in the NT and over 100 times in the LXX.[6] Of these numerous references one of the clearest comes in 1 Cor. 2:9-11: "'What no eye has seen, nor ear heard . . . what God has prepared for those who love him' — these things God has revealed to us through the Spirit . . . no one comprehends what is truly God's except the Spirit of God."

It would be a mistake, however, to limit such passages to those in which the word "revelation" explicitly occurs. At the beginning of Hebrews the author states, "Long ago God spoke to our ancestors in many and various ways by the prophets, but in these last days he has spoken to us by a Son" (Heb. 1:1-2). In the words of H. B. Swete, "The Old Testament, more especially the Prophets of the OT formed the text-book of the primitive preacher."[7] He continues, "The Holy Scriptures were regarded as the writings of the Holy Spirit."[8] The example of the prophetic writings brings together revelation in terms of their context, and inspiration in terms of their transmission of the Word of God.

In spite of this, there appear to be only two explicit references to *inspiration,* namely in the word "God-breathed" (*theopneustos*) in 2 Tim 3:16 and in the phrase "moved by the Holy Spirit" in 2 Pet. 1:21. The Vulgate correctly rendered the Greek *theopneustos* by the Latin *divinitus inspirata.* Bruce Vawter comments, "The author would also have had in this purview those writings of the apostolic Church that were already being equated with the Biblical canon: in 1 Tim 5:18 the author cites as Scripture

3. Barth, *Church Dogmatics* 1:1, see esp. 1.88-124 in the English translation.

4. Barth, *Church Dogmatics,* 1.55, 120 (1:1).

5. F. Gerald Downing, *Has Christianity a Revelation?* (London: SCM, 1964).

6. HR, 1.133-34.

7. Henry B. Swete, *The Holy Spirit in the New Testament* (London: Macmillan, 1921), p. 381.

8. Swete, *The Holy Spirit in the New Testament,* p. 383.

alongside an OT passage what is apparently a *logion* of Jesus . . . a saying now found in Matt. 10:10 and Luke 10:7."[9] The explicit reference to inspiration of the prophets by the Holy Spirit in 2 Peter deserves inclusion in full: "No prophecy ever came by human will, but men and women moved by the Holy Spirit (Greek *pheromenoi,* lit. 'carried along'; Vulgate *inspirati*) spoke from God." The phrase "the Holy Spirit, who spoke by the prophets" found its way into the Creed of Jerusalem (A.D. 348, after the Lectures of Cyril of Jerusalem), and subsequent creeds.

In the NT there are numerous repeated assertions that the Holy Spirit was active in inspired revelation. For example, "David spoke in the Holy Spirit" occurs in Mark 12:36 and in Acts 1:16 and 4:25. Paul stated that the (OT) Scriptures were "written for our instruction" (Rom. 15:4), or "were written down to instruct us" (1 Cor. 10:11); but not all of these passages refer specifically to the Holy Spirit. The action of the Spirit is assumed rather than spoken. There are also other Greek words than *apokalyptō* that are used to convey what God revealed. The word *phaneroō,* "reveal," "cause to become visible," is used of the revelation or appearance of Christ in Heb. 9:26 and 1 Pet. 1:20. In 1 John 1:2 in "this life was revealed" (twice). A third Greek word is *chrēmatizō,* "reveal" or "warn," as in Luke 2:26: "warned (NRSV 'revealed to him') by the Holy Spirit." The majority of NT examples use *apokalyptō:* "revealed . . . to infants" (Matt. 11:25 // Luke 10:21); "anyone to whom the Son chooses to reveal him" (Matt. 11:27 // Luke 10:22); "revealed this to you [Peter]" (Matt. 16:17). The theme also occurred in the epistles: "the righteousness of God is revealed" (Rom. 1:17); "revealing of the children of God" (Rom. 8:19); "the revelation of the mystery that was kept secret for long ages" (Rom. 16:25); "these things God has revealed to us through the Spirit" (1 Cor. 2:10, as noted above); "to reveal his Son to me" (Gal. 1:16); and "the revelation of Jesus Christ" (Rev. 1:1; using the noun *apokalypsis*).

In the history of Christian thought, we may note, *inspiration* by the Holy Spirit was especially emphasized from Clement of Rome and Ignatius to the third century. On the other hand, *revelation* by the Holy Spirit received special attention from John Calvin and in the post-Reformation period. Both aspects remain biblical principles, but they received special emphasis in different eras. Christopher Forbes also emphasizes "prophecy and inspired speech" in early pagan religions and in early Christian proph-

9. Bruce Vawter, *Biblical Inspiration* (Philadelphia: Westminster, 1972), p. 8.

ecy. More importantly, however, he concludes that parallels between the two cannot be supported.[10] Max Turner and Roger Stronstad focus on inspiration by the Spirit in Judaism and Luke–Acts.[11]

As early as the end of the first century, Clement of Rome wrote, "You have studied the Holy Scriptures which are true, and given by the Holy Spirit."[12] Elsewhere Clement quoted Paul, declaring, "Let not the wise man boast in his wisdom" (cf. 1 Cor. 1:31).[13] Clement also wrote, "The apostles went forth in the Holy Spirit, preaching the good news that the Kingdom of God is coming."[14] We might think that at least one of the quotations refers to revelation, but Swete comments, "Inspiration, in fact, is the function most commonly attributed by Clement to the Holy Spirit."[15] Ignatius (c. 108) and the *Didachē* share Clement's view.

The late sub-apostolic writings also emphasized the inspiration of the Holy Spirit. The *Epistle of Barnabas* (c. 98–c. 150) avers that "Moses spoke in the Spirit," alluding to Deut. 4:1-5.[16] The Ten Commandments were "written by the finger of the hand of the Lord in the Spirit."[17] The *Shepherd of Hermas* (date uncertain) understood that the Holy Spirit inspired contemporary prophecy. He carried Hermas through the wilderness to show him the "open heavens."[18] Among the apologists, Justin (c. 100–c. 165) spoke of the OT prophets "who spoke by the Holy Trinity only the things which they heard and saw when they were filled with the Spirit."[19] He quoted 1 Cor. 2:10 in support of this. Baptismal new creation, he wrote, entails "illumination" and "the Spirit of understanding."[20] Those who follow Christ receive "the

10. Christopher Forbes, *Prophecy and Inspired Speech in Early Christianity and Its Hellenistic Environment* (Tübingen: Mohr Siebeck, 1995), pp. 132-47 and throughout.

11. Max Turner, *Power from on High: The Spirit in Israel's Restoration and Witness in Luke–Acts* (Sheffield: Sheffield Academic Press, 1996); Roger Stronstad, *The Charismatic Theology of St. Luke* (Peabody, MA: Hendrickson, 1985); idem, *The Prophethood of All Believers* (Sheffield: Sheffield Academic Press, 1999).

12. *1 Clement* 45:2 (in Lake, *Apostolic Fathers*, 1.84-87).

13. *1 Clement* 13:1 (in Lake, *Apostolic Fathers*, 1.28-29).

14. *1 Clement* 42:3 (in Lake, *Apostolic Fathers*, 1.80-81).

15. Henry B. Swete, *The Holy Spirit in the Ancient Church* (London: Macmillan, 1912), p. 13.

16. *Barnabas* 10:2 (in Lake, *Apostolic Fathers*, 1.374-75).

17. *Barnabas* 14:2 (in Lake, *Apostolic Fathers*, 1.390-91).

18. *Hermas, Vision* 1:13 and 21:1; cf. *Similitudes* 9:12.

19. Justin, *Dialogue with Trypho* (*ANF*, 1.198).

20. Justin, *First Apology*, 61 (*ANF*, 1.183).

Spirit of prophecy . . . in word and truth."[21] Athenagoras (c. 180) said that Word and Wisdom flow from God as "light from fire," and that the Holy Spirit works in those who deliver genuine prophecies (or possibly pastoral preaching).[22] Theophilus of Antioch (later second century) identified the Spirit with divine Wisdom, and associated the Spirit with God's Word. He wrote, "The Word, being the Spirit of God . . . came down on the Prophets."[23]

Among the church fathers, Irenaeus of Lyons (c. 130–c. 200) regarded the Spirit as the agent of OT prophecy and also identified him with divine Wisdom, who worked in parallel with the Word.[24] He wrote, "The Scriptures are indeed perfect, since they were spoken by the Word of God and his Spirit."[25] He dismissed the self-styled *gnosis* of the Gnostics, insisting on a *public,* not private or "inner," tradition. The Holy Spirit works through normal rational processes of evaluation. A believer who received the Spirit will acknowledge the witness of both OT prophets and NT apostles.[26] Clement of Alexandria (c. 150-215) wrote, "It was God who promulgated the Scriptures by his Son."[27] Specifically, "The Spirit . . . prophesies by Isaiah."[28] Origen of Alexandria (c. 185–c. 254), possibly the greatest scholar of the third century, insisted that both the OT and NT were "inspired by the Holy Spirit."[29]

From the time of Origen onward, the agency of the Holy Spirit in inspiration became a common Christian presupposition, rather than the subject of explicit statements. This held sway until a confrontation occurred in the nineteenth century between skeptical liberal theologians and two groups of conservatives. B. B. Warfield and A. A. Hodge took an uncompromising conservative position. James Orr, P. T. Forsyth, George Smeaton, and Abraham Kuyper adopted a more moderate position. All of the writers stressed the role of the Holy Spirit in the inspiration of Scripture. But the more conservative stressed the inspired *words* of Scripture, the latter group of writers, the inspired *meaning* of Scripture. Many credit John Calvin with making this careful distinction earlier.

---

21. Justin, *First Apology,* 6, 13 (*ANF,* 1.164).
22. Athenagoras, *Embassy,* 6; and idem, *Laws,* 10.
23. Theophilus, *Autolycus,* 1:7, 14; 2:9.
24. Irenaeus, *Against Heresies,* 4.20.3-4 (*ANF,* 1.488).
25. Irenaeus, *Against Heresies,* 2.18.2-4 (*ANF,* 1.384).
26. Irenaeus, *Against Heresies,* 3.24.1 (*ANF,* 1.458).
27. Clement, *Miscellanies,* 5.4 (*ANF,* 2.464).
28. Clement, *The Instructor,* 1.5.13 (*ANF,* 2.215).
29. Origen, *On First Principles,* 1.3.1 (*ANF,* 2.252).

Calvin (1509-64) stressed the role of the Holy Spirit in *revelation.* This is not surprising, since Calvin emphasized the Spirit's communication of *knowledge of God* and *truth.* Calvin wrote in his *Institutes* (1536 ed.): "If we regard the Spirit of God as the sole fountain of truth, we shall neither reject the truth nor despise it wherever it shall appear, unless we wish to dishonour the Spirit of God."[30] In book I, chapter 6, Calvin addressed our *need* of Scripture; in chapter 7, the testimony of the Spirit to its *authority;* and in chapter 8, the *credibility* of Scripture. In I.6.1, he stated, "With great insult to the Holy Spirit, it is asked, 'Who can assure us that the Scriptures proceeded from God . . .'? . . . The Church is 'built on the foundation of the apostles and prophets' (Eph. 2:20)."[31] He added, "Our conviction of the truth of Scripture must be derived from a higher source than human conjectures, judgments, or reasons, namely, the sacred testimony of the Spirit."[32] In other words, the basis is revelation by the Holy Spirit; not purely enquiry and discovery as such. Anticipating Barth, Calvin asserted, "God alone can bear witness to his own words. . . . They are sealed by the inward testimony of the Spirit. The same Spirit . . . who spoke by the mouth of the prophets must penetrate our hearts."[33] Of various biblical narratives, Calvin added, "Shall we say that he (a character in the narrative) spoke his own natural feelings, or that he obeyed the command of the Holy Spirit?"[34] He concluded, "Scripture . . . is founded on the *inward persuasion of the Holy Spirit.*"[35]

John Owen (1616-83), both Vice-Chancellor of Oxford and a leading Puritan, argued for exactly the same basis for revelation and Scripture. Many contend that Calvin and Owen regard the Spirit as revealing the meaning of Scripture, but, again, not in the word-by-word way of Warfield and Hodge, although some may question this.[36] In our day Norman Snaith and many others follow this path. We have written enough, however, in this shorter book, to indicate the main outlines of the work of the Holy Spirit in revelation and inspiration.

---

30. John Calvin, *Institutes of the Christian Religion* (1536 edition) II.7.5.

31. Calvin, *Institutes,* I.7.1-2 (in Beveridge, ed., 1.69).

32. Calvin, *Institutes,* I.7.4 (in Beveridge, ed., 1.71).

33. Calvin, *Institutes,* I.7.4 (in Beveridge, ed., 1.72).

34. Calvin, *Institutes,* I.8.4 (in Beveridge, ed., 1.77).

35. Calvin, *Institutes,* I.8.13 (in Beveridge, ed., 1.83; my italics).

36. J. K. S. Reid, *The Authority of Scripture* (London: Methuen, 1958), pp. 48-49, 156-76; and Orr, *Revelation and Inspiration,* pp. 201-15.

CHAPTER 12

The Holy Spirit and Sanctification

It is not surprising that the Holy Spirit (*to pneuma to hagion*) is linked with the word "sanctification" (*hagiasmos;* verb, *hagiazō*), since "holy" (*hagios,* verb, *hagiazō*) preeminently characterizes God and the Holy Spirit. The Hebrew word for holy (*qādōš, √qdš*) in the first instance means "set apart," "separate," "not common," or "belonging to God." The word can be applied to things ("holy day," Isa. 58:13; "holy bread," 1 Sam. 21:4; "holy vessels," 1 Sam. 21:5; "holy mountain," Ezek. 20:40). But primarily it denotes the holy name of God (Lev. 20:3) or the holy God, who is the Holy One (Hos. 11:9). In the OT, Vriezen declares, "The Holy God" is the "*Wholly Other One*" (his italics), a phrase used also by the early Barth.[1] The concept of holiness, Vriezen continues, shows that God is different from human beings. One classic reference in the OT comes in Isaiah's vision, in which the angels covered their faces and cried, "Holy, holy, holy, is the Lord of hosts" (Isa. 6:3). In the NT, Danker regards *hagiazō* as denoting to "set aside," "sanctify," "reverence," and *hagios* as meaning "being dedicated or consecrated to the service of God."[2] A key verse is: "You shall be holy, for I am holy" (1 Pet. 1:16, citing Lev. 11:44; 19:2).[3]

This may lead to some confusion about the sense in which God through his Spirit "sanctifies" believers. There is a sense in which it can constitute an *event,* as when Hannah "lent" Samuel at birth "to the Lord":

---

1. T. G. Vriezen, *Old Testament Theology* (Oxford: Blackwell, 1962), p. 149.
2. Danker, BDAG, p. 10; similarly, for the OT, Francis Brown, S. R. Driver, and C. A. Briggs, *Hebrew and English Lexicon,* rev. ed. (Lafayette: Associated Publishers, 1980), pp. 871-74.
3. O. Procksch, "*hagios, hagiazō, hagiasmos, hagiotēs, hagiōsynē,*" in *TDNT,* 1.88-115, here 1.101.

"he is given to the Lord" (1 Sam. 1:28). But the overwhelming majority of uses of "sanctification," at least in the NT, refer to the *long and gradual process of becoming* holy, or like Christ. This is the regular meaning of "sanctification," being made holy, in the NT. Famously, in one of his earliest writings, Paul declares, "This is the will of God, your sanctification" (1 Thess. 4:3). He then spells out its ethical content: "that you abstain from fornication; that each one of you should know how to control your own body in holiness and honor, not with lustful passion, like the Gentiles who do not know God" (1 Thess. 4:3-5).

Holiness for the Christian, however, implies far more than abstinence from sexual sin, or indeed from any sin. In another early writing Paul contrasts the "works of the flesh" with "the fruit of the Spirit." The works of the flesh, he says, are "fornication, impurity, licentiousness, idolatry, sorcery, enmities, strife, jealousy, anger, quarrels, dissensions, factions, envy, drunkenness, carousing, and things like these" (Gal. 5:19-21). He then declares, "By contrast, the fruit of the Spirit is love, joy, peace, patience, kindness, generosity, faithfulness, gentleness, and self-control" (Gal. 5:22-23). The Holy Spirit does not merely prevent evil; he nurtures qualities such as love, patience, kindness, faithfulness, and gentleness, which are positive qualities of the holy life, produced by the Spirit. Moreover, patience, love, and faithfulness are qualities or dispositions which depend on the duration of time.

The philosopher Ludwig Wittgenstein shows how such qualities as love entail time and duration, whereas human feelings do not. He imagines someone saying "This pain is terrible! — Oh, it's all right — it's gone off now." But could someone, he asks, "say credibly, 'I love you deeply' — Oh it's all right — it's gone off now"?[4] Both Wittgenstein and O. R. Jones regard these qualities as *dispositions*.[5] Dispositions become manifested in particular and appropriate situations, and show themselves in appropriate conduct, attitudes, and actions. Hence Paul begins the section in Gal. 5:16, 18, with the words: "Live by the Spirit . . . if you are led by the Spirit, you are not subject to the law." He adds in 5:25: "If we live by the Spirit, let us also be guided by the Spirit." The NEB brilliantly renders Gal. 5:25: "If the Spirit is the *source* of our life, let the Spirit also direct our *course*" (my italics). "Direct our course" renders the Greek *stoichōmen* (from *stoicheō*),

---

4. Ludwig Wittgenstein, *Zettel* (Oxford: Blackwell, 1967), §504.

5. Wittgenstein, *Zettel*, §491; O. R. Jones, *The Concept of Holiness* (London: Allen & Unwin / New York: Macmillan, 1961), pp. 41, 44, 69, 89, and throughout.

which Danker renders: "following a standard of conduct," or "holding to it," as a *process*, like a *course*.[6] It is like "walking" the Christian life, or as the Jews called it, *halakah*, from the verb "walk," *halak*. Jewett explains how this exhortation can be addressed equally to libertines and to legalists in Galatians. It is the climax of his initial question, "Are you so foolish? Having started with the Spirit, are you now ending with the flesh?" (Gal. 3:3). Both the legalists and the libertines trust "the flesh" in different ways, ultimately as self-seeking, and need to be renewed by the Spirit.[7]

In 1 Corinthians Paul makes it clear that absence of the work of the Holy Spirit leads to such antisocial qualities as "jealousy and quarreling," and "behaving according to human inclinations" (1 Cor. 3:3). On the other hand, he declares, "you (plural) are God's temple, and . . . God's Spirit dwells in you" (1 Cor. 3:16). This temple of God is "holy, and you are that temple" (3:17). In 1 Cor. 6:19 the language about God's temple is applied to individuals: "Do you not know [i.e., introducing a familiar piece of teaching] that your body is a temple of the Holy Spirit within you, which you have from God, and that you are not your own?" In 2 Cor. 6:16 Paul repeats, "We are the temple of the living God."

In addition to this Albert Hogeterp points out: "Paul uses cultic imagery derived from temple services, such as references to priestly service (1 Cor. 9:13; Rom. 15:16), incense offerings (2 Cor. 2:14-16; Phil. 4:18), libations (e.g. Phil. 2:17), sacrifices (1 Cor. 10:18; Phil. 2:17; Phil. 4:18), and the offering of the Gentiles (Rom. 15:16)."[8] Parallels with pagan temples are often exaggerated. Sandmel called this tendency "parallelomania."[9] To repeat: as Hogeterp and Danker observe, the rhetorical question "Do you not know that . . . ?" introduces "a well-known fact that is generally accepted."[10] What is well known is the connection between God's holy temple and the indwelling presence of the Holy Spirit. There is also a link between the temple and God's Holy Spirit through the concept of the wisdom of the Spirit. This alluded originally to Solomon in 1 Kings 8:29, then was explored by Proverbs and other OT Wisdom literature, and finally by numerous references in early Jewish writings, including Josephus.[11] 1 Corinthians 5:1-5 also regards the case of incest as one of impurity that is

---

6. Danker, BDAG, p. 946.

7. Robert Jewett, *Paul's Anthropological Terms* (Leiden: Brill, 1971), pp. 95-114.

8. Albert L. A. Hogeterp, *Paul and God's Temple* (Leuven: Peeters, 2006), p. 1.

9. S. Sandmel, "Parallelomania," *JBL* 81 (1962), pp. 1-13.

10. Hogeterp, *Paul and God's Temple*, p. 326; Danker, BDAG, p. 693.

11. Hogeterp, *Paul and God's Temple*, pp. 328-30.

incompatible with claims to be a practicing Christian. In 1 Cor. 5:6-8 such impurity stands in contrast with "the unleavened bread of sincerity and truth," which is amplified in 5:9-13.

Many claim that 2 Cor. 6:14–7:1 deals with purity and defilement. W. O. Walker and others suggest that this section is a non-Pauline interpolation, but many also argue strongly for its Pauline character. Romans 12:1-2 also enjoins Christians not to be molded by the world (v. 2), while Rom. 12:4-21 addresses the ethical life, with further echoes in Romans 13–15. The offering of the Gentiles is "sanctified by the Holy Spirit" (15:16). Paul's temple imagery remains "a normative model."[12] Paul's language is echoed in 1 Pet. 1:2, "Chosen . . . by God the Father, and sanctified by the Spirit of God to be obedient to Jesus Christ."

Soon after the close of the NT era there is a striking account of the difference between Christian standards of holiness and those of the Greco-Roman world in which Christians lived. *The Epistle to Diognetus* was anonymous, but is probably to be dated not later than around A.D. 130. In chapters 5–6 we receive a moving picture of the lives of Christians: "Christians are distinguished from other people neither by country nor language . . . following the customs of the natives in respect of clothing, food, and the rest of their ordinary conduct (but they) display to us their wonderful and confessedly striking method of life."[13] They regard themselves as sojourners in a land of strangers, although they still marry and beget children. But "They have a common table, not a common bed. . . . They love all men, and are persecuted by all. . . . They are poor, yet make many rich, they lack all things, yet abound in all. . . . They are dishonored, and yet in their very dishonor are glorified."[14] The writer adds, "Christians . . . love those who hate them."[15]

Swete comments, "The Holy Spirit is not mentioned, but it is the life of the Spirit which is depicted. It was a new thing on the earth."[16] The *Shepherd of Hermas* speaks of the Holy Spirit as a sanctifier of Christians, enabling them "to walk in righteousness and truth."[17] Clement of Alexandria (c. 150–c. 215) declares that the Spirit unites himself mysteriously with

---

12. Hogeterp, *Paul and God's Temple*, p. 384.

13. *The Epistle to Diognetus*, 5 (*ANF*, 1.26).

14. *The Epistle to Diognetus*, 5 (*ANF*, 1.27).

15. *The Epistle to Diognetus*, 6 (*ANF*, 1.27).

16. Henry B. Swete, *The Holy Spirit in the Ancient Church* (London: Macmillan, 1912), p. 401.

17. *Hermas, Similitudes*, 9:25:2 (*ANF*, 2.52).

the believer who is "united to the Spirit through the love that knows no bounds."[18] Clement writes, "The Spirit of the Lord is a lamp . . . the more . . . a man becomes by doing right, the nearer is the illuminating Spirit to him."[19] Clement's successor, Origen (c. 185–c. 254), declares that the Holy Spirit brings "increasing sanctification."[20] In the same passage he explains that the Holy Spirit makes Christians "purer and holier," and gives "increasing sanctification." This last phrase conclusively shows that he thinks of sanctification as a *process, not an event.* For all Christians, "Their holiness [comes] from the Holy Spirit. . . . [They are] sanctified by the Spirit."[21] The Holy Spirit, he says, enables souls to be "purified by the gospel."[22]

In the post-Nicene period of the fourth century on the whole, the sanctifying work of the Holy Spirit remained a Christian presupposition, but, in reaction to the times, Athanasius, Basil, Hilary, and Ambrose concentrated overtly on the status and person of the Holy Spirit as "not a thing" (not an "it"), but a Trinitarian reality. The NT teaching was assumed rather than further explicated. There was, however, one important qualification to all this. Several of the church fathers had spoken of "deification" (*theōsis* or *theopoiēsis*), or "becoming God," not in the sense of identification, but in the effect of God-like grace. In the Eastern Orthodox Church the term became eventually formalized by Gregory Palamas (c. 1296-1358) as the Eastern equivalent to the Western sanctification. If there is any biblical support for the term, it is perhaps in 2 Pet. 1:4, "participants of the divine nature." Among the earlier fathers, Irenaeus had spoken of sharing the divine life in the context of God's becoming like us, that we may become like him. It becomes more prominent in Athanasius. He spoke of partaking of his Spirit that we might be deified.[23] The theme is repeated by Cyril of Alexandria, and steadily becomes more common in the East, to reach a formal climax in Gregory Palamas.

The sanctifying power of the Spirit next came into special prominence in the Reformation and post-Reformation periods. Martin Luther (1483-1546) has much to write about the Spirit, as Regin Prenter, especially, has demonstrated in modern times.[24] Unlike some of the medieval

18. Clement, *The Instructor*, 2.2 (*ANF*, 2.245).

19. Clement, *Miscellanies*, 4.17 (*ANF*, 2.429).

20. Origen, *On First Principles*, 1.3.8 (*ANF*, 4.255).

21. Origen, *On First Principles*, 1.3.8 (*ANF*, 4.255).

22. Origen, *Against Celsus*, 7.8 (*ANF*, 4.614).

23. Athanasius, *De Decretis*, 14.

24. Regin Prenter, *Spiritus Creator: Luther's Concept of the Holy Spirit* (Philadelphia: Muhlenberg, 1953).

mystics, he stresses the gift of the Holy Spirit for all "ordinary" Christians, including those in "secular" vocations. In the *Small Catechism* of 1529, he asserts: "The Holy Spirit sanctifies me [makes me holy] by bringing me to . . . lead a godly life."[25] He urges that *every* Christian will possess "special miraculous gifts." Similarly, in his *Large Catechism* Luther writes, "The Holy Spirit . . . makes us holy. . . . [He] has sanctified and still sanctifies us. . . . The Holy Spirit must be called *Sanctifier,* the One who makes us holy. . . . He first leads us into this holy Community . . . the church."[26] Kärk-käinen comments, "Similarly to Augustine . . . Luther took the designation Holy Spirit to mean the sanctifying work."[27]

Luther believes that sanctification through the Holy Spirit provokes conflict. He appeals especially to John and Paul. The Spirit "convicts" (*el-enchō,* NRSV, "proves wrong") "the world . . . about sin and righteousness and judgment" (John 16:8). In Paul, we have to overcome what is evil: "I do not do what I want" (Rom. 7:15), and even for the Christian, "Those who are in the flesh cannot please God" (Rom. 8:8). The Christian must destroy the last remnants of self-reliance. Temptations, "assaults," or testing, are all part of growth and sanctification.

Second, Luther finds, according to Atkinson, that his "worst enemy was not Catholicism but rather the left-wing radicalism associated with fanaticism."[28] Andreas Karlstadt and Thomas Müntzer ridiculed theological learning, preached against vows, clerical robes, and various State laws, all in the name of *private revelations* from the Holy Spirit. To Luther and Heinrich Zwingli they were the self-styled "Zwickau prophets." In 1525 Luther wrote *Against the Celestial Prophets.*[29] He reflects, "All my enemies have not hit me as hard as I have been hit by my own people." Indeed, he describes these self-styled prophets as "Satanic," especially when they encouraged the peasants to fight the princes, supposedly under the direction of the Holy Spirit. The war was a disaster, in which many of the peasants were

---

25. Martin Luther, *The Small Catechism* (Philadelphia: Concordia, 2005), article 3 of the Creed.

26. Luther, *The Large Catechism* (Philadelphia: Fortress, 1959), part 2, article 3 of the Creed, §§35-37 (italics his).

27. Veli-Matti Kärkkäinen, ed., *Holy Spirit and Salvation: The Sources of Christian Theology* (Louisville: Westminster/John Knox, 2010), p. 154.

28. James Atkinson, *Martin Luther and the Birth of Protestantism* (London: Penguin, 1968), p. 221.

29. Martin Luther, *Against the Celestial Prophets,* in *Luther's Works,* 55 vols. (St. Louis and Philadelphia: Concordia and Fortress, 1955-86), 40.79-97.

killed. For Luther, Spirit and Word speak together in harmony, or we do not hear the voice of the Spirit. The "enthusiasts'" view of sanctification as a sudden event, Luther insists, actually undermines his teaching on justification by sheer grace through faith alone. Prenter calls it "a peculiar type of piety different in principle from his [Luther's] own view."[30]

The relevance of Luther's critique for today is that some (but not all) Pentecostals regard themselves as heirs to the radical Reformers. It should be noted that Kärkkäinen, a leading Pentecostal, shares many of Luther's concerns about them. Zwingli equally opposed them, but Melanchthon held a more mediating approach.

Among other major Reformers, Martin Bucer (1491-1551) also saw the Holy Spirit as primarily the bringer of sanctification. He writes, "At every point it is the Spirit who is the key to the doctrine of sanctification."[31] John Calvin (1509-64) declares, "Believers are 'elect' through sanctification of the Spirit unto obedience and sprinkling of the blood of Jesus Christ" (1 Pet. 1:2).[32] Calvin does speak of the Holy Spirit's ministry of sanctification, but there are two reasons why this is not as prominent as it is in Luther and Bucer. First, he comments, "Faith is his [the Spirit's] principal work."[33] The Spirit is chiefly active in bringing us salvation through faith. Second, he insists, "The Scriptures . . . of which we speak aim chiefly at . . . the love of righteousness . . . implanted in our minds."[34] It is mainly through obedience to the Word that we find sanctification. But this does not exclude the application of the Word to our hearts by the Holy Spirit.

John Owen (1616-83), however, Vice-Chancellor of Oxford and Puritan theologian, insists at length on sanctification by or through the Holy Spirit. Like Luther, he warns us against "unduly pretending into supernatural agitations from God, when they were really acted by the devil."[35] He notes that 2 Pet. 2:1 warns us against "false prophets," and similarly 1 John 4:1 instructs us, "Do not believe every spirit."[36] In *The Holy Spirit*, book 2, Owen tells us that the Holy Spirit increases graces of holiness, even if believers "differ in degrees," for God works in us "both to will and to do his

---

30. Prenter, *Spiritus Creator,* p. 248.

31. Cited in W. Peter Stephens, *The Holy Spirit in the Theology of Martin Bucer* (Cambridge: Cambridge University Press, 1970), p. 74.

32. Calvin, *Institutes of the Christian Religion,* III.1.1 (in Beveridge, ed., 1.463).

33. Calvin, *Institutes,* III.1.4 (in Beveridge, ed., 1.465).

34. Calvin, *Institutes,* III.6.2 (in Beveridge, ed., 2.2).

35. John Owen, *The Holy Spirit* (Grand Rapids: Kregel, 1954), p. 25.

36. Owen, *The Holy Spirit,* p. 52.

good pleasure" (Phil. 2:13). Sanctification remains the Spirit's primary gift, and we should not become distracted with "more occasional" gifts, given for special purposes. The work of sanctification is *progressive.*[37] There may even be "delays" in growth in holiness.[38] He warns us against undue introspection. On the basis of Christ's work, "We are purged and purified from sin by the Spirit of God," until righteousness becomes habitual.[39] Owen combines constant reference to the NT with common-sense realism.

In the years following Owen, many Pentecostals found earlier roots in George Fox (1624-91) and the earliest Quakers. More often and more controversially they found them in John Wesley (1703-91) and others. Wesley's view of sanctification and "sinless perfection" is hotly debated, and it is recognized that his assistant John Fletcher went further in this direction than Wesley. Jonathan Edwards (1703-58) shared the critical dimension of Owen, as well as his use of Scripture and reason. The Spirit, in Edwards, certainly "sanctifies" and leads us to be *"Christ-like."*[40] Charles Hodge (1797-1871) concluded, "Predominantly sanctification is referred to the Holy Spirit, as his peculiar work in the economy of redemption."[41] George Smeaton (1814-89) largely follows the church fathers and Reformers, including John Owen. Abraham Kuyper (1837-1920), the eminent Dutch Calvinist, provides a comprehensive discussion, and argues that through the Holy Spirit, "Sanctification *inheres* in man," flows from the Spirit, and requires *time, patience, struggle, and perseverance.*[42] He attacks both "pietist" accounts (except Spener) and "sinless perfection." Edward Irving (1792-1834), Benjamin H. Irwin (c. 1854), and Albert B. Simpson (1843-1919) are sometimes regarded as anticipations of aspects of Pentecostalism (discussed in Part III).

This brings us to the twentieth century, in which it becomes difficult to identify "schools" of thought. Henry B. Swete (1835-1917) provided full

---

37. Owen, *The Holy Spirit* (longer version: *The John Owen Collection: A Discourse concerning the Holy Spirit* [Rio, WI: Ages Software, 2004]), p. 461.

38. Owen, *The Holy Spirit* (longer version), p. 468.

39. Owen, *The Holy Spirit* (longer version), pp. 507, 544, 549.

40. Jonathan Edwards, *A Treatise Concerning Religious Affections,* in *Select Works of Jonathan Edwards,* vol. 3 (London: Banner of Truth, 1961), §8 (his italics); also in Thomas Kepler, ed., *An Anthology of Devotional Literature* (Nappanee, IN: Evangel, 2001), p. 467.

41. Charles Hodge, *Systematic Theology,* 3 vols. (Grand Rapids: Eerdmans, 1946), 3.216.

42. Abraham Kuyper, *The Work of the Holy Spirit* (New York: Funk & Wagnalls, 1900), p. 446 (his italics in the quotation).

surveys of the NT and the church fathers. Karl Barth (1896-1968) insisted that the Spirit cannot be separated from the Word of God. He regarded sanctification as a process of struggle. His work can be found mainly in *Church Dogmatics* IV.2 §§62, 66-68, and IV.3 §73. We discuss Moltmann, Congar, and Pannenberg elsewhere.

CHAPTER 13

The Holy Spirit and Eschatology

To imagine that the Holy Spirit would support, sustain, and sanctify us forever without any change of form, i.e., to suggest that we simply drift into "immortality" without radical change, would be a denial of everything in the NT, of church tradition, and of the indications of reason. When Paul considered the resurrection of Christ, he wrote, "If the Spirit of him who raised Jesus from the dead dwells in you, he who raised Christ from the dead will give life to your mortal bodies also through his Spirit that dwells in you" (Rom. 8:11). In other words, every Christian will face death, but then be raised from death by the power of God through the Holy Spirit and union with Christ.

(1) This is confirmed by Paul's language about the "spiritual body" (1 Cor. 15:44). It is clear that the adjective *pneumatikos* ("spiritual") means "of the Holy Spirit," especially in 1 Corinthians. In 1 Cor. 2:13 Paul speaks of "interpreting spiritual things to those who are spiritual (*pneumatikois*)"; in 2:15 "those who are spiritual discern all things" (unless he means ironically "those who *claim to be* of the Spirit"); in 3:1 "spiritual people" stands in contrast to "people of the flesh," or ordinary people; in 14:1 Paul discusses "spiritual gifts" (clearly gifts bestowed by the Spirit); and in 15:44, Paul famously writes of the "spiritual body" (*sōma pneumatikon*), which functions in contrast to *sōma psychikon,* or "ordinary body" — all these passages refer to the action of the Holy Spirit. The NRSV has made here one serious mistake by translating *psychikos* as "physical," which is not its meaning here; "ordinary" or "ordinary human" would be a more accurate translation. I have pressed this argument since 1964, and endorse it in both my commentaries, together with N. T. Wright.[1] Wright does not mince

---

1. Anthony C. Thiselton, *The First Epistle to the Corinthians: A Commentary on the*

his words. He declares, "The Revised Standard Version and its successor the New Revised Standard Version . . . brazenly made them [the two kinds of body] 'a physical body' and 'a spiritual body.' "[2] This implies a contrast which Paul does not wish to make.

Wright correctly renders the Greek *sōma pneumatikon* "a body animated by, enlivened by, the Spirit of the true God, exactly as Paul has said more extensively in several other passages."[3] In my shorter commentary I commented, "The raised body is characterized by the uninterrupted, transforming power of the Holy Spirit of God. It stands in contrast with the ordinary human body that has been open to the influence of the Holy Spirit, but in partial ways, still marred by human failure, fallibility, and self-interest."[4] It emphatically does not mean "composed of nonmaterial spirit." Pannenberg, also correctly, declares, "The Spirit, then, is the creative source of the resurrection life."[5]

The implications of this are profound. It is often said that the presence and gift of the Holy Spirit is an ever-new, ever-fresh, source of life, like a flowing fountain or gushing spring.[6] Moltmann describes it with "movement metaphors" in which he includes tempest, fire, and love. The Spirit is the inexhaustible "well of life." Biblical writers regard "living water" as flowing, running water, in contrast to stagnant, dead pools or cisterns. Helmut Ringgren has provided an extensive essay on "live," "life," "living" (Hebrew *ḥāyâ, ḥay, ḥayyîm,* respectively), and related terms in *TDOT.*[7] "Life," he writes, may mean activity or well-being. "Living water" (*mayim ḥayyîm*), he asserts, "is fresh *running* water or *spring* water, in contrast to the still water in cisterns (Lev. 14:5-6, 50-52; 15:13; Num. 19:17)."[8] These passages are based on movement, activity, or functioning. The verb *ḥāyâ* means "not only 'be or stay alive', but also to enjoy a full, rich and happy

---

Greek Text (Grand Rapids: Eerdmans, 2000), pp. 1274-81; idem, *1 Corinthians: A Shorter Exegetical and Pastoral Commentary* (Grand Rapids: Eerdmans, 2006), pp. 283-84; N. T. Wright, *The Resurrection of the Son of God* (London: SPCK, 2003), pp. 351-55.

2. Wright, *The Resurrection,* p. 348.

3. Wright, *The Resurrection,* p. 354.

4. Thiselton, *1 Corinthians,* p. 283.

5. Wolfhart Pannenberg, *Systematic Theology,* 3 vols. (Edinburgh: T&T Clark / Grand Rapids: Eerdmans, 1994), 3.622.

6. Jürgen Moltmann, *The Spirit of Life: A Universal Affirmation* (London: SCM, 1982), pp. 268-89 and throughout.

7. Helmut Ringgren, *"chāyāh, chai, chaiyîm, chaiyāh, michyāh,"* in *TDOT,* 4.324-44.

8. Ringgren, *"chāyāh, chai,"* 4.333 (my italics).

life."[9] Hence it also denotes *revive* or *revival.* Proverbs 4:4 and 7:2 enjoin: "Keep my commandments and live."

This becomes especially striking in the OT in the phrase "the living God" (*'ĕlōhîm ḥayyîm,* 1 Sam. 17:26; Deut. 5:26; Jer. 10:10; 23:36; Dan. 6:20). It excludes the notion of a static inactive God.[10] Further, the OT speaks of the Tree of Life, and the Book of Life (Gen. 2:9; 3:22, 24; Ps. 69:28; Exod. 32:32). In the OT the narrative of the Tree of Life explains why human beings are mortal, but in the NT it becomes the source of endless imaginative imagery.

Exactly the same meaning is found in the NT in the Greek terms for "life," "living," "live" (*zōē, zōon, zao,* respectively). Bultmann provides the long essay on these terms in *TDNT.*[11] *Zōē* stands in contrast with *bios,* which denotes human life in the merely biological sense. *Zōē* is of a higher, more *dynamic* quality, as exemplified in the fourth gospel. Jesus himself is the life (John 11:25; 14:6). Further, Bultmann rightly insists, "*zōē* is *not* understood in the *timeless,* ideal sense."[12]

The Johannine writings provide abundant examples of this theme. For example, "in him was life" (John 1:4); "that everyone who believes in him may . . . have eternal life" (3:16); "a spring of water gushing up to eternal life" (4:14); "passed from death to life" (5:24); "as the Father has life in himself" (5:26); "the words . . . are Spirit (NRSV 'spirit') and life" (6:63); and "I am the way, and the truth, and the life" (14:6). In the first epistle of John we encounter such expressions as "the word of life" (1 John 1:1); "declare to you the eternal life" (1:2); "passed from death to life" (3:14); and "whoever has the Son has life" (5:12). In the book of Revelation we may compare "to eat from the tree of life" (Rev. 2:7); "the crown of life" (2:10); "the book of life" (3:5; 13:8; 17:8; 20:15); "springs of the water of life" (7:17; cf. 21:6; 22:1).

Because the Spirit is the cause of the resurrection (Rom. 8:11), the Holy Spirit will also sustain the post-resurrection life. This can therefore never be "timeless" (in Plato's sense), i.e., dull, repetitive, boring, in the sense of static "perfection." It would be more accurate to say "not characterized by human time." There remain purposiveness, sequence, and the unfolding of God's will. In earthly terms, we may note, there are many

---

9. Ringgren, *"chāyāh, chai,"* 4.334.

10. Ringgren, *"chāyāh, chai,"* 4.338-39.

11. Rudolf Bultmann, *"zao, zōē (bioō, bios), anazao, zōon, zōogoneō, zōopoieō,"* in *TDNT,* 2.832-75.

12. Bultmann, *"zao, zōē,"* 2.870 (my italics).

kinds of time: *clock time,* measured by astronomy and chronometers; *narrative time,* constructed by the purpose of the plot in literary theory; *subjective time* measured by human perceptions of duration, as in Martin Heidegger; and *space time,* as modified by massive changes in speed approximating towards the speed of light in the sciences. In the same way, there may be *new dimensions of time,* which are as yet uncreated, but will allow for purposive advances in eternity. If this environment is created by the Holy Spirit in accordance with his nature, it will be *dynamic and ever-fresh,* like a fountain or spring of life. It will be *living* and *vibrant,* like the Spirit himself. How could the Spirit's work cease at the end of the world-as-we-know-it? The Spirit belongs to God; he is not a created being, along with the universe.

(2) None of this is mere guesswork, because Paul tells us that in the present the Holy Spirit constitutes the first fruits (*aparchē*) of more of the same kind to come. In Rom. 8:23 Paul declares, "We ourselves, who have the first fruits of the Spirit, groan inwardly while we wait for . . . the redemption of our bodies." In his book *The Holy Spirit and Eschatology in Paul,* Hamilton comments on this verse, "The gift of the Spirit in the present is to be understood as only the beginning of the harvest proper that will occur in . . . the future age."[13] He further explains, "Because the centre of gravity lies in the future, the sons of God groan in the present. The harvest of redemption has only just begun."[14] This passage carries forward the thought of Rom. 8:9-11.

Paul switches his metaphor of the future from first fruits (*aparchē*) to "guarantee" (NRSV, Greek *arrabōn*) in 2 Cor. 5:5. The same Greek word is translated differently by the NRSV in 2 Cor. 1:22, "Giving us his Spirit in our hearts as a *first installment* (*arrabōn*)" (my italics). Hamilton remarks on this, "The Spirit is our assurance that God's promises (v. 20) will be fulfilled."[15] The term *arrabōn* also occurs in Eph. 1:14, where the NRSV correctly gives it a different translation again, namely, "pledge." Ephesians 1:13-14 read, "you also . . . were marked with the seal of the promised Holy Spirit; this is the pledge of our inheritance toward redemption as God's own people." Eduard Schweizer sums up the point: The Holy Spirit, he says, is "a guarantee of the reality of what is to come."[16] Zwiep observes

---

13. Neill Q. Hamilton, *The Holy Spirit and Eschatology in Paul* (Edinburgh: Oliver & Boyd, 1957), p. 19.

14. Hamilton, *Holy Spirit and Eschatology,* p. 19.

15. Hamilton, *Holy Spirit and Eschatology,* p. 20.

16. Eduard Schweizer, *"Pneuma, pneumatikos, pneō, empneō, pnoē, ekpneō, theopneus-*

128

that in both Paul and Acts "Pentecost is . . . an anticipation . . . of eschatological promises."[17]

The ideas conveyed by the term *arrabōn* are numerous. Danker renders the word "payment of part of a purchase price in advance, first instalment, deposit, down payment, pledge."[18] Commerce and ordinary purchases in stores have made familiar the idea of paying a deposit to secure the possession of an article. Sometimes the industrial language of "prototype" is used. Gunkel speaks of "a preliminary payment," and Friedrich Horn uses the German word *Angeld,* deposit, in a whole book on the subject.[19] The well-worn academic language of the "break-in of the future into the present" may sometimes seem more theoretical than practical, but the opposite is probably the case. For one thing, this stresses the "newness" of life in the Spirit as a new creation, which is in principle *untarnished by the past.* For another, it shows that the Kingdom of God, in which people are obedient and righteous, is imperfectly anticipated in the fallible and sinful church by the Holy Spirit, who anticipates what God has promised.

It is helpful and inspiring to see the larger picture which Paul began in Rom. 8:9-11 and then developed in 8:18-30. "Creation waits with eager longing (*apokaradokia*) for the revealing of the children of God" (8:19). Danker notes that this word is unique among Christian writers, deriving from *kara,* "head" and *dokeō,* "imagine," as in the English idiom "cranes the neck in anticipation," or as J. Fison suggests, "stands on tip-toe." [20] The whole creation longs to see God's finished redemption. In 8:20-21 Paul concedes that currently creation suffers in bondage to decay. But, in Cranfield's words, "The whole magnificent theatre of the universe together with . . . all the chorus of sub-human life" longs to see the full restoration of humankind.[21] Some are distracted by whether this implies some notion of a cosmic fall. But an excellent treatment of what is usually called the "cosmic fall" is provided by John Bimson, in both theological and scientific

---

tos: E. The New Testament," in *TDNT,* 6.396-451, here 422 (also in idem, *Bible Key Words: Spirit of God* [London: Black, 1960], p. 64).

17. Arie Zwiep, *Christ, the Spirit, and the Community of God* (Tübingen: Mohr, 2010), p. 111; and Robert Menzies, *Power: Foundations of Pentecostal Experience* (Grand Rapids: Zondervan, 2000), p. 101.

18. Danker, BDAG, p. 134.

19. Friedrich W. Horn, *Das Angeld der Geistes* (Göttingen: Vandenhoeck & Ruprecht, 1992).

20. Danker, BDAG, p. 112.

21. C. E. B. Cranfield, *Romans 1–8* (Edinburgh: T&T Clark, 1975), p. 414.

terms.[22] All that this means is that the present gift of the Spirit is somehow *less than complete,* amidst the pressures and temptation of the world. In the future this experience will be *brought to perfection.* This future will include "the redemption of our bodies." Paul therefore argues in v. 24 that if everything had been carried forward toward the future, logically there could be no such quality as *hope:* "Hope that is seen is not hope. For who hopes for what is seen?"

Paul speaks of "inheriting" (*klēronomein*) five times (1 Cor. 6:9, 10; 15:50; Gal. 5:21; Eph. 5:5). What Christians inherit includes a fuller experience of the Holy Spirit after the resurrection of the dead. Hester and Wright, among others, have explored this concept.[23] We may also compare what Harrisville has written on newness.[24] The upshot of all this is well summed up by Swete: "The resurrection of the body is so far from being the last work of the indwelling Spirit that it will be the starting point of a new creativity of spiritual life."[25] It is not only, as Harrisville argues, that newness and the heavenly life reflect contrast and continuity with the earthly; they also indicate dynamic, progressive, and untarnished newness. Paul also suggests that *love,* the supreme fruit of the Spirit, characterizes the last state (1 Cor. 13).[26] Paul writes, "Love never ends. . . . But when the complete comes, the partial will come to an end. . . . Then we will see face to face . . . then I will know fully" (13:8, 10, 12).

(3) One further way of understanding the Holy Spirit's action on the individual and the Church is to regard the Spirit as lifting us "above" the realm of sin, the law, death, and the flesh, as Paul expounds in Rom. 5–8. Yet the problem remains that on this side of the grave, as Cullmann expresses it, Christians still sin and Christians still die. It is a long-standing paradox to state categorically that Christians have been delivered and freed from the flesh, death, the law, and sin, and yet to admit that all these forces still exercise an influence — although not in a sovereign manner. A popular

22. John J. Bimson, "Reconsidering a 'Cosmic Fall'," *Science and Belief* 18 (2006), pp. 63-81.

23. James D. Hester, *Paul's Concept of Inheritance* (Edinburgh: Oliver & Boyd, 1968); N. T. Wright, "The New Inheritance according to Paul," *Bible Review* 14 (1998), pp. 16, 47, mainly on Romans.

24. R. A. Harrisville, "The Concept of Newness in the New Testament," *JBL* 74 (1955), pp. 69-79.

25. Henry B. Swete, *The Holy Spirit in the New Testament* (London: Macmillan, 1921), p. 355.

26. Harrisville, "The Concept of Newness," pp. 73, 79.

analogy has been suggested by Dennis Whiteley. Christians, he suggests, are like those who have decisively transferred from the severe cold and ice and transferred into a warm room. Yet, he says, pockets of ice and cold still exercise an influence on our limbs. We still need to be thawed out, although no one can doubt that the heat of the warm room is *decisive,* and will *win over the cold.*[27]

Oscar Cullmann, however, rightly modified and challenged mere spatial language to describe the situation. Whiteley partially acknowledges this by commenting, "It is usual to say that the Christians were 'living at the same time in each of two overlapping ages'. This simply means that the Christians were subject to two sets of 'forces', those of the old age of evil and those of the 'new age' of the new creation."[28] But Cullmann expresses this much more strongly. He declares, "The Holy Spirit is nothing else than the anticipation of the end of the present."[29] He adds that Paul's use of such terms as "first fruits" (*aparchē*) of the Spirit or "first installment" (*arrabōn*) makes this clear. Equally strongly he states, "Primitive Christian faith and thinking do not start from the spatial contrast between the Here and the Beyond, but from the *time* distinction between Formerly and Now and Then."[30] Thus Cullmann concludes, "On the basis of the Holy Spirit . . . man *is* that which *he will become only in the future.*"[31] The believer, as justified, is already sinless, though this reality is fully actualized only in the future. Cullmann then coins his famous metaphor, which was derived from World War II. He explains: "The decisive battle in a war may have already occurred . . . and yet the war still continues."[32]

This goes a long way to explain why although he calls his book *The Holy Spirit and Eschatology in Paul,* Hamilton spends so many chapters comparing A. Schweitzer's "consistent" eschatology, C. H. Dodd's "realized eschatology," and Rudolf Bultmann's "reinterpreted eschatology." It is largely because he wants to provide a *purposive* frame, wherein the Holy Spirit may precisely lead us toward the *goal* of history. Moltmann remarks, "Schweitzer shrank back and . . . rebutted the eschatology of

27. D. E. H. Whiteley, *The Theology of St Paul,* 2nd ed. (Oxford: Blackwell, 1971), pp. 126-27.

28. Whiteley, *The Theology of St Paul,* p. 126.

29. Oscar Cullmann, *Christ and Time: The Primitive Christian Conception of Time and History* (London: SCM, 1951), p. 72.

30. Cullmann, *Christ and Time,* p. 37.

31. Cullmann, *Christ and Time,* p. 75 (his italics).

32. Cullmann, *Christ and Time,* p. 84.

Jesus and the early Christians."[33] Hamilton concludes, "His [Bultmann's] re-interpretation could hardly be called Pauline."[34] Dodd stresses the present at the expense of the future, and his account of Pauline eschatology was convincingly refuted by J. Lowe.[35] Hamilton strikes the right balance in his chapter on "The Spirit and the Eschatological Tension of the Christian Life." Every Christian has the Holy Spirit in the present as a part of "being in Christ." The Holy Spirit gives us "sonship, faith, hope, prayer and glorification."[36] Yet glorification is also future, hope points to the future, and love will come to full fruition in the future. Hamilton observes, "The confidence in the present is only possible in the light of the future."[37] Thus the Spirit assists us in our "waiting" (Gal. 3:2; 5:5, 16). Even prayer is a quality which will be transformed into praise and worship in heaven. Meanwhile we must press toward the eschatological goal (Phil. 3:11-14) in the strength of the Holy Spirit.

(4) If waiting in the strength of the Holy Spirit is part of his gift, we must consider more closely what *waiting and expecting* means in practice. I have already discussed this in my recent book *Life after Death*.[38] Christians are "to wait (*anamenein*) for his Son from heaven" (1 Thess. 1:10); they "wait for the revealing of our Lord Jesus Christ" (1 Cor. 1:7); "wait for the hope of righteousness" (Gal. 5:5); "wait for adoption" (Rom. 8:23); and "wait . . . with patience" (8:25); likewise, as noted above, all "creation waits with eager longing for the revealing of the children of God" (Rom. 8:19). In 1 Corinthians, Galatians, and Romans, Paul also uses the Greek verb *apekdechomai,* "to await eagerly."[39]

Sometimes waiting may seem tedious. We may wait for trains, buses, or taxis. Waiting rooms often seem drab, colorless, and static. However, the OT may more positively speak of waiting for *God's timing*. In Ps. 37:9, "Those who wait for (*qōwê*, √*qwh*) the Lord shall inherit the land." The Psalmist again enjoins, "Wait for the Lord, and keep his way" (37:34). It would be disastrous to preempt God's timing by impatience.

33. Jürgen Moltmann, *The Coming of God* (London: SCM, 1996), p. 10.

34. Hamilton, *Holy Spirit and Eschatology*, p. 82.

35. J. Lowe, "An Examination of Attempts to Detect Development in St Paul's Theology," *JTS* 42 (1941), pp. 129-42.

36. Hamilton, *Holy Spirit and Eschatology*, p. 31.

37. Hamilton, *Holy Spirit and Eschatology*, p. 33.

38. Anthony C. Thiselton, *Life after Death: A New Approach to the Last Things* (Grand Rapids: Eerdmans, 2012); see also idem, *The Last Things* (London: SPCK, 2012), pp. 53-67.

39. Danker, BDAG, p. 100.

Many people, however, make the mistake of viewing waiting and expecting primarily as a psychological or mental state, rather than as a *disposition* or *activity*. Wittgenstein, the philosopher, suggests an excellent practical example. What does it mean in practice, he asks, to expect a guest for tea? Is it primarily a feeling of tension? No, he counters, its practical aspect is to be seen in laying the table, setting out cups and saucers, boiling the kettle, preparing a plate of cakes, and so on.[40] He thus declares, "An expectation is embedded in a situation from which it arises."[41] Finally he states (from our point of view): "'I am expecting' may be replaced by '*Be prepared* for this to happen'."[42] In the NT the best word to describe this is *readiness.* Jesus said, "You also must be ready (*hetoimos*), for the Son of Man is coming at an unexpected hour" (Matt. 24:44 ∥ Luke 12:40). In the parable of the wise and foolish maidens, "those who were ready (*hetoimos*) went with him into the wedding banquet; and the door was shut" (Matt. 25:10). The NT also uses the Greek word *hetoimazō,* "make ready," "prepare for."

In the history of the Christian Church there are numerous episodes of Christians' misunderstanding "expecting" as fervent frenzy, or even as attempting hypothetical chronological evaluations or assessments of a date. Augustine and Luther both warned their readers against such misplaced enthusiasm. Luther insisted that if he knew that the Lord would return tomorrow, he would simply continue the work to which God had called him now. According to a popular legend, he is said to have observed that he would go on planting or cultivating apple trees. One example is his stern pastoral letter to Michael Stiefel, warning him against predicting dates, which became fluctuations of expectation; rather he called for calm commitment to God's normal vocation or work.[43] The way to "be ready" is simply to do the work that God has called us to do, and to meet Jesus Christ with a cleansed and confident heart. This readiness would be the result of the work of the Holy Spirit.

(5) In addition to nurturing the final state of love, clearly the Holy Spirit conveys also *holiness,* or the *completion of his work of sanctification.*

---

40. Ludwig Wittgenstein, *The Blue and Brown Books,* 2nd ed. (Oxford: Blackwell, 1969), p. 20; and idem, *Philosophical Investigations,* 2nd ed. (Oxford: Blackwell, 1958) §444.

41. Wittgenstein, *Philosophical Investigations,* §579.

42. Ludwig Wittgenstein, *Zettel* (Oxford: Blackwell, 1967), §65 (my italics); cf. §§53-68.

43. Martin Luther, "Letter to Michael Stiefel," in T. G. Tappert, ed., *Luther: Letters of Spiritual Counsel* (London: SCM, 1955), pp. 101-3.

We must first note that holiness is *dispositional,* i.e., related to the circumstances and situation from which it arises. The key point here is one which I noted in my earlier book.[44] The situation after the resurrection will be that of closeness to God. A well-known hymn illustrates the point admirably: "When I see Thee as Thou art, I'll praise Thee as I ought." In the conditions of this present world, temptations and hindrances abound. Augustine wrote, "By the Holy Spirit their [Christians'] *will* is so much enkindled that they therefore *can*";[45] that is, by the Holy Spirit Christians have the capacity for holiness. Conditions of glory, perfect service, and perfect worship offer appropriate conditions for holiness. How could sin seem to be attractive in such an environment? The corollary of this is that notions of "purgatory" become irrelevant, either for "purification," or somehow to supplement the all-sufficient work of Christ. In Rev. 22:3, the seer proclaims, "Nothing accursed will be found there anymore."

44. Thiselton, *Life after Death,* pp. 132-36.
45. Augustine, *On Rebuke and Grace,* 38 (*NPNF,* ser. 2, 5.487, my italics).

PART III

Experience and Global Origins and Current Issues among Pentecostals

CHAPTER 14

The Origin and Development of Pentecostalism

We must be cautious about identifying the origins of Pentecostalism with Charles F. Parham (1873-1929) and William J. Seymour (1870-1922) alone, as is often done. Pentecostal churches have become a global phenomenon, and many point to revivals in Korea, Wales, and South America as Pentecostal in flavor; the movement was never entirely restricted to the United States. Moreover, some identify a series of earlier movements as "proto-Pentecostalism." Such movements range from Montanism in the second century to the Radical Reformers, Andreas Karlstadt and Thomas Müntzer, in the sixteenth century. Some also include in a broad sense George Fox (1624-91) and the early Quakers, Edward Irving (1792-1834), A. B. Simpson (1843-1919), and Benjamin Irwin (d. 1854).

1. Origins and Development, Mainly in America

(1) With these two provisos, it is customary to trace the main origin of the movement to Charles F. Parham and William J. Seymour. Some focus on Seymour rather than on Parham, partly because Parham adopted a racist tone in his theology and practice. Originally a Methodist minister in Kansas, he founded a Bible school in Topeka. Here he taught the "five-fold" or "full" gospel of justification, sanctification, Spirit baptism, divine healing, and the imminence of the return of Christ. The fifth feature was combined with a "premillennial" eschatology. Premillennialists believe that the millennium of a thousand years will *follow* the return of Christ, i.e., that the Parousia *predates* the millennium. This is usually based on a particular interpretation of Rev. 20:1-10, sometimes in conjunction with

1 Cor. 15:22-28. Revelation 20:2 speaks of the binding of the devil for a thousand years. Dayton argues, "These . . . themes are well-nigh universal within the Movement."[1]

Parham's work was closely connected with hopes of revival for Christians. He believed that new healings and miracles would follow a period of dryness, because, like A. B. Simpson, he looked for "the latter rain" of a new Pentecost in accordance with Joel 2:23 (AV/KJV). In June 1901 this hope and experience passed to one of his students in Topeka, and then to half of the student body. Parham further insisted that "speaking in tongues" was "an inseparable part of the Baptism of the Holy Spirit."[2] Parham's view of sanctification as an "event," rather than a long process, was held in common with many in the Holiness movement, including D. L. Moody and Charles Finney. A final constituent element was Parham's belief that the narrative of the Acts of the Apostles should be replicated today, and was in no sense a descriptive account of the unique age of the earliest Church. His movement seemed to reach its height in 1905-6. Several thousand experienced this revival, especially from 1903, in the Kansas revival. Afterward the movement spread to Texas, where it gained many new converts, including Seymour.

William J. Seymour is especially remembered as pastor of the Apostolic Faith Mission, Azusa Street, Los Angeles. The so-called Azusa Street Revival took place in 1906-9. Seymour's parents had been African-American slaves. He apparently left the Methodist Episcopal Church because it did not hold premillennial views and did not endorse contemporary "prophecies." He traveled to Houston in 1902-3 and studied under Parham in 1905. Because of his race, Parham had him study outside the window of the lecture room. He experienced "baptism in the spirit" and was called to become pastor of the Azusa Street Holiness mission in 1906.

From 1906-9 the Azusa Street Mission became a center of revival. Seymour used the "call and response" method of preaching familiar in many black churches. He often appealed to such standard Pentecostal texts such as "the Spirit of the Lord is upon me" (Luke 4:18, quoting Isa. 61:1); the "longer ending" of Mark: "They will cast out demons; they will speak in new tongues; they will pick up snakes . . ." (Mark 16:17-18); and,

---

1. Donald Dayton, *Theological Roots of Pentecostalism* (Grand Rapids: Baker Academic, 1987), p. 22.

2. Charles F. Parham, *A Voice Crying in the Wilderness* (Baxter Springs: Apostolic Faith Bible College, 1902), p. 35; Yongnan Jeon Ahn, *Interpretation of Tongues and Prophecy in 1 Corinthians 12–14* (Blandford Forum, UK: Deo, 2013), pp. 14-25.

"All of them were filled with the Holy Spirit and began to speak in other languages" (Acts 2:4). It is arguable that Seymour's emphasis on all nationalities was "boundary-breaking."

Surprisingly, when Parham visited the Mission in October 1906, he reacted with disgust at "animal noises, trances, shaking, jabbering," and so forth.[3] In fact, Seymour himself disowned some of these phenomena, preferring to emphasize the fruit of love. Tragically, there began a series of power struggles and splits, which marred claims to the unity of the Spirit among Pentecostals from the earliest days of the movement. Parham founded a rival community only five blocks away from Seymour, although Seymour was gracious and self-effacing, and encouraged critical responses from his congregation. By this time some 50,000 readers took the *Apostolic Faith* newspaper (first published in 1906 by Seymour and the Azusa Street Mission).

In spite of Seymour's plea for unity, splits tragically continued, most having more to do with personality clashes than with doctrine. In 1908 Seymour married, and Florence Crawford, editor of *Apostolic Faith,* moved to Portland with the paper's mailing list. At the same time William Durham again set up a rival church, although this time there was a difference in doctrinal emphasis. Seymour traveled to Alabama and Illinois, but over the years his congregation dwindled. He saw himself as forsaken "by the people he had been called to serve."[4]

(2) A phase of increased development began with Alfred G. Garr (1874-1944), Frank J. Ewart (1876-1947), Eudorus N. Bell (1866-1923), Aimee Semple McPherson (1890-1944), and Ivan Q. Spencer (1888-1970). We shall shortly consider Pentecostals in Africa, Japan, Brazil, Chile, and Korea.

(i) Originally a Baptist, Garr received "baptism in the Holy Spirit" in the Azusa Street Revival in 1906. He entered Asbury College, in Wilmore, Kentucky, and experienced a call to undertake missionary work in India. He had endorsed Parham's principle that the "initial experience" of baptism in the Spirit was speaking in tongues. This became a standard feature of "classical" Pentecostalism.[5] He traveled to Calcutta where a Pentecostal revival was in process. But a crucial factor now entered some circles of

3. C. M. Robeck, "Seymour, William Joseph," in *NIDPCM*, pp. 1053-58, here pp. 1055-56.

4. Robeck, "Seymour," p. 1057.

5. Gary B. McGee, ed., *Initial Evidence: Historical and Biblical Perspectives* (Eugene, OR: Wipf & Stock, 2007).

Pentecostalism. To his surprise, Garr discovered that his gift of tongues proved to have no significance for his learning the Bengali language, just as his wife, Lillian, discovered that, for her, "tongues" had nothing to do with learning Tibetan or Mandarin Chinese. They henceforth regarded speaking in tongues as an expression of praise and prayer, and possibly a sign of empowerment.

(ii) Two years after Garr's experience at Azusa Street, in 1908, Frank Ewart received "baptism in the Spirit." In 1911 he became assistant pastor to Durham in Los Angeles, and pastor a year later. He also encountered Robert McAlister in 1913. This led to a second departure from the "classical" Pentecostalism of Parham and Seymour. In the light of these collaborations, Ewart began to anticipate the "Oneness" movement, which insisted on baptism in the name of Christ, not the Trinity. It emphasized the centrality of Christ, but also moved away from Trinitarian theology, perceiving other Pentecostals as preoccupied with the Holy Spirit at the expense of Christ. The movement persisted within the Pentecostal Assemblies of God. Their outlook was at the time known as "the new issue" or the "Jesus only" emphasis, and looked back especially to Durham.

(iii) Eudorus Bell and the Assemblies of God (founded 1913) originally came out of the Baptist churches. He issued a public "call" to share in a Council of Pentecostal Churches at Hot Springs, Arizona, which brought about the Assemblies. From 1917 to 1919 he edited the *Pentecostal Evangel,* and was officially Chairman of the Assemblies of God in 1920. Bell went as far as to be re-baptized, this time in the name of Christ. Moreover, his understanding of Trinitarian theology seems to have varied, and later he returned to a more Trinitarian faith, although retaining his Pentecostal roots.

(iv) Aimee Semple McPherson was ordained in the Assemblies of God in 1919 as an evangelist, although she resigned three years later to join William Durham's community. She married Robert Semple, and they became missionaries in China until Robert's death in 1921. She returned to Los Angeles and published *The Second Coming of Christ.* Most important for Pentecostals, during the early 1920s she began to teach and preach the "Four-Square Gospel," reflecting A. B. Simpson's earlier "fourfold gospel."

In 1923 Aimee Semple McPherson founded the Lighthouse of International Foursquare Evangelism (LIFE) Bible Training College. She preached there the four cardinal principles of Pentecostal thought: (1) Christ as Savior (John 3:16); (2) Christ as Baptizer in the Spirit (Acts 2:4); (3) Christ as Healer (James 5:14-15); and (4) Christ as Coming King

(1 Thess. 4:16-17).[6] During the 1920s she had an influential ministry, which, especially through the radio, reached several million people. But alongside this were various controversies, and in 1930 she suffered what was then called "a nervous breakdown." In 1936 she wrote *Give Me My Own God.*[7]

(v) Ivan Quay Spencer founded the Elim Fellowship of Churches in 1933.[8] He was originally from the Methodist Episcopal Church, and he received "baptism in the Holy Spirit" in 1912. In 1915 he became minister of Elim Tabernacle Church. He joined the Assemblies of God in 1919 in New York and founded the Elim Bible Institute in 1924. It is not always easy to distinguish between "Pentecostal" and "Elim Fellowship." The latter includes the former, but is probably more open to other traditions. Its web site tells us that it is "of Pentecostal conviction and charismatic orientation," but it is also "Christ-centred" and seeks to edify "all followers of Christ, no matter what their church background." Its mission is primarily "Christ's mandate to preach the gospel" and its purpose is "to manifest the Spirit of Christ." It includes "restoring broken lives."[9]

We shall consider the main significance of Pentecostal theology and practice when we have examined part of the broader international picture.

2. Pentecostalism in the Two-Thirds World: Latin America and Asia

We must observe a warning offered by Allan Anderson. He writes, "Historians of Pentecostalism have reflected a bias interpreting history from a predominantly white American perspective, neglecting . . . the vital work of Asian, African . . . and Latin-American Pentecostal pioneers."[10] This area constituted a serious gap in my larger book, *The Holy Spirit* (2013). Yet a writer from the West must tread very carefully here. Either he or she is accused of neglecting a vital area, or the writer may well be accused of writing "from the outside," as a white Westerner, located in the Northern

---

6. Aimee Semple McPherson, *The Four-Square Gospel,* compiled by Raymond Cox (Los Angeles: Heritage Committee, 1969), p. 9; and Ahn, *Interpretation of Tongues,* pp. 26, 32.

7. Aimee Semple McPherson, *Give Me My Own God* (New York: H. C. Kinsey, 1936).

8. E. E. Warner, "Elim Fellowship," in *NIDPCM,* p. 598.

9. www.elimfellowship.org.

10. Allan Anderson, *An Introduction to Pentecostalism: Global Charismatic Christianity* (Cambridge: Cambridge University Press, 2004), p. 166.

Hemisphere. Hence we attempt simply to describe the explosion of Pentecostalism as it has been over the last twenty years, and to correct some assumptions about its origins in the two-thirds world.

(1) *Latin America: Brazil and Chile.* Perhaps of all the areas involved, the most spectacular growth has occurred in Latin America. The respected linguistic scholar Eugene Nida has claimed that in Brazil some 87 percent of the Protestant community is either Pentecostal or charismatic. Even some years ago in 1974, he calculated the Brazilian Assemblies of God at around 22 million.[11] Hollenweger calculated Brazilian Assemblies of God at 13,000 in 1930, 600,000 in 1950, 1.5 million in 1967; by 1972 it was the largest Protestant church in Brazil.[12] In 2003 E. A. Wilson argued that between two-thirds and three-fourths of the 40 million evangelical Christians in Brazil were Pentecostal, and that Brazil represented the largest number in South America.[13] Brazil has 47 percent Pentecostals in a population of 170 million. Second comes Chile, with 36 percent of 15 million; third comes Colombia with 29 percent of 24 million.

In Chile, Wilson calculates, 95 percent of all Protestants are Pentecostals. Juan Sepúlveda traces the origins of Pentecostalism in Chile only partly to the Azusa Street Revival of 1906, on the basis of testimony written on behalf of Willis C. Hoover.[14] Hoover mentions "pre-Pentecostal" meetings in Valparaiso, based on a study of Acts that resulted in daily prayer meetings. Hoover recounts: "Laughter, weeping, shouting, singing, foreign tongues, visions and ecstasies, during which the individual fell to the ground and felt himself caught up into another place, to heaven, to Paradise . . . with various kinds of experience: conversations with God, the angels, or the devil. Those who experienced these things were . . . filled with praises, the spirit of prayer and love."[15] Nellie Laidlaw was a new convert, who in 1909 was known for her gift of prophecy. Her preaching or "prophecy" is regarded as the foundation day of Chilean Pentecostalism.

11. Eugene A. Nida, *Understanding Latin Americans with Special Reference to Religious Renewal Movements* (Pasadena: William Carey Library, 1974); and idem, "The Indigenous Churches in Latin America," *Practical Anthropology* 8 (1961), pp. 97-105.

12. Walter J. Hollenweger, *The Pentecostals* (Peabody, MA: Hendrickson, 1972).

13. E. A. Wilson, "Latin America," in *NIDPCM*, pp. 157-67.

14. Juan Sepúlveda, "Indigenous Pentecostalism and the Chilean Experience," in Allan H. Anderson and Walter J. Hollenweger, eds., *Pentecostals after a Century: Global Perspectives* (Sheffield: Sheffield Academic Press, 1999), pp. 111-34, here p. 113.

15. Sepúlveda, "Indigenous Pentecostalism," p. 116 (quoting Willis C. Hoover, *Historia* [Valparaiso: Excelsior, 1948], p. 33).

In 1909-10 the Methodist Church of Santiago withdrew from Hoover's and Laidlaw's meetings, but Hoover appealed to Wesley's writings. Yet Sepúlveda comments, "In fact Chilean Pentecostalism accepts the 25 faith articles of the Methodist Episcopal Church with no alteration, practises infant baptism . . . This closeness to Methodism differentiates Chilean Pentecostalism from USA-born Pentecostalism."[16] He calls this a "clash between two 'mentalities' or 'cultures' . . . developing within Chilean Pentecostalism."[17] These came to relate to what he called an official, educated, rational culture and a popular, oral, traditional culture. Today he sees "a complex relation of continuity and discontinuity between the Protestant tradition received from missionaries, popular Catholicism, and the local culture."[18]

Chilean Pentecostalism therefore differs in several respects from the "classical" Pentecostalism of Parham. Speaking in tongues may be *one* gift of the Holy Spirit, but it does not constitute "initial evidence" of baptism in the Spirit. Indeed, the latter may be identified with conversion. Infant baptism is also practiced. Sepúlveda concludes that its manifestation in Chile is indeed genuine Pentecostalism, but "broader" than that of the USA. In his response, Andrew Kirk first agrees about independent or indigenous development. But then he also calls the relation to the Methodist Church "ambiguous," and points to such phenomena as processions, healing, multiple weddings, and attitudes to healing and illness as mirroring popular Catholicism. He argues that by 2010 it would have become likely that non-Catholics will exceed the number of Catholics in South America.[19]

Returning to Brazil, Hollenweger reminds us that Brazilian Pentecostals do not rely on printed books or radio programs but "rely entirely on the personal testimony of their members." They do not "employ any pastors in the traditional sense. . . . The elders and deacons carry on the preaching. . . . During the service, anyone can give testimony or prophesy, but the community passes judgment on everything (1 Cor. 14:29)."[20] Women, he says, dress carefully for worship, and people often endure persecution with silent suffering. Thus, although there is a significant overlap

16. Sepúlveda, "Indigenous Pentecostalism," p. 119.
17. Sepúlveda, "Indigenous Pentecostalism," p. 122.
18. Sepúlveda, "Indigenous Pentecostalism," p. 129.
19. J. Andrew Kirk, "Response," in Allan H. Anderson and Walter J. Hollenweger, eds., *Pentecostals after a Century: Global Perspectives* (Sheffield: Sheffield Academic Press, 1999), pp. 135-37, here p. 137.
20. Hollenweger, *The Pentecostals,* p. 85.

with liberation theology, the two movements are not entirely similar, let alone the same. As in African Pentecostalism, in Latin American Pentecostalism the world is "full of supernatural and invisible powers, where miracles and divine healing are not only happening, but are made to happen."[21] Like practitioners of liberation theology, Latin American Pentecostals reflect solidarity with the poor, and they do not confine themselves to soul-saving. Healing the sick through prayer is a regular feature of Brazilian Pentecostalism. Hollenweger concludes that their experience "is not carried on in rational categories," and they have changed much of their attitude to Catholicism since Vatican II (1962-65).

Jürgen Moltmann shares the view that Pentecostalism in Latin America, Asia, and Africa does not simply spring from Parham and Seymour in North America. He writes, "Pentecostal churches are not sects steered by US capital . . . they have sprung out of the ground everywhere. . . . They are an independent popular movement of the poor. They have something to say to the whole of Christendom on earth, and have liberating experiences to pass on."[22]

(2) *Asia, Korea, India (Kerala), and the Chinese House Churches.*

(i) Paulson Pulikottil argues that in the 1920s, the southern Indian state of Kerala witnessed the encounter between "native Pentecostalism" and the Pentecostalism "introduced by missionaries from the West."[23] Pulikottil in fact traces the initial involvement with Pentecostalism to the Syrian church fathers of the early centuries and even to the mission of Thomas to India in the first century. As a "postcolonial" writer he is keen to provide a history "from the edges," in contrast to the more conventional or traditional history. In "traditional" history the mission of Thomas to India largely rests on a reference in Eusebius (*Ecclesiastical History,* 3.1) to Thomas's missionary work in Parthia, and to the Acts of Thomas, which, in the words of Susan Myers, "purports to tell the story of the travels of the apostle Thomas in the 'land of the Indians'." She adds, "The Acts of Thomas provides some of the earliest evidence available for the Christianity that flourished among Syrian-speaking Christians. . . . Chris-

21. Hollenweger, *The Pentecostals,* p. 101.

22. Jürgen Moltmann, "Preface," in Veli-Matti Kärkkäinen, ed., *The Spirit in the World: Emerging Pentecostal Theologies in Global Contexts* (Grand Rapids: Eerdmans, 2009), pp. viii-xii, here p. ix.

23. Paulson Pulikottil, "One God, One Spirit, Two Memories: A Pentecostal and Native Pentecostalism in Kerala," in Kärkkäinen, ed., *The Spirit in the World,* pp. 19-88, here p. 69.

tian ascetics from Northern Mesopotamia became famous for their enthusiasm . . . a life of celibacy . . . renouncing sexual activity."[24] The apocryphal book, in origin a gnostic writing from the fourth century in Syriac and Greek, should be distinguished from the Gospel of Thomas, also an apocryphal book, which probably dates much earlier, from around AD 150, and was found among the largely gnostic Nag Hammadi writings in c. 1945, written in Coptic.

Certainly the Mar Thoma Church believes not only in its early Syrian origins, but also in its foundation by Thomas the apostle. In favor of this tradition, Rome had set up trade routes from Rome to India, and travel to India was quite possible. The Syrian Orthodox Church was earlier than any Roman Catholic influence. *Mar* is Syrian for "Lord" and is the title regularly given to saints. On the other hand, Burgess also asserts concerning Thomas and India, "There is [a] question about the historicity of this tale."[25]

Pulikottil does acknowledge the influence of Topeka and the Azusa Street Revival, but he sees two types of Pentecostalism arriving in India. He insists, however, that a postcolonial approach "focuses on locality and particularity."[26] Pentecostalism shared "with Syrian Orthodox tradition before the arrival of the Portuguese in India in the fifteenth century."[27] The Syrian church in its reformed form was called the Mar Thomas Church. Pastor K. E. Abraham, Pulikottil argues, led Holiness churches in 1918, and then the South India Pentecostal Church of God. Meanwhile George Berg arrived in Kerala in 1909 representing Parham and Seymour's teaching on baptism in the Spirit, and his work was consolidated by Robert F. Cook in 1912. By 1923, he concludes, there were "three important Pentecostal movements in Kerala."[28] The first was the South India Pentecostal Church of God descended from Abraham; the second was the Assemblies of God; the third was the South India Full Gospel Church, still led by Cook. In 1926 two of these merged to preserve the "two memories" to which he refers. The history of all this is preserved in Abraham's autobiography.

---

24. Susan E. Myers, "Thomas, Acts of," in *NIDB*, 5.582-84.

25. Stanley M. Burgess, *The Holy Spirit: Eastern Christian Traditions* (Peabody, MA: Hendrickson, 1989), p. 86; similarly Michael von Brück and J. Paul Rajashekar, "India," in Erwin Fahlbusch et al., eds., *The Encyclopedia of Christianity*, vol. 2 (Grand Rapids: Eerdmans / Leiden: Brill, 2001), pp. 683-90, here p. 686.

26. Pulikottil, "One God," p. 71.

27. Pulikottil, "One God," p. 72.

28. Pulikottil, "One God," p. 75.

In essence the original Pentecostal movement in India refused "to reinvent the Holy Spirit" as Parham had taught. Revivals had taken place in Kerala in 1873, 1895, and 1908. Pulikottil concludes, "Pentecostal scholars from the non-Western countries need to explore ways in which they write the natives back into history . . . reconstructing the history . . . from the edges."[29] Although some of the claims of Pulikottil may remain controversial, Moltmann speaks of the importance of Pyongyang, Korea, Kerala, and a number of places in Africa as pointing to, or underlining, Pentecostalism as "a religion of the people."[30]

(ii) Korea: Pyongyang and *minjung* culture. The Korean Pentecostal experience is also controversial. Two Korean writers, Lee Hong Jung and Yongnan Jeon Ahn, are both thoroughly versed in their Korean world, but they received doctorates from two British universities, Birmingham and Nottingham, respectively. Lee Hong Jung argues that after 1960, "Korean Pentecostalism" was materially "distorted in the process of syncretism with Korean shamanism and North American capitalism," especially in the light of its relations to Korean *minjung* — those exploited and "alienated socially, uneducated in cultural and intellectual matters."[31] Ahn makes no such claims, focusing on more specific theological issues, including speaking in tongues, spiritual gifts, and biblical hermeneutics.[32]

Both would agree, however, that the outpouring of the Holy Spirit in Pyongyang, now in North Korea near the border with South Korea, was an indigenous experience for Korea, and of major importance for Pentecostalism. This was preceded by the martyrdom of a Welsh missionary in 1866 and the "Wansan Revival" of 1904. Over the next three years, 30,000 became Christians. But the "Great Revival" took place in Pyongyang from January 1907 to 1910. Initially 50,000 were converted to Christian faith, and most met daily in prayer for an outpouring of the Holy Spirit. Under the leadership of Yong Do Lee, many spent ten days in prayer and fasting on Kam Kang Mountain, during which the voice of God was heard, and some "cast out demons." The Yongmuh Mountain movement commenced again following the defeat of Japan in 1945. The Pentecostal concern for the Holy Spirit spread to Seoul; meanwhile a

---

29. Pulikottil, "One God," p. 87.

30. Moltmann, "Preface," p. x.

31. Lee Hong Jung, "*Minjung* and Pentecostal Movements in Korea," in Anderson and Hollenweger, eds., *Pentecostals after a Century*, pp. 138-63, here p. 138 and n. 1.

32. Ahn, *Interpretation of Tongues*.

missionary, Jonathan Gosforth, then revisited China and Manchuria with the news of the Korean revival.

My own experience of South Korea came about in May 2007, when I was invited to Seoul for the celebration of one hundred years since the Pyongyang Great Revival. At this conference they expected 5,000 participants. I was also invited to speak in at least six or seven seminaries, some of which were Pentecostal. Their hospitality was magnificent, and their church life impressive.

The huge impact of Pentecostalism in Korea cannot be denied, nor could it be true to deny that many generations of Koreans before 1945 have been oppressed, in turn, by Japanese, Russian, and probably Chinese conquests. But whether this confirms the influence of *minjung* on Korean Pentecostalism may refer more readily to past rather than present experiences. Today the population of South Korea is around 50 million, of whom Protestants number around 20 percent, Buddhists some 15 percent, and Confucians some 11 percent. Undoubtedly Pentecostal and other churches show concern for the urban poor, and the so-called *minjung* movement has prospered since 1970. It is said that the Protestant and Pentecostal emphasis on biblical authority owes something to the Confucian stress on authoritative texts. Lee Hong Jung states, "*Historically speaking,* a dynamic dialectical interaction of the Pentecostal movement and the reality of the Korean *minjung,* are integral parts of the reality of Korea."[33] But today it seems that Pentecostalism includes people from many backgrounds in a variety of seminaries.

The size of Pentecostal congregations in Korea is staggering. Anderson recounts that "the largest Christian congregation in the world, with an estimated 800,000 members in 1995, has been a Pentecostal one, the Yoido Full Gospel Church in Seoul, Korea."[34] He compares it with "the second largest congregation in the World," namely the Temple of Brazil Para Cristo in São Paulo. I witnessed enormous Pentecostal congregations in Seoul and Daejeon, South Korea. Undoubtedly these represent a mixture of highly educated and socially deprived people, and oppression under Japan, Russia, and perhaps China has played a part in shaping the subsequent mind-set. But we should be cautious about sociological, rather than theological, explanations of that growth.

33. Jung, "*Minjung* and the Pentecostal Movement in Korea," p. 141 (first italics mine).

34. Anderson, "Introduction: World Pentecostalism at the Crossroads," in Anderson and Hollenweger, eds., *Pentecostals after a Century,* pp. 19-31, here p. 27.

3. African Pentecostalism

The voices of many African Pentecostals can be typified in the emphatic assertion of Ogbu Kalu, when he writes: "African Pentecostalism did not originate from Azusa Street and is not an extension of the American electronic church."[35] In view of opinions to the contrary, it may be tempting to regard this as an overstatement. But Kalu has impressive academic credentials as a historian of Pentecostalism. In 1974 he was Professor in the University of Nigeria, and in 2001 Professor of McCormick Theological Seminary. Clifton Clarke regards Kalu as "the most accomplished African scholar in North America today," although in fact he died in 2009.[36]

Kalu insists on three fundamental principles: (i) the continuity of African Christianity with African primal religion; (ii) the church as more than an institution with restrictive walls; and (iii) an ecumenical perspective which appreciates "grass-roots" experience and people. The first principle is heavily influenced by African cosmology. This emphatically includes the reality of witchcraft, ecstatic prophets, and numerous spirits as permeating the everyday world, often bringing sickness, disease, and poverty. It also privileges oral testimony over written documents, and narrative over argumentation. Hence the oral testimony of Pentecostals, together with a key emphasis on healing and often prosperity, makes a ready appeal. Participatory "call and response" preaching is a phenomenon of most black churches, together with drumming, singing, and often dancing, which includes "a spontaneous verbal and non-verbal interaction between speaker and listener in which statements ('calls') are punctuated by expressions ('responses') from the listener."[37]

The African "context" of the spirit world constitutes the "underside of history," which David Bosch calls "an epistemological break" from the traditional, often Christological, approach "from above."[38] The traditional

---

35. Ogbu Kalu, *African Pentecostalism: An Introduction* (Oxford: Oxford University Press, 2008), p. viii.

36. Clifton R. Clarke, "Ogbu Kalu and Africa's Pentecostalism: A Tribute Essay," in idem, ed., *Pentecostal Theology in Africa* (Eugene, OR: Pickwick, 2014), pp. 7-18, here p. 7.

37. G. Smitherman, *Talkin and Testifyin: The Language of Black America* (Detroit: Wayne State University Press, 1977), p. 104; and Clifton R. Clarke, "Call and Response: Toward an African Pentecostal Theological Method," in idem, ed., *Pentecostal Theology in Africa,* pp. 21-39, here p. 28.

38. David Bosch, *Transforming Mission: Paradigm Shifts in the Theology of Mission* (Maryknoll, NY: Orbis, 1991), p. 423; and Clarke, "Call and Response," p. 33.

approach is allegedly elitist. Kalu talks of "unshackling" theology from rationalistic or scientific ways of thinking.[39] Thus the so-called spiritual dimension of reality includes not only prayers, but folktales, songs, myths, proverbs, riddles, healing, demons, tongues, and even the tactile symbols of popular Catholicism. African cosmology views life holistically. In conclusion, W. Hollenweger declares, "The [Pentecostal] Movement has more members and is theologically more important outside the United States."[40]

(1) *West Africa* contains some of the largest countries, by population, on the continent. Nigeria claims 130 million people, of which 43 percent are supposedly Christian. Ghana has 20 million, of which 57 percent claim to be Christian. J. K. Olupona writes, "Prayer alone is the panacea for all needs, with the Bible."[41] Many independent, "prophetic" churches have been founded by prophets. African cosmology, as we noted, assumes the reality of witchcraft, ecstatic prophecy, and the role of the "big man," or authoritative, charismatic, leader; predestination and increasingly today what is called "the prosperity gospel" have made great advances, on the ground that the spiritual and material worlds are one. Leaders, Olupona suggests, are "compulsive rather than persuasive."[42] Physical or quasi-physical symbols remain important, including water, holy oil, dreams, songs, and more. They are judged to have more importance than books, magazines, teaching, or biblical commentaries. No single theory, Olupona insists, can account for rapid Pentecostal growth.[43] "Healing is at the core" of the movement, he adds, and the Full Gospel Business Men's Fellowship and Deeper Christian Life movements have influence.

David Ogungbile argues that the most radical challenge within Pentecostalism, especially in Nigeria, is the "prosperity gospel." He carefully demonstrates how an earlier emphasis on "other worldly affirmation" and an acceptance of earthly poverty have given way to a "sudden shift" to "craving for material prosperity."[44] Ogungbile shows how, for example, the traditional application of the parable of the Rich Man and Lazarus of

39. Kalu, *African Pentecostalism,* p. 250.

40. Walter J. Hollenweger, "Pentecostalism," in Erwin Fahlbusch et al., eds., *The Encyclopedia of Christianity,* vol. 4 (Grand Rapids: Eerdmans / Leiden: Brill, 1997), pp. 144-51, here p. 146.

41. J. K. Olupona, "Africa, West," in *NIDPCM,* pp. 11-31, here p. 11.

42. Olupona, "Africa, West," in *NIDPCM,* p. 14.

43. Olupona, "Africa, West," in *NIDPCM,* p. 15.

44. David Ogungbile, "African Pentecostalism and the Prosperity Gospel," in Clarke, ed., *Pentecostal Theology in Africa,* pp. 132-49, here pp. 134-35.

Luke 16 has been completely reversed. "Whereas the poor beggar Lazarus was once held up as a paradigm of blessing, the Adeboye-led Redeemed Church of God in Nigeria regards Lazarus as merely residing in Abraham's bosom in the absence of entry to the Kingdom of God, while Abraham himself was extremely rich, on the basis of Genesis 13:2: 'Abraham was very rich in cattle, in silver, and in gold'" (AV/KJV).

Ogungbile also maintains that the prosperity gospel has spread to Egypt, Ethiopia, Kenya, Sudan, Tanzania, and Zambia. Yet Nigeria remains the most prominent, largely because of the "declining economic performance as a result of heavy reliance on it, deepening corruption among the political elite, misrule leading to the non-performance of the state."[45] Ogungbile regards Archbishop Benson Idahosa as the recognized pioneer of the prosperity gospel in Africa.[46] He also cites as leaders Pastor Enoch Adejare Adeboye and Ayodele Joseph Oritsejafor. He quotes Benson Idahosa as declaring, "My God is not the God of the poor. . . . See by the podium here my computerized Mercedes Benz. In six months time, I am riding my jet. . . . You are having the multiple of ten of what you are offering."[47]

The prosperity gospel, like exorcisms, healing, and deeds of power, illustrates the pragmatic attitude to human needs which some describe as "contextualization." It is not surprising that some theologians have grave reservations about this approach.

(2) *East Africa* is said to have a combined population of around 260 million, of which up to 61 percent claim to be Christian. The larger countries include Ethiopia (66 million), Kenya (35 million), Tanzania (35 million), Uganda (23 million), and Zambia (12 million). The largest number of Christians probably live in Kenya (about 80 percent), and Uganda and Zambia (both between 67 percent and 80 percent).

Kenya has about two million Pentecostals, including a very large church, the Valley Road Pentecostal Church, in Nairobi. It witnessed the Mau Mau uprising in 1952, but in 1963 Jomo Kenyatta became prime minister, then president in 1964. Daniel arap Moi succeeded him in 1978. This brought a measure of stability. In 2000 the Catholic Church organized eighteen dioceses, and the Anglican Province of Kenya was formed in 1960. For many years the African Inland Mission and Bible Churchman's

---

45. Adoyi Onoja, "The Pentecostal Churches: The Politics of Spiritual Deregulation since the 1980s," in Julius O. Adekunle, ed., *Religion in Politics: Secularism and National Integration in Modern Nigeria* (Trenton, NJ: Africa World, 2009), pp. 263-73, here p. 263.

46. Ogungbile, "African Pentecostalism," p. 138.

47. Ogungbile, "African Pentecostalism," p. 141.

Missionary Society had been active. The Kenyan Assemblies of God had half a million adherents in 1943. The 1969 constitution guarantees religious liberty. The Nairobi Pentecostal Church also reaches out to abandoned and abused "street children," providing guardians, schools, Bible classes, and apprenticeships for them.

In Uganda, Idi Amin took power in 1971, serving as president for eight years. In 1975 he closed twenty-seven Christian denominations, allowing only Anglican, Roman Catholic, and Eastern Orthodox Churches to survive. Between 100,000 and 500,000 were killed, and many fled to other countries. In 1979 Amin was ousted and Obote resumed as president. Armed struggles took place until relative security in 1993. There has been a resurgence or maintenance of primitive or tribal religion including establishing relations with spirits, performing exorcisms, and reverence for ancestors and for the mystical powers of nature.

On the other hand, Pentecostal churches have been flourishing and active, notably the Kampala Pentecostal Church. The AIDS crisis in Uganda created two million orphans, and the Kampala Pentecostal Church "initiated an innovative response."[48] The Kampala Church built small villages rather than "Western-style" orphanages with hundreds of children in residence. They also created schools with teachers resident on the campus, and invented a "Father's Heart Ministry" where men could visit every weekend, especially to families with a widowed or divorced woman at their heart. The "fathers" also prayed together during the week.

(3) *South Africa* has a population of 46 million, with supposedly 80 percent Christians, of whom 34-45 percent belong to indigenous churches — 28 percent Protestant and 8 percent Catholic. The executive government is in Pretoria, the National Assembly in Cape Town, and Constitutional Court in Johannesburg. The nineteenth century saw conflict between the British and Afrikaners. Diamond and gold mining led to industrialization and urbanization of many. Africans supported apartheid from 1948, with increasing poverty and unemployment in rural areas. But in 1990 apartheid was overthrown by F. W. de Klerk, and the African National Congress gained a majority in parliament in 1994 when Nelson Mandela was elected president. Missionaries had earlier come to South Africa (Moravians in the late eighteenth century, the London Missionary Society in 1799, and the

---

48. Donald E. Miller and Tetsunao Yamamori, *Global Pentecostalism: The New Face of Christian Social Engagement* (Berkeley: University of California Press, 2007), p. 68, cf. pp. 68-70.

Wesleyan Methodist Mission in 1816). Several European groups founded schools.

Meanwhile the African churches sought a style and worship that was more suited to African expectations and needs. Healing through prayer became central. After 1969 black theology related to the black consciousness movement. But transition to New South Africa was largely peaceful, especially the Truth and Reconciliation Commission under Archbishop Desmond Tutu. Yet an undercurrent of unemployment, violence, and crime, together with AIDS, remains an urgent problem.

In 1991 South African Pentecostal churches accounted for 30 percent of the total population. Anderson calculates that the 6,000 Pentecostal churches represent some ten million people.[49] But he also argues that the "dangerous memories" of which he speaks arose from an anomalous situation in about 1908. To begin with, the Apostolic Faith Mission had partly modeled itself on the Azusa Street Revival. The movement began mainly with disenfranchised black people and poor white Afrikaners after the Boer War of 1899-1902. In the earliest years races were integrated. But by 1908 the Executive Council of the Apostolic Faith Mission pronounced that "the baptism of natives" should take place only *after* the baptism of white people, and in 1925 that the superintendent in charge of the work must be white.[50] Even in the 1950s, Anderson comments, "African pastors . . . (as well as) the A. F. M. pioneer Elias Letwaba . . . raised no objection to the indignities place upon him."[51]

Meanwhile the Zion Christian Church, founded by Engenas Lekganyane practiced baptism in the Spirit and healing, and became one of South Africa's leading independent churches. They stressed the oral and narrative tradition of Pentecostals, together with healing, exorcism, and prophecy. Today three streams of Pentecostals continue, which have been founded by Western missionaries: Assemblies of God and the Apostolic Faith Mission, each of about a quarter of a million adherents, and the smaller Full Gospel Church of God. Only in 1985 did the Apostolic Faith Mission accept "the Biblical principles of unity" and reject apartheid. In 1990 black adherents become legal members. But the Full Gospel Church of God continued with separatist practices. Anderson concludes, "Pente-

---

49. Allan Anderson, "Dangerous Memories for South African Pentecostals," in Anderson and Hollenweger, *Pentecostals after a Century,* pp. 89-107, here p. 89.

50. Anderson, "Dangerous Memories," p. 95.

51. Anderson, "Dangerous Memories," p. 96.

costals were seldom in the forefront of the 'freedom struggle','" with a few exceptions.[52] One such exception was Frank Chikane. African Pentecostalism nevertheless has its roots in a marginalized and underprivileged society.

Many of these aspects caused much heart-searching and "self-awareness" in British and other Pentecostal groups, as a large quantity of web correspondence testifies. On the internet we can find numerous Pentecostal web sites, which encourage not only correspondence, but also letters that reflect criticisms and misgivings, as well as constructive comments, from fellow Pentecostals. In particular the "prosperity" gospel was especially criticized in Britain.

52. Anderson, "Dangerous Memories," p. 103.

CHAPTER 15

The Self-Awareness and Diversity
of Pentecostals Today

Pentecostalism has undoubtedly reached a new stage in its development. The movement now boasts such world-class theologians as Amos Yong, Veli-Matti Kärkkäinen, Frank D. Macchia, Allan Anderson, Donald Miller, Ogbu Kalu, Simon Chan, and many more. Pentecostal New Testament scholars include Gordon Fee, Roger Stronstad, and Robert P. Menzies. But what is most impressive is the plethora of contributions to several Pentecostal web sites by many ordinary Pentecostals, whose insights are beginning to address issues that have plagued Pentecostal circles for some thirty years. I have seen nothing like this commendable self-awareness and even self-criticism among leaders of the renewal movement in the major denominations, who can presumably shelter behind the main denominations while subtly or openly changing the tone of their worship and practices.

As I have read the messages in these web sites and the increasing spate of books on the diversity of global Pentecostalism, I have come across no less than two dozen issues which are now openly debated among Pentecostals. This does not mean that Pentecostals have lost their "heart" or their core beliefs. For example, Yongnan Jeon Ahn has a substantial chapter on "Debates in Contemporary Hermeneutics," but nevertheless refers to the "Spiritual Ethos" of Pentecostals and the generally shared belief that "the first Pentecost can be repeated in the lives of all Christians."[1] Even then, as James Dunn writes as a sympathetic observer of the movement, in one sense "Pentecost can never be repeated"; in another sense,

---

1. Yongnan Jeon Ahn, *Interpretation of Tongues and Prophecy in 1 Corinthians 12–14* (Blandford Forum, UK: Deo, 2013), pp. 37-66 and 32-53.

154

"Pentecost can and must be repeated in the experience of all who would become Christians."[2] Many Pentecostals would also now agree with this.

1. Some Important Pentecostal Thinkers

Before we enumerate some of these two dozen or so issues, we may note the shift in perspective which characterizes the views of several leading thinkers. Of all the thinkers whom we might consider, the most striking is probably Amos Yong, followed closely by Veli-Matti Kärkkäinen and several others.

(1) Amos Yong was born in Malaysia but holds a PhD from Boston University. He has served as President of the Society for Pentecostal Studies (2008-9) and coeditor of *Pneuma*. Since 2014 he has been Professor of Theology and Mission at Fuller Theological Seminary, in Pasadena. His range of books and articles is impressive, together with the wide array of subjects and issues which each of these addresses. In 2002 he published *Spirit–Word–Community: Theological Hermeneutics in Trinitarian Perspective*. Here he shows how Spirit, Word, and community can be interrelated in a Pentecostal hermeneutic within a Trinitarian framework. He seeks to fill "the lacuna that is detected in the recent triadic methodologies proposed by Kevin Vanhoozer and by Stanley Grenz and John Franke."[3]

Yong then published *The Spirit Poured Out on All Flesh* (2005), which explores a systematic theology from a Pentecostal perspective. In effect it constitutes a systematic theology, including salvation, God, creation, and other topics including biblical hermeneutics. Yong also considers constraints between Luke–Acts and Paul, and Pentecostals in the two-thirds world ("all flesh") and relations to other faiths. In 2007 and 2011, Yong considered disabilities from a Pentecostal perspective: *Theology and Down Syndrome: Reimagining Disability in Late Modernity* (2007); and *The Bible, Disability, and the Church: A New Vision for the People of God* (2011). In 2008 he published *Hospitality and the Other: Pentecost, Christian Practices, and the Neighbor,* which relates to other religions and even includes material on performatives or speech acts. In 2010 he turned to political theory with *In the Days of Caesar: Pentecostalism and Political Theology.* In 2011 he examined Pentecostalism in the light of interdisciplinary dialogue in *The*

---

2. James D. G. Dunn, *Baptism in the Holy Spirit* (London: SCM, 1970), p. 53.

3. Amos Yong, *Spirit–Word–Community: Theological Hermeneutics in Trinitarian Perspective* (Burlington, VT: Ashgate, 2002), p. 10.

Spirit of Creation: Modern Science and Divine Action in Pentecostal-Charismatic Imagination, and in 2012 addressed Buddhism in *Pneumatology and the Christian-Buddhist Dialogue: Does the Spirit Blow through the Middle Way?* Finally, he compared the importance of love and the questionable claims of "powers," respectively, in *Spirit of Love: A Trinitarian Theology of Grace* (2012). The Fuller web site suggests that he has written at least thirty volumes. Work on his theology and philosophy includes Volfgang Vandey and Martin Mittelstadt, eds., *The Theology of Amos Yong and the New Face of Pentecostalism* (Leiden: Brill, online e-book, 2013); and a substantial section of Christopher A. Stephenson, *Types of Pentecostal Theology* (2013).[4]

(2) Veli-Matti Kärkkäinen graduated from Fuller Theological Seminary, holds a ThD and Habilitation from the University of Helsinki, and joined the Fuller faculty as Professor in 2003. He has taught in Finland, Thailand, and North America. He has published or edited more than twenty books. These include *One with God: Salvation as Deification and Justification* (2004); *Trinity and Religious Pluralism: The Doctrine of the Trinity in Christian Theology of Religions* (2004); and especially *Holy Spirit and Salvation: The Sources of Christian Theology* (2010). He has also published *Christ and Reconciliation: A Constructive Christian Theology for the Pluralistic World,* vol. 1 (2013) and *Trinity and Revelation: A Constructive Christian Theology for the Pluralistic World,* vol. 2 (2014). He edited the important volume *The Spirit in the World: Emerging Pentecostal Theologies in Global Contexts* (2009), to which Jürgen Moltmann contributed the preface. He participates in working groups in the World Council of Churches.

Kärkkäinen distinguishes today between several types of Pentecostals. First, the traditional or "classical" type includes Assemblies of God or Foursquare Gospel, and themes and practices from the Azusa Street Revival. Second, charismatic churches within major traditions usually call themselves the charismatic renewal movement, the largest of which is within the Roman Catholic Church. Third, there have emerged "neo-charismatic movements" such as the Vineyard Fellowship in the USA, Africa "initiated" Churches, and the China House Church movement. Charismatic movements now number around 200 million worldwide.[5] Kärkkäinen's main fo-

---

4. Christopher A. Stephenson, *Types of Pentecostal Theology: Method, System, Spirit* (Oxford: Oxford University Press, 2013), pp. 82-110.

5. Veli-Matti Kärkkäinen, "Introduction: Pentecostalism and Pentecostal Theology in the Third Millennium: Taking Stock of the Contemporary Global Situation," in idem, ed., *The Spirit in the World: Emerging Pentecostal Theologies in Global Contexts* (Grand Rapids: Eerdmans, 2009), pp. xiii-xxiv, here pp. xv-xvi.

cus is on the first of these, in which "Jesus is perceived as Savior, Sanctifier, Healer, Baptizer with the Spirit, and the Soon-returning King."[6]

One decisive conference at which Kärkkäinen and Frank Macchia were keynote speakers was "The Spirit in the World: The Dynamics of Pentecostal Growth and Experience," held in October 2006 at the University of Southern California in Los Angeles, hosted by the Centre for Religion and Civic Culture, and sponsored by the John Templeton Foundation. I listened to the papers and responses on the internet, and was fascinated by some unexpected outcomes. Several leading speakers (including, I think, Kärkkäinen) stated either that they had never spoken in tongues, or that they ascribed to them little importance. Macchia, as we shall note, gave a new emphasis to, or explanation of, baptism in the Spirit. Paulson Pulikottil argued against "Western" interpretations of Indian Pentecostal phenomena, as we noted in the previous chapter. Koo Dong Yun of Korea discussed the significance of *minjung,* as we also noted there. The Nigerian Ogbu Kalu discussed African Pentecostalism and its distinctive worldview, and Amos Yong spoke of the Chinese-Malaysian experience.[7]

In *Holy Spirit and Salvation* Kärkkäinen devotes his first one hundred pages to the apostolic fathers, the apologists, and the Ante-Nicene and Post-Nicene fathers. He considers medieval pneumatologies from Eastern and Western traditions, and in the Reformation era. The post-Reformation and nineteenth century also appear, before he turns to Africa, Asia, and Latin America. Much of the material takes the form of extracts from primary sources.

(3) Frank D. Macchia is editor of *Pneuma,* took master's degrees from Wheaton College and Union Theological Seminary, and holds a ThD from the University of Basel. His publications include *Justification in the Spirit: Creation, Redemption, and the Triune God* (2010), *The Trinity, Practically Speaking* (2010), and *Baptized in the Spirit: A Global Pentecostal Theology* (2006). Macchia insists in *The Trinity* that the Holy Trinity is an explicitly biblical doctrine, citing not least John 3:16, "God so loved the world that he gave his one and only Son."[8] The Trinity constitutes God's identity. The Father, the Son, and the Holy Spirit all work together for our salvation. All are vital to the reality of salvation.

6. Kärkkäinen, "Introduction," p. xvii.
7. Kärkkäinen, "Introduction," pp. xxi-ii.
8. Frank D. Macchia, *The Trinity: Practically Speaking* (Downers Grove, IL: Intervarsity / Colorado Springs: Biblica, 2010), p. 1.

We shall look more closely at *Baptized in the Spirit* when we consider the first of the issues now widely debated among Pentecostals. Here, however, he argues, "The global Pentecostal affirmation of Spirit baptism is a critical theological concern," i.e. among Pentecostals.[9] But we shall see that he broadens the "classical" definition. In *Spirituality and Social Liberation* he draws much inspiration from Johann and Christoph Blumhardt (respectively 1805-80 and 1842-1919). Macchia is especially concerned with the coming Kingdom of God as an aspect of the doctrine of the Holy Spirit. The Blumhardts believed that the Kingdom of God is manifested in history, especially in the healing of the sick and the liberation of the poor. Macchia regards this as also legitimizing social concern. In more traditional terms, he relates speaking in tongues to the presence of God, focusing on theophanies and on "sighs too deep for words" in Rom. 8:26. Thus glossolalia is characterized by God's spontaneous self-disclosure. Glossolalia, Stephenson comments, "is a continuing reminder of the Spirit's ability to conform humans in dramatic ways that . . . change their outlooks."[10] Macchia also associates justification with the Kingdom of God. Moreover, he resists an over-sharp distinction between the Kingdom and the Church, but neither does he identify one with the other.

(4) Stephen J. Land and Simon K. H. Chan explore systematic theology from a Pentecostal viewpoint and seek to integrate it with the practical "walk" of the Christian life. Land is president of the Pentecostal Seminary in Cleveland, Tennessee, and wrote *Pentecostal Spirituality* in 1993. He believes that in Pentecostalism belief and practice shape each other. He promotes the "fivefold gospel" described in the last chapter and sees apocalyptic, or eschatology, as part and parcel of this.

Simon Chan is Professor of Systematic Theology at Trinity Theological College, Singapore, after graduating with a PhD from Cambridge in 1986. He published *Spiritual Theology: A Systematic Study of the Christian Life* (1998); *Pentecostal Theology and the Christian Spiritual Tradition* (2000 and 2011); *Liturgical Theology: The Church as Worshiping Community* (2006); and *Pentecostal Ecclesiology: An Essay on the Development of Doctrine* (2011). On the Spirit and the Church, Chan considers Barth's theology, Catholic theologies, and ecclesial practices as the work of the Spirit.[11] In

---

9. Frank D. Macchia, *Baptized in the Spirit: A Global Pentecostal Theology* (Grand Rapids: Zondervan, 2006), p. 21.

10. Stephenson, *Types of Pentecostal Theology,* p. 62; cf. pp. 59-81.

11. Simon Chan, *Pentecostal Ecclesiology: An Essay on the Development of Doctrine,* (Blandford Forum, UK: Deo, 2011), pp. 32-49.

Pentecostal Ecclesiology Chan comments, "God's Spirit was typically related to God's covenantal activities in and on behalf of Israel," as Max Turner had previously observed.[12] Moreover, "the earliest Christian understanding of the Holy Spirit is that he is the Spirit-in-the-Church."[13] He appeals here to Zizioulas, as well as to Scripture. Further, he observes, "Deification is a sharing in the divine nature."[14] On the subject of the Trinity, Chan follows Moltmann, Pannenberg, and Eugene Rogers in regarding the best approach to the Trinity as flowing from the Trinitarian Narrative in the NT. This includes the baptism of Jesus (Matt. 3:11-12; Mark 1:8; Luke 3:16; John 1:26-27, 33) and such passages as Rom. 8:14-17 in Paul.[15] The Church is the communion of the Holy Spirit, as L. S. Thornton and others argue.[16] All this is broadly orthodox. But he concludes, "Pentecost is an experience not a denomination," in which "experience is both theologically formative and is itself formed by previous experiences."[17] This precisely accords with the approach of the Korean scholar Yongnan Jeon Ahn.

(5) In my larger book on the Holy Spirit I outlined the approach of two NT Pentecostals, Gordon Fee and Roger Stronstad.[18] Gordon Fee is a NT scholar first and Pentecostal second, so he is nearer to the mainline churches. Indeed, he dissents from most fellow Pentecostals in *not* following their standard teaching on baptism in the Spirit. This now introduces a string of issues for which we must trace a diversity of Pentecostal opinions. Because this book is designed to meet requests for a "shorter" book on the Holy Spirit, these issues will be summarized briefly and also be selective.

2. Some Important Pentecostal Issues

(1) *Baptism in the Spirit.* The first of these issues is baptism in the Spirit, which has long been regarded as the hallmark of Pentecostals. Frank Macchia writes, "The centrality of Spirit baptism to Pentecostal theology is

---

12. Chan, *Pentecostal Ecclesiology*, p. 23.
13. Chan, *Pentecostal Ecclesiology*, p. 24.
14. Chan, *Pentecostal Ecclesiology*, p. 42.
15. Chan, *Pentecostal Ecclesiology*, pp. 51, 55.
16. Chan, *Pentecostal Ecclesiology*, pp. 74-92.
17. Chan, *Pentecostal Ecclesiology*, pp. 93.
18. Anthony C. Thiselton, *The Holy Spirit — in Biblical Teaching, through the Centuries, and Today* (Grand Rapids: Eerdmans / London: SPCK, 2013), pp. 373-79.

revealed in part by the fact that Pentecostal theological discussion cannot ignore the topic," even if some recently "attempt to decentralize the metaphor as a functional center for theological reflection."[19] Kärkkäinen agrees with this.[20]

Yet clearly there remains deep disagreement about the meaning of the term. Elsewhere Macchia writes, "Some Trinitarian Pentecostal groups (e.g. in Chile and Germany) have identified Spirit baptism as Christian regeneration, separate from water baptism."[21] Yong also adopts a broad approach. Not everyone would agree with Macchia that baptism in the Spirit is a distinctive Pentecostal issue. Significantly, Russ Spittler, an Assemblies of God writer from Fuller Theological Seminary, describes it as a "non-issue" for many today, while even early Pentecostals did not regard it as "a new *ordo salutis.*"[22] Gordon Fee argued that the doctrine or phrase has very little support, even if the experience that often goes by that name is authentic. Hollenweger traces its roots to the Holiness movements associated with Charles Finney, Dwight Moody, R. A. Torrey and others, but stresses the need today for "Rethinking Spirit Baptism."[23] Donald Dayton traces it farther back, to the revival of 1857-58 and to Phoebe Palmer, to Asa Mahan in 1870, and earlier to Wesley's assistant John Fletcher, though Dayton comments on the earlier ambiguity about whether this signified the gift of empowerment or holiness.[24]

This last comment provides the clue as to how Macchia can make so much of Spirit baptism as a distinctive badge of Pentecostals both in his book *Baptized in the Spirit* (2006) and in his classic essay of the same name (2009). He rightly concludes, "The Spirit baptism metaphor in the scriptures *is fluid,* referring to judgment (Matt. 3:12), cleansing (Acts 15:8-9), empowerment (Acts 1:8), incorporation into the life of the church (1 Cor.

---

19. Macchia, *Baptized in the Spirit,* p. 20.

20. Veli-Matti Kärkkäinen, *Spiritus ubi vult spirat: Pneumatology in Catholic–Pentecostal Dialogue (1922-89)* (Helsinki: Luther Agricola Society, 1988), p. 198.

21. Frank D. Macchia, "Baptized in the Spirit: Towards a Global Theology of Spirit Baptism," in Kärkkäinen, ed., *The Spirit in the World*, pp. 3-20, here p. 9.

22. Russ Spittler, "Suggested Areas of Further Research in Pentecostal Studies," *Pneuma* 5 (1983), pp. 39-57, here p. 43.

23. Walter J. Hollenweger, "Rethinking Spirit Baptism," in Allan H. Anderson and Walter J. Hollenweger, eds., *Pentecostals after a Century: Global Perspectives* (Sheffield: Sheffield Academic Press, 1999), pp. 164-96.

24. Donald W. Dayton, *Theological Roots of Pentecostalism* (Grand Rapids: Baker Academic, 1987), pp. 87-113.

12:13), and the final new creation (Acts 2:17-21).[25] This comment does justice to exegesis and to recent global Pentecostal history.

This certainly takes much of the pressure away from those of us who have always believed that Pentecostals place more weight on the noun-phrase in 1 Cor. 12:13, which does indeed signify "incorporation into the life of the church." The problem, however, seems to remain that whether the term signifies holiness, commitment and dedication, or even empowerment, the emphasis seems to lie on *event* rather than process. Yet, by way of reply, most traditions emphasize "event" in baptism, and where relevant also in confirmation and ordination. It is clear, however, that these events are *incomplete* until they are implemented by a long faithful process of living them out. This seems to me to hold the most constructive way forward for universally recognizing the validity of the event as that which can be authenticated over time in struggle and faithful discipleship. Frank Macchia has opened the door to constructive dialogue. Sepúlveda precisely asks for a "broader definition," when in Chile "often the baptism of the Holy Spirit is identified with the experience of conversion, yet Chilean Pentecostals remain true Pentecostals."[26]

(2) *Divine Healing.* Margaret M. Poloma asserts, "Healing had been and remained a central belief and practice of Pentecostal believers throughout the twentieth century."[27] One possible shift in the twenty-first century is away from the earlier idea that this was often through the agency of "famous healing evangelists — well-known anointed men and women like William Branham, Kathryn Kuhlman, Oral Roberts, and Benny Hinn."[28] J. G. Lake introduced "healing rooms" in which ordinary people became agents of healing, although there remained healing leaders such as John Wimber of the Vineyard churches. Healing showed the "interweaving of soul, mind, body and spirit" and more recently the context of closeness to God, perhaps in "inner healing."[29]

To most Christian traditions this emphasis has one strong positive factor and two which invite reservation. First, the utter rejection of a

---

25. Macchia, "Baptized in the Spirit," p. 17 (my italics).

26. Juan Sepúlveda, "Indigenous Pentecostalism and the Chilean Experience," in Anderson and Hollenweger, eds., *Pentecostals after a Century*, pp. 111-34, here p. 133.

27. Margaret M. Poloma, "Divine Healing, Religious Revivals, and Contemporary Pentecostalism: A North American Perspective," in Kärkkäinen, ed., *The Spirit in the World*, pp. 21-39, here p. 25.

28. Poloma, "Divine Healing," p. 25.

29. Poloma, "Divine Healing," pp. 27, 29-30.

mechanistic or materialist worldview is greatly to be affirmed. To confuse/confess mechanistic *methods* with a mechanistic *worldview* is emphatically *not* "scientific." But at least two or perhaps three features call for examination. First, Hollenweger, Donald Miller, Tetsunao Yamamori, and many others call attention to the implied dualism of the natural and supernatural which too often accompanies this emphasis. "Many," Miller and Yamamori write, "are dualists at heart, separating body and mind, heaven and hell, good and evil."[30] To greater effect, Hollenweger declares, "'Supernatural' is in my view biblically and scientifically untenable. Biblically it is untenable because the list of the charismata in the New Testament includes 'extraordinary' gifts . . . and so-called 'ordinary' gifts (management, teaching, giving money to the poor)."[31] Elsewhere he comments, "Miracles are ambiguous and not specifically Christian. . . . To define a miracle as a breaking of the laws of nature is inadmissible both theologically and scientifically."[32] An extreme version of "God of the gaps" almost suggests that everything is caused either by God or by demons, spirits, and Satan.

The second huge difficulty is the expectation, sometimes encouraged, that prayer and faith for healing will *always* result in a positive deliverance from sickness. For those whom God does not choose to heal, such a general expectation is damning, especially if they or their champions are accused of inadequate faith or inadequate prayer. It is downright cruel, exaggerating the problem of evil and suffering for them. Admittedly Keith Warrington hastens to say, "These perspectives are not supported by many Pentecostals, but where they are held, they can cause immense pastoral difficulties."[33] Some Pentecostals do see the part played by medicine. The vast number of biblical commentators down the years have seen Paul's reference to the gifts of healing as involving what J. A. Bengel, the Pietist, called "natural remedies." The important truth guarded by Pentecostals is the *possibility* of divine action in the world, when God chooses, and what means he chooses to use. But to give the last word to Hollenweger, "Third Wavers [i.e., Wimber Charismatics; see chapter 17] . . . see the world as a

---

30. Donald Miller and Tetsunao Yamamori, *Global Pentecostalism: The New Face of Christian Social Engagement* (Berkeley: University of California Press, 2007), p. 217.

31. Hollenweger, "Rethinking Spirit Baptism," pp. 169-70.

32. Walter J. Hollenweger, *The Pentecostals* (Peabody, MA: Hendrickson, 1972), cf. pp. 353-77, here pp. 371-72.

33. Keith Warrington, *Pentecostal Theology: A Theology of Encounter* (London: T&T Clark, 2008), cf. pp. 265-308, here pp. 285.

cosmic and moral duality. There is no room for the natural. Everything is either divine or demonic."[34]

(3) *The Prosperity Gospel.* We have discussed this with special reference to Nigeria and to some North American communities. I have to admit that many Pentecostals are seriously troubled about this abuse, and personally I can feel nothing but shock when I read of the experience in parts of Nigeria (though this does not detract from my realization of extreme poverty in Nigeria). By way of reminder, David Ogungbile notes practices in the Redeemed Church of God in Nigeria under the leadership of Benson Idahosa and others and the "Deeper Life Bible Church." They reversed the application of the parable of the Rich Man and Lazarus, while the preacher referred to his computerized Mercedes Benz with the promise that those who gave generously would also become prosperous.[35] Ogungbile comments, "Branding and rebranding are constantly done to make the message and practice of the prosperity gospel acceptable to members and to persuade members to make financial commitments out of their insufficient earnings."[36]

Ogungbile explains that widening poverty in Africa created a ready market for the prosperity gospel industry. It has, he says, "some measure of positive impact but a great deal of negative impact."[37] But on the other side, he says, it makes people view the gospel message "as a commodity to be invested upon in any way possible."[38] There have even been allegations of fraud among prosperity pastors. Abogunrin called it a "health and wealth" gospel. We find parallel narratives that concern several American TV evangelists. The encouraging feature, however, is the self-awareness and self-criticism voiced by many ordinary Pentecostal Christians. Ogungbile refers to preachers beyond Africa, including a "charismatic megachurch in Kiev, Ukraine, and another in Botswana.[39]

(4) *Syncretism.* This problem is acute in many parts of the two-thirds world, especially in Africa, India, as well as in Korea. The complaint is

---

34. Walter J. Hollenweger, "Current Issues for Pentecostals," in Anderson and Hollenweger, eds., *Pentecostals after a Century,* pp. 176-91, here p. 180.

35. David Ogungbile, "African Pentecostalism and the Prosperity Gospel," in Clifton R. Clarke, ed., *Pentecostal Theology in Africa* (Eugene, OR: Pickwick, 2014), pp. 132-49, here pp. 141-42.

36. Ogungbile, "African Pentecostalism," p. 143.

37. Ogungbile, "African Pentecostalism," p. 145.

38. Ogungbile, "African Pentecostalism," p. 147.

39. Ogungbile, "African Pentecostalism," p. 149.

often voiced that Western missionaries propagate patronizingly "Western" versions of Pentecostalism and should pay more attention to indigenous churches and indigenous culture. One of many examples is the *minjung* ethos in Korea (i.e. the mind-set of the oppressed), which Moltmann contends that he never saw.[40] Koo Dong Yun discusses not only *minjung*, but Shamanic aspects in Korean Pentecostalism.[41] Similarly Harvey Cox, who is sympathetic with much in Pentecostalism, claims, "Pentecostalism in Korea seems to be able to incorporate many of the characteristics of shamanism."[42] Cox views this positively as a preparation for political and economic survival. He cites the huge mega-church, the Yoido Full Gospel Church of 800,000 members, querying whether it verges towards an amalgamation of "shamanism, Buddhism, and Confucianism."[43] He admits, however, that this troubles Pentecostals elsewhere.

In Africa the issue especially hangs on whether an indigenous cosmology is imported. Opoku Onyinah discusses ways of confronting witchcraft in contemporary Africa. He argues that the Christian gospel proclaims victory over witchcraft and demons because God alone is sovereign. Nevertheless, some methods of confronting witchcraft have "negative effects," which make the ministry "quite alarming."[44] He claims that there is too great a deference to witchcraft and demons, involving "affirmation of the old order." This focuses on gods, fetishes, dwarfs, and demons.

On the other hand, Amos Yong applauds attempts in India to build bridges with Buddhism. We should not simply dismiss it as false. Particularly in Sri Lanka he sees value in interreligious dialogue. He asks, "How might a pneumatological theology serve as a springboard for a Pentecostal dialogue with Buddhism?"[45]

40. Lee Hong Jung, "*Minjung* and Pentecostal Movement in Korea," in Anderson and Hollenweger, eds., *Pentecostals after a Century,* pp. 138-63; Jürgen Moltmann, "Preface," in Kärkkäinen, ed., *The Spirit in the World,* pp. viii-xii, here p. x.

41. Koo Dong Yun, "Pentecostalism from Below: *Minjung* Liberation and Asian Pentecostal Theology," in Kärkkäinen, ed., *The Spirit in the World,* pp. 89-114.

42. Harvey Cox, *Fire from Heaven: The Rise of Pentecostal Spirituality* (Cambridge, MA: Da Capo, 1995), p. 219.

43. Cox, *Fire from Heaven,* p. 221.

44. Opoku Onyinah, "Deliverance as a Way of Confronting Witchcraft in Contemporary Africa: Ghana as a Case Study," in Kärkkäinen, ed., *The Spirit in the World,* pp. 181-202, here p. 201.

45. Amos Yong, "From Azusa Street to the Bo Tree and Back . . . in the Pentecostal Encounter with Buddhism," in Kärkkäinen, ed., *The Spirit in the World,* pp. 203-26, here p. 220.

The situation in parts of Africa, however, raises concerns. For example, Ogbu Kalu, the respected church historian, believes that "African Christianity is essentially rooted in African primal religion."[46] Elsewhere he comments, "It is a revaluation of culture to transform it into an instrument for building *ubantu*" (i.e., "availability to others," as defined by Desmond Tutu).[47] Pentecostals, he insists, must respond "to the system of meanings embodied in the symbols and world-views of indigenous African religions and cultures."[48] "*Sankofa*" is a Twi symbol in Ghana which belongs to the Ghanaian cultural heritage, namely a bird who returns backwards to move in the reverse direction. Thus Pentecostals, Kalu claims, should return back to their cultural roots in Africa.

Deidre Helen Crumbley is sympathetic with the need to take account of African cultural practices, but argues that the issue is far more complex than is generally appreciated. It becomes especially sensitive in the case of gender practices.[49] Paul Clifford shows how confronting evil, witchcraft, and deliverance is essential to African Pentecostalism.[50] This includes such experiences as "being bewitched" and being the victim of curses. Examples can be multiplied from African Pentecostalism. The least that we may say is that this issue of evangelism or syncretism demands urgent discussion and examination. Certainly many Pentecostals today are acutely aware of both sides of this problem.

(5) *Hermeneutics.* This issue belongs to the agenda for urgent discussion and debate in almost every book and many articles on contemporary Pentecostalism. Amos Yong, Lee Roy Martin, Donald Dayton, Yongnan Jeon Ahn, Jacqueline Grey, Kenneth Archer, Walter Hollenweger, and a host of other writers make this point.[51] So unanimous is this consensus that we postpone the issue to a separate chapter, which follows this.

46. Ogbu Kalu, *African Pentecostalism: An Introduction* (Oxford: Oxford University Press, 2008), pp. 3-11.

47. Ogbu Kalu, "Sankofa: Pentecostalism and African Cultural Heritage," in Kärkkäinen, ed., *The Spirit in the World*, pp. 135-52, here pp. 139.

48. Kalu, "Sankofa," p. 136.

49. Deidre Helen Crumbley, "Sanctified Saints — Impure Prophetesses: A Cross-Cultural Study of Gender and Power," in Kärkkäinen, ed., *The Spirit in the World*, pp. 115-34.

50. Paul Clifford, "Evil, Witchcraft, and Deliverance in African Pentecostal Worldview," in Clarke, ed., *Pentecostal Theology in Africa*, pp. 112-31.

51. Yong, *Spirit–Word–Community*, pp. 297-316 and throughout; Lee Roy Martin, ed., *Pentecostal Hermeneutics* (Leiden: Brill, 2013); Dayton, *Theological Roots of Pentecostalism*, pp. 23-26; Ahn, *Interpretation of Tongues*, pp. 6-93, Jacqueline Grey, *Three's a Crowd: Pentecostal Hermeneutics and the O.T.* (Eugene, OR: Pickwick, 2011); Kenneth Archer,

(6) *Political Attitudes.* Harvey Cox discusses varying attitudes to politics in Brazil and America. He tells of testimonies in the Brazilian Assemblies of God which tell of the culture of Brazilian society, corrupt politics and big business.[52] Many in Brazil sponsored a Workers' Party and in 1994 one ran for president. In America, he tells us, Pat Robertson attempted to mobilize political forces, especially with his book *The New World Order.* He sees demons behind oppressive structures. Cox points out, however, that Robertson is Baptist rather than Pentecostal, but he ties it to his "pre-millennial" approach. Robert Beckford associates "black consciousness" with political power in Britain and Africa, which opposed "the political question of a previous generation."[53]

What most impresses me, however, is those Pentecostal web sites in which many raise profound questions about the relation between their Quietist roots and such issues as military service, pacifism, poverty, and related matters. Clearly some profound questions and thinking is taking place at grass-roots level.

(7) *Eschatology.* The same debate is taking place among ordinary communities about eschatology. Outside America not everyone has the "coming soon" presupposition which drove many "classic" Pentecostals. To be sure, throughout the world the Return of Christ as Coming King remains crucial and central. But "expectation" need not be what Stendahl calls a "high voltage" state of mind. I have often appealed here to Wittgenstein. If I "expect" a visitor to tea, a sense of excitement is secondary. The emphasis is on "being ready," i.e., laying a table, setting out cups, saucers, and plates, providing cakes, and so on. A number of Pentecostals are questioning whether the import of "millennial" theories from the Holiness movement or many in the USA can genuinely be supported by biblical evidence. This applies all the more to "the rapture" and associated phenomena. The key point about eschatology, as Yong expresses it, is: "Eschatologically, the final truth will account for all provisional beliefs insofar as these are true."[54]

These seem to me to be the seven issues for current debate which

---

"Pentecostal Hermeneutics: Retrospect and Prospect," in Martin, ed., *Pentecostal Hermeneutics,* pp. 131-48; and Walter J. Hollenweger, "Crucial Issues for Pentecostals," in Anderson and Hollenweger, eds., *Pentecostals after a Century,* pp. 176-91.

52. Cox, *Fire from Heaven,* pp. 162-65.

53. Robert Beckford, "Black Pentecostals and Black Politics," in Anderson and Hollenweger, *Pentecostals after a Century,* pp. 48-59.

54. Yong, *Spirit–Word–Community,* p. 171.

command the greatest consensus. But we could go on for many more pages listing the issues which have appeared for debate on Pentecostal web sites. Nevertheless we are committed to write a shorter book on this subject. With more space, we could list and expand on: (8) orality versus written texts; (9) signs and wonders; (10) missiology; (11) the pragmatic nature of truth; (12) ethics; (13) spontaneity and reflection; (14) perfectionism; (15) charismatic gifts; (16) prophecy and preaching; (17) gender; (18) ecumenical issues; (19) the Bible and tradition; and many more.

What is clear is the willingness of Pentecostals to debate these issues. This compares most favorably in general with the charismatic renewal movement in established denominations on the other hand (discussed in chapter 17). Some, although not all, charismatics seem to live in a world of pure practice for much of the time, unencumbered with the different problems of Christian theology or ethics.

At the recent Anglican and Pentecostal Consultation, which was the first of its kind, held at High Leigh in April 2014, a number of key points were identified. The present book seeks to address these, especially in the present chapter. We identify their numbers in the Consultation by # before the designated number or paragraph, and follow their sequence in the Consultation:

i. All were concerned to avoid suspicions on either side (#9).
ii. Each side was keen to emphasize the diversity of its traditions (#18).
iii. Clarification was sought on baptism in the Spirit and gifts of the Spirit (#26).
iv. The crucial need for serious discussion of, and attention to, hermeneutics was stressed (#43).
v. The groups raised issues about prophecy (#48).
vi. Pentecostals asked whether they were too dualist in their view of the supernatural (#49).
vii. The importance of preaching as the climax of worship in Pentecostalism was noted.

Anglicans might well have acknowledged how preaching has unwittingly followed a downward curve in many Anglican churches to their disadvantage. All seven points have featured in this book, and especially this chapter.

CHAPTER 16

The Holy Spirit and Hermeneutics

This chapter concerns both hermeneutics in general, and specifically Pentecostal claims that "Pentecostal Hermeneutics" constitutes a distinctive approach with its own unique methods and aims. One problematic idea that sometimes surfaces in Pentecostal hermeneutics is the claim that the Holy Spirit cannot be fully operative in all mainline hermeneutics, even when interpreters seek to be open to the leading of the Holy Spirit.

This is not the case for every Pentecostal believer or writer. Amos Yong, for example, thoroughly integrates both explicitly Pentecostal approaches and more constructive "mainline" approaches in his book *Spirit–Word–Community*. He offers us, rightly, a Trinitarian hermeneutics, which "undercuts once for all any hermeneutical claim based on a single principle."[1] He also declares, again rightly, "The task of developing theological hermeneutics cannot be separated from the question of hermeneutical theology."[2] The latter is what I attempted to achieve in *The Hermeneutics of Doctrine* and in my other half-dozen volumes on hermeneutics.[3] But some reviewers and critics suspect that my work and other similar approaches do not take full account of the Holy Spirit, but that we should add an extra "layer," lens, or technique of inquiry. Some urge a correct exhortation to prayer and openness to God, but I hope these already operate in my hermeneutics, rendering such a critique otiose. Some urge the exclusion

---

1. Amos Yong, *Spirit–Word–Community: Theological Hermeneutics in Trinitarian Perspective* (Burlington, VT: Ashgate, 2002), p. 311.

2. Yong, *Spirit–Word–Community*, p. 311.

3. Anthony C. Thiselton, *The Hermeneutics of Doctrine* (Grand Rapids: Eerdmans, 2007).

of some particular tradition of inquiry, as if "academic" and "of the Spirit" constitute mutually incompatible approaches.

The heart of the issue seems to depend on two wider questions. First, is the work of the Holy Spirit an *alternative* to rational reflection by a mind fully committed to God and his authority, or does the Holy Spirit work *through* such a mind which is also committed to argument, truth, and fair-mindedness? Second, does the hermeneutical tradition since Schleiermacher, Heidegger, Bultmann, and Gadamer suggest that the "subjective" notion of "pre-understanding" allows any presupposition to direct the rest of our inquiry in a predetermined way, or is it a way of completing a fuller understanding, which can be both negotiated with, and take full account of, texts, readers, traditions, and the Church? In contrast to Gadamer, who rightly emphasizes "listening," Ricoeur stresses both a listening or "post-critical naïveté" and also a widespread array of critical tools and controls.[4] Many feminist writers, liberation theologians, and some Pentecostals regard "subjective" pre-understanding as a license to depart from good, balanced scholarship, and also to privilege the same range of predictable, selected texts.

1. Hermeneutics in the Christian Tradition: My Personal Testimony

Because among many Pentecostals and charismatics the mode of testimony sometimes appears more convincing and trustworthy than that of argument, I have chosen to give a personal account of my own development in hermeneutical inquiry. Before this, however, two or three general principles must be explained and asserted.

First, I was and am concerned to rescue the term "pre-understanding" from the subjectivity with which it is often equated among those whose knowledge of hermeneutics is less thorough than might be desired. For Gadamer, the term relates precisely to the dethronement of Descartes's self-centered human consciousness, as reminiscent of the Enlightenment.[5]

---

4. Hans-Georg Gadamer, "Reflections on My Philosophical Journey," in Lewis E. Hahn, ed., *The Philosophy of Hans-Georg Gadamer* (Chicago: Open Court, 1997), pp. 3-63, here p. 17; and Paul Ricoeur, *Freud and Philosophy: An Essay on Interpretation* (New Haven: Yale University Press, 1970), pp. 24-28.

5. Hans-Georg Gadamer, *Truth and Method,* 2nd Eng. ed. (London: Sheed and Ward, 1989), pp. 270-85, esp. pp. 275-77; cf. also pages 19-24, 101-10, 299-309.

This is what many liberation theologians, many feminists, and many Pentecostals ultimately seek. But frequently this term is not at all used in the way that might be associated with the term "presupposition." It simply signifies a preliminary or partial understanding, which constitutes the starting point towards a fuller understanding of the text or of another person. As Friedrich Ast and Friedrich Schleiermacher pointed out about the hermeneutical circle, it is not a fixed presupposition, or a permanent "lens," but a provisional way forward, which has to be negotiated with a fuller understanding, in turn, of the text or the "Other" concerned.[6] It can indeed be corrected by fuller understanding of the text.

The dimensions of the reader and the Church are also important. Reader-response criticism is a crucial addition to the tools of the interpreter. Such writers as Stanley Fish and Richard Rorty can press this approach into a postmodern and extreme elevation of the "success" of a particular community and a pragmatic concept of truth, over against the text (even if they themselves fail to recognize it as a given text). Even "success" can be assessed only in the light of a very wide spread of communities who use different criteria for what counts as "success."[7]

Reception theory and reception history can help us here. Admittedly, sometimes reception history sinks to the level of mere description. This might sometimes be taken to imply that any interpretation is as good as another. But it allows for more than mere comparison. As H. R. Jauss, its modern founder, conceived it, it can bring our attention to social formation. For Christians this in practice means how Scripture shapes communities, for good or ill.[8] The effect of such shaping enriches our criteria for interpretation. Having laid down these two principles, I shall now resume my testimony as author of some seven books on this subject. I wrote under what I regarded, and still regard, as the leading of the Holy Spirit.

First, in order precisely to avoid imposing a self-centered view upon the text, I stressed the distinctiveness of the horizon of the text from the horizon of the reader. That is why I entitled my first book on

---

6. Friedrich Schleiermacher, *Hermeneutics: The Handwritten Manuscripts,* ed. Heinz Kimmerle (Missoula, MT: Scholars Press, 1977), pp. 99-115.

7. Stanley Fish, *Doing What Comes Naturally* (Oxford: Clarendon, 1989), pp. 1-39, 68-86, 103-40, 471-502; Richard Rorty, *Truth and Progress* (Cambridge: Cambridge University Press, 1998) pp. 21, 25, and throughout.

8. Hans Robert Jauss, *Toward an Aesthetic of Reception* (Minneapolis: University of Minnesota Press, 1982); David P. Parris, *Reception Theory and Biblical Hermeneutics* (Eugene, OR: Pickwick, 2009).

the subject *The Two Horizons.*[9] I also examined precisely what is meant by "preunderstanding" or preliminary understanding. I then attempted to explore the value of the term "horizon" as against "presupposition." The latter usually denotes a fixed, non-negotiable, entrenched position, as opposed to a horizon that moves with us as we move. Gadamer stresses this, while Pannenberg rightly calls attention to the virtually infinite capacity of horizons to expand.[10] In Pannenberg's view, the horizon of the Christian theologian is probably broader and more comprehensive than that of any other discipline. Finally in this first major work, I attempted to show that genuine hermeneutics demands an interdisciplinary approach which calls upon linguistics, philosophy, theology, history, and linguistic philosophy.

Second, twelve years later I expressed my concern that while many biblical specialists conceived of hermeneutics perhaps too narrowly (at times as if it were exegesis), many theologians tended merely to generalize about "the biblical writings," without treating the biblical writings as a God-given library of many different books and genres. Neither reading the Bible nor the Bible itself is simply one thing. Hence I attempted to match different hermeneutical strategies and methods with different kinds of biblical texts. I also regarded the goal of hermeneutics, in accordance with the work of the Holy Spirit, as aiming at the transformation of readers. Hence the main title *New Horizons in Hermeneutics* received the subtitle *The Theory and Practice of Transforming Biblical Reading.*[11]

Hence I examined the capacity of readers to transform texts, perhaps too often rendering them into mirrors of themselves, as well as the capacity of biblical texts to transform readers. I digressed into a debate with postmodernity and Derrida, which in some ways I now partly regret because of its complexity and difficulty for readers. I attempted to show that the clarity of Scripture at the Reformation constituted a working clarity, which enabled all readers to take the next step, not an exemption from writing commentaries or offering clarifications of passages.[12] I then stressed how the logic of self-involvement made far better sense than Bultmann's

9. Anthony C. Thiselton, *The Two Horizons: New Testament Hermeneutics and Philosophical Description* (Grand Rapids: Eerdmans / Exeter: Paternoster, 1980).

10. Gadamer, *Truth and Method*, pp. 302-7.

11. Anthony C. Thiselton, *New Horizons in Hermeneutics: The Theory and Practice of Transforming Biblical Reading* (London: HarperCollins / Grand Rapids: Zondervan, 1992; repr., 2012).

12. Thiselton, *New Horizons*, pp. 179-94.

misguided attempt at "demythologizing."[13] This ultimately, I argued, was self-contradictory. I also attempted to introduce speech acts as a paradigmatic way of transforming readers' statuses and roles in the sight of God.[14] I noted some strengths of feminist and liberation hermeneutics, but regretted their selective and often pragmatic reading of Scripture.[15]

The key chapters, however, embodied a hermeneutics of pastoral theology, in which some dozen hermeneutical models were specifically related to particular kinds of biblical texts and genres.[16] Hence the controversial notion of "intention" I renamed "directedness," as Paul Ricoeur might say, on the part of the will. As is well known, "mainline" hermeneutics explores multiple models of interpretation. What has often been less clear is that specific models need to be matched with the exposition of specific texts. Many systematic theologians simply talk about "the biblical text" without making sufficiently explicit distinctions between specific biblical genres and specific methods of interpretation that fit the diverse functions of these various texts. Thus I have not only explored reader-response models, existentialist models, narrative-grammar and narrative-world models, but I have shown what types of biblical texts are illuminated by each distinctive model. I have even discussed "believing reading" with the help of some sociological analysis. For example, while some assume that the narrative in Acts functions only as historical report, I have distinguished between several functions of narrative. To such writers as Ricoeur, many narrative theorists, and exponents of the New Hermeneutic, all this seems self-evident. Such biblical material as the book of Revelation demands also the appreciation of symbolism. Northrop Frye has discussed such symbols as city, mountain, river, garden, tree, fountain, bread, wine, bride, and sheep. Tillich calls these "depth" archetypes, and Ricoeur calls them double-meaning symbols.[17]

The last chapter considers speech-act models, which include acts of authorization, acts of forgiveness, acts of liberation, and especially acts of promise, including the promissory acts of God. The reformer William Tyndale had hinted at this. I draw on Alfred Schutz's criteria of relevance,

13. Thiselton, *New Horizons,* pp. 272-83.

14. Thiselton, *New Horizons,* pp. 283-307.

15. Thiselton, *New Horizons,* pp. 411-63.

16. Thiselton, *New Horizons,* pp. 558-619.

17. Paul Ricoeur, *Interpretation Theory* (Fort Worth: Texas Christian University Press, 1976), pp. 55-57; and idem, *The Conflict of Interpretations* (Evanston, IL: Northwestern University Press, 1976), pp. 287-334.

to consider "believing reading," and the power of the cross and the resurrection of Jesus Christ.[18] From the standpoint of the social sciences, Karl-Otto Apel and Jürgen Habermas are also relevant. From the standpoint of theology, Wolfhart Pannenberg and Jürgen Moltmann, as well as others, offer valuable insights to hermeneutics.

Third, in *The Promise of Hermeneutics*, written jointly with Roger Lundin of Wheaton College and Clarence Walhout of Calvin College, we addressed problems of the Cartesian tradition (Lundin) and of much literary theory (Walhout), while I examined "promise" as the paradigmatic example of speech acts.[19] I also included a critique of human autonomy, an assessment of different kinds of reader-response theories, an exploration of polyphonic discourse, and an elucidation of differences between chronological time and narrative time. This exploration of narrative greatly affects supposed problems of sequence in the synoptic gospels and elsewhere. Chronological sequence is not a key concern for narrators who use narrative time to organize a plot. Such clarification still seems to me to constitute a hermeneutic prompted by the leading of the Holy Spirit.

After my exhaustive commentary of some 1500 pages on the exegesis and hermeneutics of the Greek text of 1 Corinthians,[20] I produced an almost equally large volume of forty-two essays under the title *Thiselton on Hermeneutics*.[21] These were mainly research articles, to which I added fresh introductions and explanations, and retrospective reappraisals. Ashgate called this series Ashgate Contemporary Thinkers on Religion: Collected Works, and Eerdmans published it simultaneously with Ashgate. This included both old (reprinted) and new essays, including an early exploration of semantics and a critique of word-magic in my article reprinted from the *Journal of Theological Studies* (vol. 25, 1974), "The Supposed Power of Words in the Biblical Writings." In another essay I related speech-act theory to Christology, to explain Jesus' acts of forgiveness or other illocutions. In another I used hermeneutical and exegetical tools to explain Titus 1:12-13, which might *seem* to endorse the racist generalization that "all Cretans are liars"; but *in fact* wittily uses a well-known logical paradox

18. Thiselton*, New Horizons,* pp. 597-619.

19. Roger Lundin, Clarence Walhout, and Anthony C. Thiselton, *The Promise of Hermeneutics* (Grand Rapids: Eerdmans, 1999).

20. Anthony C. Thiselton, *The First Epistle to the Corinthians* (Grand Rapids: Eerdmans, 2000).

21. Anthony C. Thiselton, *Thiselton on Hermeneutics: Collected Works with New Essays* (Burlington, VT: Ashgate / Grand Rapids: Eerdmans, 2006).

to make an entirely different point about avoiding purely speculative arguments, and about ensuring that words match deeds. Subjects included speech-act theory, conceptual grammar, reception history and exegesis, narrative worlds, reader-response theories, philosophy and language, and hermeneutics and history.

Once again, the peril of this testimony mode is that it too easily seems to merge into self-advertisement. But in this chapter, I want to ask potential Pentecostal critics how such approaches to Scripture and hermeneutics as these could be brushed aside as "academic and objective," in contrast to hermeneutics prompted by the Holy Spirit.

That following year, 2007, my *Hermeneutics of Doctrine* attempted to approach themes in systematic theology from a hermeneutical perspective.[22] Shortly thereafter I produced a shorter book on hermeneutics, simply entitled *Hermeneutics: An Introduction*.[23] This consisted of seventeen chapters on the main issues and thinkers in hermeneutics to date, including suggestions in each chapter for further reading. Predictably this includes chapters on Gadamer, Ricoeur, liberation and postcolonial hermeneutics, feminist and womanist hermeneutics, and finally postmodernism and hermeneutics.

My commentary *1 and 2 Thessalonians* accorded with the explicit aim of the Wiley-Blackwell series on reception history down the centuries.[24] Much is admittedly descriptive, but this also enlarges our horizons and allows us to call on a wide range of insights. I also commented more critically, however, on "the Rapture" and "pre-millennialism" in 1 Thess. 4:13-17, as well as on repeatedly made claims that Paul's words "we who are alive and remain" (4:17) indicate that Paul believed that Christ would return during his lifetime.[25] I think that this belief is profoundly mistaken, on grounds of both exegesis and logic. If Paul had used "those who are alive," it would compromise his solidarity with readers, and repeated opinion makes a logical confusion between *assertion* and *presupposition,* which has been well exposed by the philosopher P. F. Strawson.

In 2012 I developed several of these insights further in my book *Life after Death* (published simultaneously by SPCK under a different title:

22. Anthony C. Thiselton, *Hermeneutics of Doctrine* (Grand Rapids: Eerdmasn, 2007).

23. Anthony C. Thiselton, *Hermeneutics: An Introduction* (Grand Rapids: Eerdmans, 2009).

24. Anthony C. Thiselton, *1 and 2 Thessalonians through the Centuries and Today* (Chichester & Oxford: Wiley-Blackwell, 2011).

25. Thiselton, *1 and 2 Thessalonians,* pp. 116-20, 143-48.

The Last Things: A New Approach).[26] One of many conceptual clarifications includes the notion of "expectation." This does *not* primarily involve excited mental states at all. As the philosopher Wittgenstein points out, to expect a visitor for tea involves first and foremost "being ready," e.g., by laying the table, putting out cakes, and so on. The NT and Luther make precisely the same point. We must be "ready" for the return of Christ, even if this means going on in obedience to God's will, not nurturing a fever of excitement. Similarly in the light of other comments by Wittgenstein (and, later, Gilbert Ryle), I drew a distinction between "participant" language and "observer" language. I suggested a homely illustration. On Christmas Eve we often say to small children, using participant language, "The sooner you fall asleep, the sooner Christmas morning will come." Meanwhile in terms of observer language, the family has much to do, including perhaps wrapping presents, attending church, and making culinary preparations for the next day. This is closely parallel to the "participant" experience of being *immediately with* Christ at death, and the "observer" or theological sequence of judgement, resurrection, and the events of the end.

The next book, *The Holy Spirit,* was not merely a larger version of the present study, but was intended to consider the work of the Holy Spirit comprehensively in the Bible, in the history of the church, and today, also aiming to facilitate mutual respect and dialogue with Pentecostals.[27] Among some weaknesses, in retrospect, this book was inadequate on global Pentecostalism in the two-thirds world, which I hastened to correct in this small volume. Indeed while the biblical material may be similar, doctrinal and experiential material is new and different. Finally, Eerdmans has published *The Thiselton Companion to Christian Theology* (called in Britain *The SPCK Dictionary of Theology and Hermeneutics*).[28] This includes more than 600 essays and articles on various subjects, including hermeneutics. As would be expected, it includes essays on Gadamer, Ricoeur, and Pannenberg, as well as some forty pages on the Holy Spirit. Admittedly all this owes more to reflection and argument than to "spontaneity," but I cannot see how "spontaneity" could be an invariable of sign of the Holy Spirit,

---

26. Anthony C. Thiselton, *Life After Death: A New Approach to the Last Things* (Grand Rapids: Eerdmans, 2012), esp. pp. 53-99.

27. Anthony C. Thiselton, *The Holy Spirit — in Biblical Teaching, through the Centuries, and Today* (Grand Rapids: Eerdmans / London: SPCK, 2013).

28. Anthony C. Thiselton, *The Thiselton Companion to Christian Theology* (Grand Rapids: Eerdmans, 2015).

especially when he bestows such gifts as administration and faithfulness. As Amos Yong and others observe, the work of the Spirit is always in conjunction with hearing the Word of God.

2. Pentecostal Hermeneutics

In a reconciling and irenical manner, we must first admit that there are varieties of Pentecostal hermeneutics, and further that there is considerable overlap between traditional Christian hermeneutics and distinctively Pentecostal hermeneutics. Christians generally agree with Luther and Calvin that the ultimate aim of the interpretation of Scripture is to glorify Christ, and that the main task of readers is to listen to the voice of God through Scripture (Ps. 95:7) and be judged by him (Heb. 4:12). In terms of listening to the text, few have appreciated this more urgently than Gadamer, who was a major contributor to contemporary hermeneutics. He writes: "Hermeneutics is above all a practice. . . . In it what one has to exercise above all is the ear."[29]

I could not have hoped to address such a subject as Pentecostal hermeneutics without the aid of the fifteen essays in Lee Roy Martin's book *Pentecostal Hermeneutics* (2013), the relevant sections in Keith Warrington's *Pentecostal Theology* (2008), Yongnan Jeon Ahn's *Interpretation of Tongues and Prophecy in 1 Corinthians 12–14* (2013), and many similar books, as well as especially the earlier volumes of the *Journal of Pentecostal Theology* (especially vol. 1 [1992], vols. 5-8 [1997-2000], and vol. 15 [2006]), and also the journal *Paraclete*. The broadest and most congenial source written by a Pentecostal but accessible to other thinkers is probably Amos Yong's book, *Spirit-Word-Community* (2002).

Two features of Pentecostal hermeneutics may strike readers. One is the sheer *diversity* of Pentecostal hermeneutics. The book edited by Lee Roy Martin illustrates this, together with the varied contributions to the *Journal of Pentecostal Theology* and *Pneuma*. On the other hand, several key phrases characterize nearly every Pentecostal essay. The favorite terms are: "experience," "supernatural," and seeing through a predetermined "lens."[30] Correspondingly the two most frequently used negative terms

---

29. Gadamer, "Reflections on My Philosophical Journey," p. 17.

30. On "experience," see Lee Roy Martin, ed., *Pentecostal Hermeneutics* (Leiden: Brill, 2013), pp. 5, 12, 33, 109, 132, 142, 168, etc.; on the "supernatural," see in the same volume

(i.e., for non-Pentecostal hermeneutics) seem to be "rational" and "objective."[31] Other terms frequently employed in the description of Pentecostal hermeneutics include "narrative," "presupposition," "apocalyptic horizon," "praxis," "prophetic," "community," "miraculous," and the paradigm of Luke–Acts (over against Paul).

Kenneth Archer, a frequent writer on this subject, declares, "What is at stake in the present hermeneutical debate is not whether Pentecostals have correctly exegeted [as if it were a verb] the Lucan corpus according to the traditional historical-critical methodologies, but *Pentecostal identity*. . . . The essence of Pentecostalism is its persistent emphasis upon the *supernatural* within the community."[32]

We have already expressed strong reservations, as Hollenweger does, about the implied dualism of natural and supernatural in the use of the term "supernatural." Hollenweger, Miller, and Yamamori claim that, as we saw in the previous chapter, Pentecostals are often "dualists at heart, separating body and mind, heaven and hell, good and evil."[33] Hollenweger, we noted, declared, "'Supernatural' is in my view biblically and scientifically untenable. Biblically — the list of *charismata* in the New Testament includes 'extraordinary gifts' . . . and the so-called 'ordinary gifts' (management, teaching, giving money to the poor . . . ."[34] Are the sovereignty and activity of God restricted to the "supernatural" realm, and excluded from the "ordinary" realm of life? This use of the term also disguises what is held in common with many evangelical Protestant exegetes and a number of Roman Catholic and Eastern Orthodox scholars, namely the firm *rejection of a mechanistic view of the universe modelled on the Enlightenment.* On these grounds we may doubt whether "belief in the supernatural" really distinguishes Pentecostals from many mainline Christians who reject a materialist view of the universe.

---

pp. 6, 67, 96, 131, 132, 141. The metaphor of "lens" seems to be used by virtually everyone who contributed to that volume, including especially Kenneth Archer.

31. On "rationalism," see Martin, ed., *Pentecostal Hermeneutics*, pp. 6, 33, 57, 62, 81, 95, etc.; on "objectivity," pp. 57, 95, 96, etc.

32. Kenneth J. Archer, "Pentecostal Hermeneutics: Retrospect and Prospect," in Martin, ed., *Pentecostal Hermeneutics,* pp. 131-48, here p. 131 (my italics).

33. Donald Miller and Tetsunao Yamamori, *Global Pentecostalism: The New Face of Christian Social Engagement* (Berkeley: University of California Press, 2007), p. 217.

34. Walter J. Hollenweger, "Rethinking Spirit Baptism," in Allan H. Anderson and Walter J. Hollenweger, eds., *Pentecostals after a Century: Global Perspectives* (Sheffield: Sheffield Academic Press, 1999), pp. 164-96, here pp. 169-70.

Yongnan Jeon Ahn also articulates a less generalizing approach to "objectivity." She rightly asserts, "The subjectivity of experience can interact with objectivity without division."[35] She stresses "experience" just as much as most other Pentecostals, regarding it as a key to Pentecostal identity.[36] But this is very different from Robert Baker's claim that academic scholarship (as if this were all one kind of thing!) "has displayed at least one of the symptoms of paranoid schizophrenia. It lacks emotion in the(ir) attempt to arrive at a scientific objective understanding of the text. . . . A rational approach . . . is in effect, then, a schizophrenic one."[37] Baker accuses most Christian scholars of "passionless objectivity," in contrast to the "pleasure" commended by Roland Barthes in his postmodern approach.[38] Is this to suggest that, for example, Tom Wright, Richard Bauckham, Francis Watson, or Joel Green always write without emotion, pleasure, or passion?

All these scholars also insist that interpretation takes place in the context of the Christian Church as a participatory *community.* It is simply untrue to many in mainline churches, including Karl Barth, to recognize that the emphasis on community context is the exclusive prerogative of Pentecostalism.

Rickie Moore, Yongnan Ahn, and others are nearer to the truth when they see *narrative* and its relation to *didactic respectability* as near the heart of Pentecostal hermeneutics. Should the narrative of Pentecost in Acts 2 *be repeated* in the lives of Christians today?[39] As Ahn points out, this matter is hotly debated among many Pentecostals themselves. She quotes both Gordon Fee and Bradley Truman Noel on one side, and Robert Menzies and Roger Stronstad on the other. She comments, "Fee argues strongly that Acts, as a historical narrative, cannot be utilized to establish norm or doctrine without the author's explicit intent, whereas Stronstad and Menzies claim that the narratives have a significant didactic value that lends support to the Pentecostal claim of 'repeatability' of historical precedence."[40] Bradley Truman Noel writes that there can never be agreement

35. Yongnan Jeon Ahn, *Interpretation of Tongues and Prophecy in 1 Corinthians 12–14* (Blandford Forum, UK: Deo, 2013), p. 49.

36. Ahn, *Interpretation of Tongues,* pp. 9-14.

37. Robert Baker, "Pentecostal Bible Reading: Toward a Model of Reading for the Formation of the Affections," in Martin, ed., *Pentecostal Hermeneutics,* pp. 95-108, here p. 95.

38. Baker, "Pentecostal Bible Reading," pp. 96, 98-100.

39. Ahn, *Interpretation of Tongues,* p. 33.

40. Ahn, *Interpretation of Tongues,* p. 41.

on the issue of "biblical precedent as historical precedent for establishing what is normative."[41] Ahn describes this as "the Pentecostal hermeneutical dilemma"; some Pentecostals seek the historicity of Acts but also see it as a theological treatise for the norm and doctrine of Pentecostal experience. It concerns "two of Pentecostalism's most cherished doctrines, subsequence [i.e., a baptism in the Spirit subsequent to conversion or regeneration] and initial evidence."[42]

In spite of the attention given by many Pentecostals to reader-response theory, postmodernism, and literary theory (e.g. by Robert O. Baker),[43] few engage with narratology, or the multiple purposes of narrative, in literary theory as represented by Paul Ricoeur and Gérard Genette. To be sure, Robby Waddell mentions Genette and Tzvetan Todorov in a footnote, and briefly alludes to the New Criticism of the 1950s, just as Martin gives a one-sentence footnote to Ricoeur. But there is no serious engagement.[44] Of all Pentecostal writers, probably Ahn gives most attention to Ricoeur and multifunctional narrative, considering also Gadamer, Conzelmann, Iser, Vanhoozer, and others.[45] Many *prima facie* "problems" of chronology are easily resolved by drawing a careful distinction between chronological time and narrative time. Clear examples include the sequence of the temptations and the cleansing of the temple in John and the synoptic gospels.

Mark uses narrative time, beginning at a very fast pace, then slowing down, then portraying the Passion in slow motion, all for the purpose of focusing on the cross, rather than providing a descriptive chronological report. Narrative worlds (like that of the Laborers in the Vineyard) are designed to draw readers into their world, with the aim of the readers experiencing shock and consternation at the employer's verdict. Robert O.

---

41. Bradley Truman Noel, "Gordon Fee and the Challenge to Pentecostal Hermeneutics: Thirty Years Later," *Pneuma* 26 (2002), pp. 60-80, here p. 79.

42. Ahn, *Interpretation of Tongues*, p. 41; cf. Gordon D. Fee, "Response to Roger Stronstad's 'The Biblical Precedent from Historical Precedent'," *Paraclete* 27 (1993), pp. 11-14, here p. 13; cf. also Gordon D. Fee, *Gospel and Spirit: Issues in New Testament Hermeneutics* (Peabody, MA: Hendrickson, 1991).

43. Baker, "Pentecostal Bible Reading," pp. 98-104.

44. Robby Waddell, "Hearing What the Spirit Says to the Churches: Profile of a Pentecostal Reader of the Apocalypse," in Martin, ed., *Pentecostal Hermeneutics*, pp. 171-204, here p. 173 n. 8; Lee Roy Martin, "Hearing the Voice of God: Pentecostal Hermeneutics and the Book of Judges," in idem, ed., *Pentecostal Hermeneutics*, pp. 205-32, here p. 223 n. 10.

45. Ahn, *Interpretation of Tongues*, pp. 45-47, 52-58, 68-72, 104-16, 120-23, and throughout.

Baker, by denouncing academic NT study as having "symptoms of paranoid schizophrenia" and lacking emotion, shows that he is unaware of the new hermeneutic of Ernst Fuchs on the parable of Jesus in Matt. 20:1-16! Fuchs makes the story throb with emotion; it is a different hermeneutic, he says, from "the pallid requirement of belief in God's kindness."[46]

An accurate assessment of the intention, or directedness and aim, of narratives in Acts can be assessed only in the light of the many options available. If they belong to the category of report, they may well simply reflect what the early Church once was, before the Holy Spirit introduced developments in its understanding, including necessary infrastructures, as it reached out into the wider Hellenistic and Gentile world.[47]

Ahn also provides one of the most sophisticated discussions of "'experience' as a hermeneutical resource."[48] Rather than simply asserting this as a self-evident fact, she discusses reader-response theory and its creative role, "pre-understanding" in Gadamer and Ricoeur, and the dialectical relation between understanding and explanation (as in Ricoeur and Karl-Otto Apel). But where many Pentecostals regard "pre-understanding" as a fixed presupposition or non-negotiable "lens," she concedes that in the constant *process* of the hermeneutical circle, "experience does not terminate in a moment of reflective knowledge, but remains open to further experiences."[49] She cites Gadamer on the anticipatory structure of understanding, and Ricoeur on the dialectical movement between "explanation" and "understanding." She values "pre-understanding, when its provisional nature is recognized."[50] As she insists, Ricoeur does not remain at the level of "the first naïveté" but passes through post-critical comprehension, with "the ascending curve of the author's subjective intention."[51]

Ahn's Pentecostal credentials and conviction cannot be doubted. My one reservation is her possible appeal to "women's experience" in feminist hermeneutics, and to the "experience" of the poor in liberation hermeneu-

46. Ernst Fuchs, *Studies of the Historical Jesus* (London: SCM, 1964), pp. 33-37; cf. pp. 21-28, 154-56; and more broadly on "narrative world," Anthony C. Thiselton, *New Horizons in Hermeneutics*, pp. 566-92; on narrative time, see in the same volume pp. 354-68, 419-27, 480-81.

47. On the purpose of God, cf. Beverly Roberts Gaventa, *The Acts of the Apostles:* (Nashville: Abingdon, 2003).

48. Ahn, *Interpretation of Tongues*, pp. 67-72.

49. Ahn, *Interpretation of Tongues,* p. 69.

50. Ahn, *Interpretation of Tongues,* p. 68.

51. Ahn, *Interpretation of Tongues,* p. 70.

tics. Although I sympathize with the plight of those who suffer oppression, I also have doubts about their over-selective use of biblical passages, and over-ready tendency to read their own agenda into almost every text, when careful examination will reveal other concerns. One example is Elizabeth Schüssler Fiorenza, who, with some generalization, attacks "the so-called objectivity and value-neutrality of academic theology," and insists that the motivation for Peter's supposed prominence over Mary Magdalene is entirely due to gender bias. She does not seem to consider Peter's restoration after failure, in contrast to Mary's more recent but consistent record of faithful discipleship.[52]

Unfortunately there is a similar pragmatic strain in all these movements, which Ahn elsewhere acknowledges in her contrast between social-critical and socio-pragmatic hermeneutical methods. Even Keith Warrington, in his section on hermeneutics, appears to say sheer "effectiveness" is the criterion for preaching, which reflects "the vibrant spontaneity of the Spirit."[53]

One remaining issue is that of eschatology. It is entirely right that the return of Jesus, or his Parousia, receives full attention. But even Kenneth Archer, a specialist in Pentecostal hermeneutics, concedes that until recently "classical Pentecostalism has a rigorous literal exegesis, e.g. handling snakes in Mark 16 [the disputed longer ending] which takes it 'at face value'."[54] This is frequently extended to the symbolism of events of the end. But in rightly looking forward to the Coming King, Baker commends "emotion," and many commend "intensity," whereas I have argued in another book that to "expect" is a *disposition,* not a mental state; as I noted above, it is best seen as a *state of readiness.* This does not exclude joy; but the emphasis lies on quietly doing God's will in readiness for Christ's return.[55] I argued this on biblical, historical, and philosophical terms.

There is much more to be said on the topic of hermeneutics, but this is supposed to be a short book, so I shall conclude. I might well have discussed the relation between prophecy and applied preaching. A refreshing Pentecostal contribution, alongside those of Yong and Ahn, is the essay by

---

52. Elizabeth Schüssler Fiorenza, *In Memory of Her: A Feminist Theological Reconstruction of Christian Origins* (New York: Crossroads / London: SCM, 1983), pp. 5-6, 332-33; cf. Thiselton, *New Horizons in Hermeneutics,* pp. 430-39, 442-50.

53. Keith Warrington, *Pentecostal Theology: A Theology of Encounter* (London: T&T Clark, 2008), pp. 184-205, here p. 194.

54. Archer, "Pentecostal Hermeneutics," p. 133.

55. Anthony C. Thiselton, *Life after Death,* pp. 58-67.

Andrew Davies, "What Does It Mean to Read the Bible as a Pentecostal?"[56] On an issue such as pre-millennialism, for example, he argues that "Pentecostal theology in its . . . more popular forms requires a degree of uncertainty. . . . It is precisely our faith and certainty against all the odds which causes us problems."[57] He also acknowledged the need for more Pentecostal systematic theologians. Similarly, Stephenson comments, "More than any other Pentecostal scholar, Yong demonstrates awareness that hermeneutics encompasses far more than simply biblical interpretation"; he uses "philosophical hermeneutics," and reflects on "theological method."[58]

To repeat: the most fundamental issue of all is the substitution of the term "supernatural" in place of "God's sovereign interaction with the world." Together with this, Pentecostal writers tend to see "*the* historical-critical method" as one single, generalized, thing, often as it was twenty or thirty years ago. Richard Bauckham, formerly Professor of New Testament at the University of St. Andrews, has argued that the Bible's metanarrative is the story of God and the world, from creation to new creation. In an article published in 2013 he argued, "New Testament scholarship has changed" since the 1960s, and that "the understanding of New Testament scholarship as an incremental science is *a misleading one. . . . The biggest mistake . . . was form criticism* and the *criteria of authenticity* that the quest of the historical Jesus . . . found it necessary to adopt"; moreover, "The literary turn in Gospel studies . . . occurred in the late twentieth century."[59] He refers to Pannenberg's reformulation of historical method to include the resurrection of Jesus.

The reaction against "value-neutral" scholarship was expressed eleven years ago by Francis Watson. He wrote, "The assumption that faith is incompatible with proper academic standards or with openness to alternative viewpoints is ultimately a mere prejudice. . . . The miracle of Pentecost is not an inner-ecclesial event, but an event in which the church addresses the world. . . . The world is the object of God's loving action."[60]

---

56. Andrew Davies, "What Does It Mean to Read the Bible as a Pentecostal?" in Martin, ed., *Pentecostal Hermeneutics,* pp. 249-62.

57. Davies, "What Does It Mean?" pp. 252-53.

58. Christopher A. Stephenson, *Types of Pentecostal Theology: Method, System, Spirit* (Oxford: Oxford University Press, 2013), pp. 107-8.

59. Richard Bauckham, "Are We Still Missing the Elephant? C. S. Lewis's "'Fernseed and Elephants' Half a Century On," *Theology* 116 (2013), pp. 427-34 (my italics).

60. Francis Watson, *Text, Church and World: Biblical Interpretation in Theological Perspective* (Edinburgh: T&T Clark, 1994), pp. 9, 10, 11.

Since the turn of the nineteenth century, biblical scholars have included such theologians as B. F. Westcott, J. B. Lightfoot, and F. J. Hort, whose Christian faith shone through their "academic" scholarship. Today they have been replaced by Tom Wright, James D. G. Dunn, Richard Bauckham, and others. I had also hoped to show through the medium of personal testimony in what hermeneutics consisted, and whether it could not constitute *as much a work of the Holy Spirit* as what is called "Pentecostal hermeneneutics." To quote Pannenberg again, "An otherwise unconvincing message cannot attain the power to convince simply by appealing to the Holy Spirit. . . . Argumentation and the operation of the Spirit are not in competition with each other. In trusting in the Spirit, Paul in no way spared himself thinking and arguing."[61]

61. Wolfhart Pannenberg, *Basic Questions in Theology* (London: SCM, 1971), 2.34, 35.

CHAPTER 17

Prayer and Worship in the Context of the Spirit and the Trinity

1. Prayer as Intra-Trinitarian Dialogue: To God through Christ by the Holy Spirit

Of the Christian experiences which conspicuously depend on the ministry of the Holy Spirit, prayer and worship constitute probably the most striking. Just as we cannot try to make ourselves holy without the aid of the Holy Spirit, so also we are disinclined to give God his due in worship, reverence, thanksgiving, and love, unless we are responding to the promptings of the Holy Spirit. Prayer is notoriously challenging and "difficult." Paul acknowledges this and explains in Romans that we cannot pray *alone* without the aid of the Holy Spirit.

This becomes abundantly clear in Rom. 8:26-27. In 8:16 Paul declares that it is the Holy Spirit who witnesses within us that we are children of God. Then in 8:26-27 he is more explicit. He writes, "The Spirit helps us in our weakness; for we do not know how to pray as we ought, but that very Spirit intercedes with sighs too deep for words. And God, who searches the heart, knows what is the mind of the Spirit, because the Spirit intercedes for the saints according to the will of God."

Every phrase here carries weight. First, Paul affirms that, if we try to pray on our own, "we [humans] do not know how to pray" appropriately. Most Christians would endorse this as true to experience. Prayer is often called a difficult subject, which is hardly solved by repeatedly using only historical formularies. This shows our "weakness." Second, God "knows what is the mind of the Spirit," and the *Holy Spirit prays within us* both individually and corporately. The Spirit prays appropriately because the Spirit knows the will of God. Hence the context of prayer is the *interactive dialogue* between the Father and the Holy Spirit, which is ultimately addressed to the Father through the Son. Hence this may correctly be called *intra-Trinitarian dialogue.* The normal or ideal, but not invariable, practice of Christians, therefore, is to pray *to* God the Father, as Provider and Sovereign, *through* Jesus Christ as Mediator and Savior, *by* (or in the power of) the Holy Spirit, who initiates, inspires, and articulates appropriate prayer, according to the will of God.

The upshot of this, as we expressed it in our Doctrine Commission Report for the Church of England, is that Christians are "graciously caught up in a divine conversation," in which they have "the experience of being 'prayed in'."[1] God is the source and goal of all things (Rom. 11:36). He is the Fatherly Provider, to whom Jesus encouraged us to direct our prayers and worship in the model prayer, "Our Father." It is also the Holy Spirit who brings to the surface of our minds what has hitherto been unconscious or hidden within our hearts. Thus Paul speaks of "the secrets of the heart" in Rom. 2:12-16; 1 Cor. 4:1-5; 14:20-25. Writers as diverse as Ernst Käsemann, Gerd Theissen, and Frank Macchia all understand "sighs too deep for words" in these verses as *glossolalia* or tongues-speech.[2] Even if we cannot be fully certain of this exegesis, clearly the Holy Spirit brings order and expression out of human confusion or from barely conscious thought. Here Freud argues that the libido and repressed wishes are at work, although the Christian would add that longings to praise God adequately, and to give him glory through Jesus Christ, also find a place in the hidden secrets of the heart. Käsemann observes, "Christians do not know by virtue of their humanity . . . what God really wants of us. . . . It comes about once more through *auto to pneuma* ['that very Spirit', NRSV] . . . directly God-inspired . . . heavenly tongues."[3]

In Rom. 8:15 Paul notes that the believer's prayer life mirrors that of Jesus, for whom "Abba! Father!" was a hallmark. This was prompted by the Spirit of adoption, who established our filial relationship with God as

---

1. Doctrine Commission of the Church of England, *We Believe in God* (London: Church House Publishing, 1987), p. 108, to which Sarah Coakley made a substantial contribution; cf. also Anthony C. Thiselton, *Life after Death: A New Approach to the Last Things* (Grand Rapids: Eerdmans, 2012), p. 213.

2. Ernst Käsemann, "Cry for Liberty in the Church's Worship," in idem, *Perspectives on Paul* (London: SCM, 1971), pp. 122-37, here pp. 131-32; Gerd Theissen, *Psychological Aspects of Pauline Theology* (Edinburgh: T&T Clark, 1987), pp. 57-114 and 320-44; Frank D. Macchia, "Sighs Too Deep for Words" *JPT* 1 (1992), pp. 47-73.

3. Käsemann, "Cry for Liberty," pp. 129-30, 132.

Father. Dunn comments on Rom. 8:15 and Gal. 4:6: *"The early Christians'
experience of Sonship was understood as an echo and reproduction of Jesus'
own experience; it is precisely the Spirit of the Son* who cries 'Abba'."[4] Later
in the same book, Dunn declares "Paul [is] describing an existential experience (the awareness of Sonship), which is a mark of the Spirit of God."[5]
He broadly follows Jeremias in asserting that *Abba* was a family word in the
time of Jesus. Christians now approach God as Father, precisely because
their Sonship derives from Christ's Sonship, and both address prayers to
God as Father in the power of the Holy Spirit. Dunn regards the pattern of
the prayer life of Jesus as due to his anointing by the Holy Spirit.[6]

The synoptic gospels spell this out. The Holy Spirit led Jesus to his
messianic trials and testing as God's Son (Matt. 4:1-11; Luke 4:1-13). During
the temptations, Luke comments, "Jesus [was] full of the Holy Spirit" (v. 1).
But John is also clear. In the dialogue between Jesus and the Woman of
Samaria, it is unfortunate that the NRSV translates John 4:24, "God is
spirit, and those who worship him must worship him in spirit and in truth."
I firmly agree with Raymond Brown when he observes, "[Jesus'] statement
has nothing to do with the worship of God in the inner recesses of one's
own spirit; for the Spirit is the Spirit of God," who gives birth from above,
and was given by Jesus "to animate the worship that replaces worship at
the Temple."[7] John draws on the theme: The Spirit is the Spirit of Jesus,
and is the Spirit of truth (14:17; 15:26), who is to guide men into truth.
Schnackenburg similarly appeals to the parallel of the Spirit from above
in the writings of Qumran.[8]

We cannot doubt that the Spirit of God motivated the extensive examples of worship through sacrifice and through the tabernacle or temple
in the Old Testament era, even if the new age superseded it in Christ. There
are impressive scenes of worship in Isaiah 6:1-13 and the throne visions of
Ezekiel (Ezek. 1:1-28 and elsewhere), just as in the Levitical regulations
about sacrifice.

---

4. James D. G. Dunn, *Jesus and the Spirit: A Study of the Religious and Charismatic
Experience of Jesus and the First Christians as Reflected in the New Testament* (London: SCM,
1975), p. 23 (his italics).

5. Dunn, *Jesus and the Spirit*, p. 319.

6. Dunn, *Jesus and the Spirit*, pp. 15-40.

7. Raymond E. Brown, *The Gospel according to John* (London: Chapman / New York:
Macmillan, 1966), p. 180.

8. Rudolf Schnackenburg, *The Gospel according to John*, 3 vols. (Freiberg: Herder,
1965-75), 2.50, 156, 300-13.

2. Is There Self-Awareness in Worship within the Charismatic Movement?

We have shown several times that the Pentecostal churches are currently entirely self-aware of a number of current issues that deserve attention. These include the so-called prosperity gospel, hermeneutics, baptism in the spirit, and several more. We have also argued that such self-awareness cannot usually be credited to the same extent in the charismatic movement as it is manifested in mainstream denominations. It is possible, of course, to identify important exceptions. Some of the leading thinkers may be identified as Tom Smail, Andrew Walker, Nigel Wright, Mark Cartledge, Mark Bonnington, Don Carson, and Andy Lord. There are no doubt others, but these come to mind most readily, especially on worship.

Tom Smail, Mark Bonnington, and Mark Cartledge speak most directly of the strengths and weaknesses of worship within the charismatic movement. One important source is the book by Smail, Walker, and Wright called *The Love of Power or the Power of Love.*[9] Among the strengths of charismatic worship, all of the writers rightly stress the dynamic intensity and personal involvement of the worship. As in Pentecostalism, there is a sense of intimacy with the living God, in contrast to experiencing thirst for God in dry places. The aim is that worship should never be dull, routine, or even predictable. Tom Smail, however, has questioned whether spontaneity always operates in the precise way that serves a charismatic goal. On the positive side, he comments "Because charismatic renewal is about our relationship to God, the renewal of our worship of God is one of its primary concerns. . . . [It seeks] immediacy, intimacy, freedom, and joy in the near presence of God."[10] Even if rational faculties are bypassed, this may well be because of the experience of divine transcendence or Otherness.

Nevertheless Smail comments, "All is not well" with charismatic worship.[11] At worst, he observes, "The high praise of God had degenerated into endless repetitive chorus-singing that was in danger of becoming a bore and burden rather than release and a joy. . . . In the midst of the noisy and exuberant striving for the spiritual mountaintops, there was little room

---

9. Tom Smail, Andrew Walker, and Nigel Wright, *The Love of Power or the Power of Love: A Careful Assessment of the Problems within the Charismatic and Word-of-Faith Movements* (Minneapolis: Bethany House, 1994), esp. pp. 95-103.

10. Smail, Walker, and Wright, *The Love of Power,* p. 95.

11. Smail, Walker, and Wright, *The Love of Power,* p. 97.

for silent listening and patient waiting upon God."[12] Furthermore, he adds, too often "*Theologia gloriae* . . . does not wrestle with a *theologia crucis,* and can engender a worship style that concentrates too one-sidedly on the triumphs of Easter and Pentecost, and does not sufficiently take into account that they can be reached only by way of the cross."[13] Smail then adds a measured comment, writing: "Worship must have a place not just for the moments when hearts lift high and eyes are shining and joy abounds, but for the dull days when we are empty and unresponsive in ourselves and can only hold out empty hands for the bread and wine, the body and blood, redeeming gift of his living but crucified self that Jesus gives us from the cross."[14] A central place, he observes, must always be given to confession of sins, deep repentance, and God's free forgiveness.

Smail also sees too often an inadequate attention to intercession. In addition to this there is often "A ministry of healing rather than engaging in prayer for healing. . . . We tend to see ourselves as standing, as it were, at God's side and exercising the power and authority that He has given us against illness and evil, armed with words of knowledge . . . that will make us the triumphant masters of the situations we encounter."[15] He also questions whether worship is "always as spontaneous and unscripted as may appear. Certain songs sung in a certain sequence can be guaranteed to produce singing in tongues that will be followed by one of five predictable 'prophecies' that we have all heard before."[16] Smail urges that freedom and liturgy should be complementary to each other, rather than regarded as mutually exclusive alternatives.

Bonnington and Cartledge make some astute positive and negative comments about the so-called "Third Wave" charismatic worship mainly associated with John Wimber, Peter Wagner, the so-called Toronto Blessing, and the Vineyard movement, founded by Wimber in 1987. Typical experiences in their worship meetings included being "slain in the Spirit," "resting in the Spirit," or "holy laughter," and "healings" regularly occurred. The phrase "power evangelism" became almost a fashion.[17] Bonnington acknowledges, "John Wimber's Vineyard movement and their so-called 'third wave' teaching are consciously attempting a synthesis of charis-

12. Smail, Walker, and Wright, *The Love of Power,* p. 97.
13. Smail, Walker, and Wright, *The Love of Power,* pp. 97-98.
14. Smail, Walker, and Wright, *The Love of Power,* p. 98.
15. Smail, Walker, and Wright, *The Love of Power,* p. 99.
16. Smail, Walker, and Wright, *The Love of Power,* p. 101.
17. Peter Wagner, "Third Wave," in *NIDPCM,* p. 1141.

matic ideas with traditional evangelical ones. 'Spirit baptism' is played down in favour of other metaphors ('filling') . . . [with] repeated fillings."[18] Cartledge regards tongues-speech and other phenomena as reflecting the experience of the "otherness" or transcendence of God.[19]

On the other hand, Bonnington observes, "The worship is often identified as . . . expressive of its own particular style of music."[20] To understand his next analogy, readers outside Britain need to know that of our main three BBC networks, Radio 4 broadcasts mainly informative talks; Radio 3 usually broadcasts classical music and is sometimes called elitist; while Radio 2 broadcasts endless pop music. In this light, Bonnington writes that many "see charismatic worship as Radio 2 worship . . . it does not suit the taste of Radio 3 purists with their high-culture commitment to classical style (choirs, robes, and liturgical precision), nor the more intellectual approach of Radio 4."[21] I have longed for many years that someone would point this out; for many such as I, it constitutes a genuine stumbling block to appreciating some positive features. It definitely smacks of a particular subculture, and underrates the continuous work of the Holy Spirit in earlier years both in theology and hymnody.

Yves Congar, the Roman Catholic theologian, writes supportively of the charismatic renewal movement. But in the context of "hand-clapping, raised hands, cries and sounds . . . dancing," he comments, "I do not believe that the Renewal [movement], in the form in which it appears now, can be extended to the whole of the Church."[22] Don Carson is also clearly supportive of charismatic renewal, but, he argues, many features call for a more moderate "middle way."[23] Andrew Walker observes, "Once words of knowledge appeared on the charismatic scene, they became *de rigueur* in the renewal and the so-called 'new' churches."[24] Most of these writers question whether the popular "word of knowledge" bears any relation to well-informed exegetical comment. Nigel Wright calls for more serious

---

18. Mark Bonnington, *Patterns in Charismatic Spirituality* (Cambridge: Grove, 2007), p. 7.

19. Mark J. Cartledge, *Charismatic Glossolalia: An Empirical-Theological Study* (Burlington, VT: Ashgate, 2002), p. 200.

20. Bonnington, *Patterns in Charismatic Spirituality*, p. 16.

21. Bonnington, *Patterns in Charismatic Spirituality*, pp. 16-17.

22. Yves Congar, *I Believe in the Holy Spirit: Lord and Giver of Life* (New York: Seabury / London: Chapman, 1983), 2.156; cf. 2.154.

23. Donald A. Carson, *Showing the Spirit* (Grand Rapids: Baker, 1987), pp. 183-88.

24. Smail, Walker, and Wright, *The Love of Power*, p. 119.

exposition of Scripture, arguing that too often so-called "prophecies" become "ensnared in mystical subjectivism."[25]

The important point to note is that all these writers are "friends" of the charismatic movement and its fervor and thirst for God, but see the need for sympathetic critiques from inside. But these critiques are the exception rather than the rule. As we have made plain, no such hesitations shackle those in the Pentecostal movement, who often display an admirable self-awareness that seems to be missing from many writers in the charismatic renewal movement. This is no mere theoretical matter, but profoundly affects how the Holy Spirit is perceived to direct our worship.

Finally, on this subject, Andy Lord concedes that the renewal movement can learn much from Roman Catholic traditions, especially regarding worship.[26] Similarly he calls for "a renewal of learning," "Trinitarian love," and "drawing more on biblical studies and . . . theological studies."[27] He also urges a more careful ecclesiology and eschatology, and such imaginative approaches as were used by Thomas Merton. He concludes, "Charismatic tradition can learn with integrity from the Roman Catholic tradition."[28] On worship he presents a careful evaluation of David Watson. He quotes Watson as writing, "The primary task of the Church is to worship God," and comments, "Worship depends on the presence of the Holy Spirit and yet links with human practices of giving worth to God."[29] There is a theological seriousness about Lord's book which could potentially transform charismatic worship. Yet in this chapter we have cited fewer than a dozen "obvious" names on transforming charismatic renewal, compared with hundreds or potentially thousands in the Pentecostal tradition, including busy correspondence on web sites.

3. The Worship Inspired by the Holy Spirit Reflects on Earth the Worship of Heaven

In the light of our first heading in this chapter, the book of Revelation eclipses the glories of God in Ezekiel, just as Hebrews eclipses the regula-

---

25. Smail, Walker, and Wright, *The Love of Power,* p. 111.

26. Andy Lord, *Transforming Renewal: Charismatic Renewal Meets Thomas Merton* (Eugene, OR: Pickwick, 2015).

27. Lord, *Transforming Renewal,* pp. 159, 161, 163.

28. Lord, *Transforming Renewal,* p. 171.

29. Lord, *Transforming Renewal,* p. 122.

tions in Leviticus about sacrifice. Christian worship has continuity. It would be odd if this were not so, for the same Holy Spirit has inspired it down the centuries. Indeed more than this, the Church seeks, through the Spirit, to reflect the worship of heaven and of the end time. Through Christ and the Holy Spirit, the writer to the Hebrews urges, "Let us therefore approach the throne of grace with boldness" (Heb. 4:16). In the Christian congregation the ministry of the Holy Spirit through preaching or prophecy has the effect of disclosing the secrets of the unbeliever's heart, and causing such people to bow down before God and worship him (1 Cor. 14:25).

Yet the book of Revelation also exposes the fully Trinitarian nature of heavenly worship.[30] Certainly the Holy Spirit fills worshipers with "exultant joy" (Greek, *agalliasis*), and the ever-fresh, ever-new work of the Holy Spirit reveals the ever-fresh dimensions of the inexhaustible glory of God. The knowledge of God's victory, sovereignty, and triumph becomes all the more wonderful and poignant because the victorious Christ still bears the wounds and scars of the cross, and is "the lamb who was slain" (Rev. 5:6, 12-13; 6:1; 7:9-10, 14; 8:1; 12:11; 13:8; 14:1; 17:14; 22:3; and elsewhere). In 5:12 the angels, living creatures, and elders cry, "Worthy is the Lamb that was slaughtered to receive power and wealth and wisdom and might and honor and glory and blessing!" And the four living creatures cried "Amen" (5:14). In 7:10 the great multitude cried out in a loud voice, "Salvation belongs to our God who is seated on the throne, and to the Lamb!" The angels and elders join in with "Amen! Blessing and glory and wisdom and thanksgiving . . . be to our God forever and ever! Amen" (7:12).

This is all due to the working together of the Holy Trinity. God — Father, Son, and Holy Spirit — receives worship from all, while the Spirit inspires such worship. The Father has purposed, planned, and provided everything. Christ, the slain Lamb, has redeemed us as our Mediator, "by the blood of the Lamb" (7:14). The Holy Spirit, who inspired earthly worship of God, inspires the worship of heaven, making all things new and ever fresh. It is also the Holy Spirit who makes and keeps Christ's people sinless as they now live in a new creation and new world. The Father has prepared this glorious destiny; the Son has made it possible through his incarnation, death, and resurrection; while the Holy Spirit activates heavenly worship, and renews the people of God continuously or "day by day," in accordance with his living nature.

30. Anthony C. Thiselton, *Life After Death: A New Approach to the Last Things* (Grand Rapids: Eerdmans, 2012), pp. 204-15.

Bibliography

Adekunle, Julius O., ed., *Religion in Politics* (Trenton, NJ: Africa World, 2009).

Ahn, Yongnan Jeon, *Interpretation of Tongues and Prophecy in 1 Corinthians 12–14*, JPTSup 41 (Blandford Forum, UK: Deo, 2013).

Allen, D. M., "The Forgotten Spirit: A Pentecostal Reading of the Letter to the Hebrews," *JPT* 18 (2009), pp. 51-66. Reprinted in Burke and Warrington, eds., *A Biblical Theology of the Holy Spirit,* pp. 226-37.

Ambrose, *On the Holy Spirit.* In *NPNF,* ser. 2, 10.91-158.

Anderson, Allan H., "Dangerous Memories for South African Pentecostals," in Anderson and Hollenweger, eds., *Pentecostals after a Century,* pp. 89-107.

———, "The Indigenous Churches in Latin America," *Practical Anthropology* 8 (1961), pp. 97-105.

———, "Introduction: World Pentecostalism at the Crossroads," in Anderson and Hollenweger, eds., *Pentecostals after a Century,* pp. 19-31.

———, *An Introduction to Pentecostalism: Global Charismatic Christianity* (Cambridge: Cambridge University Press, 2004).

Anderson, Allan H., and Walter J. Hollenweger, *Pentecostals after a Century: Global Perspectives,* JPTSup 15 (Sheffield: Sheffield Academic Press, 1999).

Anglican and Pentecostal Consultation, held at High Leigh on 7th-8th April, 2014.

Aquinas, Thomas, *Summa Theologiae,* 60 vols. (London: Eyre & Spottiswoode / New York: McGraw-Hill, 1964-81).

Archer, Kenneth J., "Crucial Issues for Pentecostals," in Anderson and Hollenweger, eds., *Pentecostals after a Century,* pp. 176-91.

———, "Pentecostal Hermeneutics: Retrospect and Prospect," in Martin, ed., *Pentecostal Hermeneutics,* pp. 131-48.

Athanasius, *First Epistle to Serapion.* In C. R. B. Shapland, *The Letter of St. Athanasius concerning the Holy Spirit* (London: Epworth, 1951).

Athenagoras, *Embassy,* or *A Plea for the Christians.* In *ANF,* 2.129-48.

Atkinson, James, *Martin Luther and the Birth of Protestantism* (London: Penguin, 1968).

Atkinson, William, "1 Corinthians," in Burke and Warrington, eds., *A Biblical Theology of the Holy Spirit,* pp. 146-59.

Attridge, Harold W., *The Epistle to the Hebrews,* Hermeneia (Philadelphia: Fortress, 1989).

Augustine, *On Rebuke and Grace.* In *NPNF,* ser. 1, 5.486-89.

———, *On the Gospel of John.* In *NPNF,* ser. 1, 7.1-447.

———, *On the Trinity.* In *NPNF,* ser. 1, 3.17-228.

Averbeck, Richard E., "Breath, Wind, Spirit and the Holy Spirit in the O.T.," in Firth and Wegner, eds., *Presence, Power, and Promise,* pp. 25-37.

Baker, Robert, "Pentecostal Bible Reading: Toward a Model of Reading for the Formation of the Affections," in Martin, ed., *Pentecostal Hermeneutics,* pp. 95-108.

Barnabas, Epistle of. In Lake, *Apostolic Fathers,* 1.335-409.

Barr, James, *The Semantics of Biblical Language* (Oxford: Oxford University Press, 1961).

Barrett, C. K., *The Holy Spirit and the Gospel Tradition* (London: SPCK, 1947).

Barth, Karl, *Church Dogmatics,* 14 vols. (Edinburgh: T&T Clark, 1957-75).

———, *The Epistle to the Romans* (Oxford: Oxford University Press, 1933).

———, *The Holy Spirit and the Christian Life* (Louisville: Westminster/John Knox, 1993).

———, *The Resurrection of the Dead* (London: Hodder & Stoughton, 1933).

———, *The Word of God and the Word of Man* (London: Hodder and Stoughton, 1928).

Basil, *On the Holy Spirit.* In *NPNF,* ser. 2, 8.1-50.

Bauckham, Richard, "Are We Still Missing the Elephant? C. S. Lewis's 'Fernseed and Elephants' Half a Century On," *Theology* 116 (2013), pp. 427-34.

———, "Scripture and Authority," *Transformation* 15 (1998), pp. 5-11.

Beare, F. W., *The First Epistle of Peter* (Oxford: Blackwell, 1961).

Beckford, Robert, "Black Pentecostals and Black Politics," in Anderson and Hollenweger, *Pentecostals after a Century,* pp. 48-59.

Bengel, J. A., *Gnomon Novi Testamenti,* 3rd ed. (Stuttgart: Steinkopf, 1866).

Berry, R. J., "The Virgin Birth of Christ," *Science and Christian Belief* 8 (1996), pp. 101-10.

Best, Ernest, *1 Peter,* NCB (London: Oliphants, 1971).

Bimson, John J., "Reconsidering a 'Cosmic Fall,'" *Science and Belief* 18 (2006), pp. 63-81.

Bittlinger, A., *Gifts and Graces: A Commentary on 1 Corinthians 12–14* (London: Hodder and Stoughton, 1967).

Block, Daniel I., "The View from the Top: The Holy Spirit in the Prophets," in Firth and Wegner, eds., *Presence, Power, and Promise,* pp. 175-207.

Bonaventura, *Itinerary.* In R. C. Perry, ed., *Late Mediaeval Mysticism* (London: SCM / Philadelphia: Westminster, 1957), pp. 132-41.

Bonnington, Mark, *Patterns in Charismatic Spirituality* (Cambridge: Grove, 2007).

Bornkamm, Günther, *Early Christian Experience* (London: SCM, 1969).

Bosch, David, *Transforming Mission: Paradigm Shifts in the Theology of Mission* (Maryknoll, NY: Orbis, 1991).

Brown, Francis, S. R. Driver, and C. A. Briggs, *Hebrew and English Lexicon,* rev. ed. (Lafayette: Associated Publishers, 1980).

Brown, Raymond E., *The Gospel according to John,* Anchor Bible (London: Chapman / New York: Macmillan, 1966).

Bruce, F. F., *The Epistle to the Hebrews* (Grand Rapids: Eerdmans, 1964).

Bruner, F. Dale, *A Theology of the Holy Spirit* (Grand Rapids: Eerdmans, 1970).

Brunner, Emil, *Dogmatics,* vol. 3: *The Christian Doctrine of the Church, Faith and Consummation* (London: Lutterworth, 1962).

———, *The Misunderstanding of the Church* (London: Lutterworth, repr. 2002).

———, *Truth as Encounter* (Philadelphia: Westminster, repr. 1964).

Bultmann, Rudolf, *"zaō, zōē (bioō, bios), anazaō, zōon, zōogoneō, zōopoieō,"* in *TDNT,* 2.832-75.

———, *Theology of the New Testament,* vol. 1 (London: SCM, 1952).

Burge, Gary M., "The Gospel of John," in Burke and Warrington, eds., *A Biblical Theology of the Holy Spirit,* pp. 104-15.

Burgess, Stanley M., *The Holy Spirit: Eastern Christian Traditions* (Peabody, MA: Hendrickson, 1989).

Burke, Trevor, "Romans," in Burke and Warrington, eds., *A Biblical Theology of the Holy Spirit,* pp. 129-45.

Burke, Trevor, and Keith Warrington, eds., *A Biblical Theology of the Holy Spirit* (London: SPCK, 2014).

Caird, George B., *The Revelation of St. John the Divine* (London: Black, 1966).

Calvin, John, *The First Epistle of Paul to the Corinthians,* Calvin's Commentaries (Grand Rapids: Eerdmans, 1960).

———, *Institutes of the Christian Religion,* ed. Henry Beveridge, 2 vols. (London: James Clarke, 1957).

Carson, Donald, *Showing the Spirit: A Theological Exposition of 1 Corinthians 12–14* (Grand Rapids: Baker, 1987).

Cartledge, Mark J., *Charismatic Glossolalia: An Empirical-Theological Study* (Burlington, VT: Ashgate, 2002).

Cartledge, Mark J., ed., *Speaking in Tongues: Multi-Disciplinary Perspectives* (Milton Keynes: Paternoster, 2006).

Catherine of Sienna, *Dialogue* (London: Kegan Paul, Trench, & Trubner, 1907).

Chan, Simon, *Liturgical Theology: The Church as Worshipping Community* (Downers Grove, IL: InterVarsity, 2006).

———, *Pentecostal Ecclesiology: An Essay in the Development of Doctrine,* JPTSup 38 (Blandford Forum, UK: Deo, 2011).

———, *Pentecostal Theology and the Christian Spiritual Tradition* (Eugene, OR: Wipf & Stock, repr. 2011).

Chrysostom, John, *Homilies on 1 Corinthians.* In *NPNF,* ser. 1, 13.3-269.

————, *Homilies on Acts.* In *NPNF,* ser. 1, 11.1-330.

Clarke, Clifton R., "Call and Response: Toward an African Pentecostal Theological Method," in idem, ed., *Pentecostal Theology in Africa,* pp. 21-39.

————, "Ogbu Kalu and Africa's Pentecostalism: A Tribute Essay," in idem, ed., *Pentecostal Theology in Africa,* pp. 7-18.

Clarke, Clifton R., ed., *Pentecostal Theology in Africa* (Eugene, OR: Pickwick, 2014).

Clement of Alexandria, *The Instructor.* In *ANF,* 2.207-298.

————, *Miscellanies.* In *ANF,* 2.299-568.

Clement of Rome, *1 Clement.* In Lake, *Apostolic Fathers,* 1.8-121.

Clifford, Paul, "Evil, Witchcraft, and Deliverance in African Pentecostal Worldview," in Clarke, ed., *Pentecostal Theology in Africa,* pp. 112-31.

Collins, R. F., *First Corinthians,* Sacra Pagina (Collegeville, MN: Glazier, 1999).

Congar, Yves, *I Believe in the Holy Spirit: Lord and Giver of Life,* 3 vols. (New York: Seabury / London: Chapman, 1983).

Cox, Harvey, *Fire from Heaven: The Rise of Pentecostal Spirituality* (Cambridge, MA: Da Capo, 1995).

Cranfield, C. E. B., *1 and 2 Peter and Jude* (London: SCM, 1960).

————, *Romans 1–8,* ICC (Edinburgh: T&T Clark 1975).

————, "Some Reflections on the Subject of the Virgin Birth," *SJT* 41 (1988), pp. 177-89.

Crumbley, Deidre Helen, "Sanctified Saints — Impure Prophetesses: A Cross-Cultural Study of Gender and Power," in Kärkkäinen, ed., *The Spirit in the World,* pp. 115-34.

Cullmann, Oscar, *Christ and Time: The Primitive Christian Conception of Time and History* (London: SCM, 1951).

Cyprian, *Treatise: On the Unity of the Church.* In *ANF,* 5.421-29.

Cyril of Jerusalem, *Catechetical Lectures.* In *NPNF,* ser. 2, 7.6-157.

Davids, Peter H., *The Epistle of James: A Commentary on the Greek Text,* NIGTC (Grand Rapids: Eerdmans, 1982).

Davies, Andrew, "What Does It Mean to Read the Bible as a Pentecostal?" in Martin, ed., *Pentecostal Hermeneutics,* pp. 249-62.

Dayton, Donald W., *Theological Roots of Pentecostalism* (Grand Rapids: Baker Academic, 1987).

Dewar, Lindsay, *The Holy Spirit in Modern Thought* (London: Mowbray, 1952).

Didachē. In Lake, *Apostolic Fathers,* 1.303-34.

Doctrine Commission of the Church of England, *We Believe in God* (London: Church House, 1987).

————, *We Believe in the Holy Spirit* (London: Church House, 1991).

Downing, F. Gerald, *Has Christianity a Revelation?* (London: SCM, 1964).

Dunn, James D. G., *Baptism in the Holy Spirit: A Re-examination of the New Testament Gift of the Spirit,* SBT 15 (London: SCM, 1970).

————, *Jesus and the Spirit: A Study of the Religious and Charismatic Experience of Jesus and the First Christians as Reflected in the New Testament* (London: SCM, 1975).

Edwards, Jonathan, *A Treatise Concerning Religious Affections in Select Works of Jonathan Edwards,* vol. 3 (London: Banner of Truth, 1961).

Edwards, T. C., *A Commentary on the First Epistle to the Corinthians: Greek Text,* 3rd ed. (London: Hodder and Stoughton, 1885).

Eusebius, *Church History.* In *NPNF,* ser. 2, 1.3-839.

Fahlbusch, Erwin, et al., eds., *The Encyclopedia of Christianity,* 5 vols. (Grand Rapids: Eerdmans / Leiden: Brill, 1998-2008).

Fee, Gordon D., *God's Empowering Presence: The Holy Spirit in the Letters of Paul* (Milton Keynes: Paternoster, 1995 / Peabody, MA: Hendrickson, 1994).

————, *Gospel and Spirit: Issues in New Testament Hermeneutics* (Peabody, MA: Hendrickson, 1991).

————, "Response to Roger Stronstad's 'The Biblical Precedent from Historical Precedent'," *Paraclete* 27 (1993), pp. 11-14.

Firth, David G., and Paul D. Wegner, eds., *Presence, Power, and Promise: The Role of the Spirit in the Old Testament* (Nottingham: Apollos, 2011).

Fish, Stanley, *Doing What Comes Naturally* (Oxford: Clarendon, 1989).

Fison, J. E., *The Blessing of the Holy Spirit* (London: Longmans, Green, 1950).

Forbes, Christopher, *Prophecy and Inspired Speech in Early Christianity and Its Hellenistic Environment,* WUNT/2 75 (Tübingen: Mohr Siebeck, 1995).

France, Richard T., *The Gospel of Mark: A Commentary on the Greek Text,* NIGTC (Grand Rapids: Eerdmans, 2002).

Friedrich, Gerhard, "*prophētēs, prophētis, prophēteuō, prophēteia, prophētikos, pseudoprophētēs,*" in *TDNT,* 6.781-862.

Fuchs, Ernst, *Studies of the Historical Jesus* (London: SCM, 1964).

Furnish, Victor P., *2 Corinthians,* Anchor Bible (New York: Doubleday, 1984).

Gadamer, Hans Georg, "Reflections on My Philosophical Journey," in Lewis E. Hahn, ed., *The Philosophy of Hans-Georg-Gadamer* (Chicago: Open Court, 1997), pp. 3-63.

————, *Truth and Method,* 2nd Eng. ed. (London: Sheed and Ward, 1989).

Gaventa, Beverly Roberts, *The Acts of the Apostles,* Abingdon New Testament Commentaries (Nashville: Abingdon, 2003).

Gee, Donald, *Spiritual Gifts in the Work of the Ministry Today* (Springfield, MO: Gospel Publications, 1963).

Gillespie, Thomas W., *The First Theologians: A Study in Early Christian Prophecy* (Grand Rapids: Eerdmans, 1994).

Goff, James R., Jr. "Initial Tongues in the Theology of Charles Fox Parham," in McGee, ed., *Initial Evidence,* pp. 57-71.

Green, Joel, *The Gospel of Luke,* NICNT (Grand Rapids: Eerdmans, 1997).

Gregory of Nyssa, *On "Not Three Gods."* In *NPNF,* ser. 2, 5.331-36.

Bibliography

Grey, Jacqueline, *Three's a Crowd: Pentecostal Hermeneutics and the Old Testament* (Eugene, OR: Pickwick, 2011).

Grudem, Wayne, *The Gift of Prophecy in 1 Corinthians* (Lanham, MD: University Press of America, 1982).

Hamilton, Neil Q., *The Holy Spirit and Eschatology in Paul*, SJT Occasional Paper 6 (Edinburgh: Oliver & Boyd, 1957).

Harlow, Hilary, "The Spirit of Yahweh in Isaiah 11:1-9," in Firth and Wegner, eds., *Presence, Power, and Promise*, pp. 220-32.

Harrisville, R. A., "The Concept of Newness in the New Testament," *JBL* 74 (1955), pp. 69-79.

Haykin, Michael A. G., *The Spirit of God: The Exegesis of 1 & 2 Corinthians in the Pneumatomachian Controversy of the Fourth Century*, Supplements to Vigiliae Christianae 27 (Leiden: Brill, 1994).

Hegel, Georg W. F., *Lectures on the Philosophy of Religion*, 3 vols. (London: Kegan Paul, Trench, & Trubner, 1895).

Hendry, George, *The Holy Spirit in Christian Theology* (London: SCM, 1966).

Hess, Richard S., "Bezalel and Oholiab: Spirit and Creativity," in Firth and Wegner, eds., *Presence, Power, and Promise*, pp. 161-72.

Hester, James D., *Paul's Concept of Inheritance* (Edinburgh: Oliver & Boyd, 1968).

Hilary, *On the Trinity*. In *NPNF*, ser. 2, 9.40-234).

Hildegard, *Scivias*, Classics of Western Spirituality (Mahwah, NJ: Paulist, 1990).

Hill, David, *New Testament Prophecy* (London: Marshall, 1979).

Hill, Wesley, *Paul and the Trinity* (Grand Rapids: Eerdmans, 2015).

Hippolytus, *Against Noetus*. In *ANF*, 5.223-31.

———, *Refutation of All Heresies*. In *ANF*, 5.9-153.

Hodge, Charles, *Systematic Theology*, 3 vols. (Grand Rapids: Eerdmans, 1946).

Hodgson, P. C., *Hegel and Christian Theology* (Oxford: Oxford University Press, 2008).

Hodson, Alan, "Hebrews," in Burke and Warrington, eds., *A Biblical Theology of the Holy Spirit*, pp. 226-37.

Hogeterp, Albert L. A., *Paul and God's Temple* (Leuven: Peeters, 2006).

Hollenweger, Walter J., *Der 1 Korintherbrief: eine Arbeithilfe zur Bibelwoche* (Kingmünster: Volksmissionarisches, 1964).

———, "Current Issues for Pentecostals," in Anderson and Hollenweger, eds., *Pentecostals after a Century*, pp. 176-91.

———, "Pentecostalism," in Fahlbusch et al., eds., *The Encyclopaedia of Christianity* 4.144-51.

———, *The Pentecostals* (Peabody, MA: Hendrickson, 1972).

———, "Rethinking Spirit Baptism," in Anderson and Hollenweger, eds., *Pentecostals after a Century*, pp. 164-73.

Hooker, Richard, *Treatise of the Laws of Ecclesiastical Polity*, ed. John Keble, 7th ed., 3 vols. (Oxford, Clarendon, 1888).

197

Horn, Friedrich W., *Das Angeld der Geistes* (Göttingen: Vandenhoeck & Ruprecht, 1992).

Hubbard, Robert L.,"The Spirit and Creation," in Firth and Wegner, eds., *Presence, Power, and Promise,* pp. 71-91.

Hudson, Neil, "Strange Words and Their Impact on Early Pentecostals," in Cartledge, ed., *Speaking in Tongues,* pp. 111-46.

Hurtado, Larry W., *Lord Jesus Christ: Devotion to Jesus in Earliest Christianity* (Grand Rapids: Eerdmans, 2003).

Hütter, R., "The Church as Public Dogma, Practice, and the Holy Spirit," *Pro Ecclesia* 3 (1994), pp. 334-61.

————, *Suffering Divine Things* (Grand Rapids: Eerdmans, 2010).

Ignatius, *To the Ephesians.* In Lake, *Apostolic Fathers,* 1.172-97.

————, *To the Philadelphians.* In Lake, *Apostolic Fathers,* 1.238-51.

————, *To the Smyrnaeans.* In Lake, *Apostolic Fathers,* 1.250-67.

————, *To the Trallians.* In Lake, *Apostolic Fathers,* 1.212-25.

Irenaeus, *Against Heresies.* In *ANF,* 1.315-567.

Jauss, Hans Robert, *Toward an Aesthetic of Reception* (Minneapolis: University of Minnesota Press, 1982).

Jeremias, Joachim, *The Central Message of the New Testament* (London: SCM, 1965).

————, *New Testament Theology,* vol. 1 (London: SCM, 1971).

Jewett, Robert, *Paul's Anthropological Terms* (Leiden: Brill, 1971).

————, *Romans: A Commentary,* Hermeneia (Minneapolis: Press, 2007).

Jones, O. R., *The Concept of Holiness* (London: Allen & Unwin / New York: Macmillan, 1961).

Julian of Norwich, *Revelations of Divine Love* (longer text; London: Penguin, 1968).

Jung, Lee Hong, *"Minjung* and Pentecostal Movement in Korea," in Anderson and Hollenweger, *Pentecostals after a Century,* pp. 138-60.

Justin, *Apology.* In *ANF,* 1.159-93.

————, *Dialogue with Trypho.* In *ANF,* 1.194-279.

Kaiser, Walter C., "The Pentateuch," in Burke and Warrington, eds., *A Biblical Theology of the Holy Spirit* (London: SPCK, 2014), pp. 1-11.

Kalu, Ogbu, *African Pentecostalism: An Introduction* (Oxford: Oxford University Press, 2008).

————, *"Sankofa:* Pentecostalism and African Cultural Heritage," in Kärkkäinen, ed., *The Spirit in the World,* pp. 135-52.

Kärkkäinen, Veli-Matti, "Baptized in the Spirit," in idem, ed., *The Spirit in the World,* p. 9.

————, *Holy Spirit and Salvation: The Sources of Christian Theology* (Louisville: Westminster/John Knox, 2010).

————, *Pneumatology: The Holy Spirit in Ecumenical, International, and Contextual Perspective* (Grand Rapids: Baker Academic, 2002).

————, *Spiritus ubi vult spirat: Pneumatology in Catholic-Pentecostal Dialogue (1922-89)* (Helsinki: Luther Agricola Society, 1988), p. 198.

Kärkkäinen, Veli-Matti, ed., *The Spirit in the World: Emerging Pentecostal Theologies in Global Contexts* (Grand Rapids: Eerdmans, 2009).

Käsemann, Ernst, "Cry for Liberty in the Church's Worship," in idem, *Perspectives on Paul*, pp. 122-37.

————, *Perspectives on Paul* (London: SCM, 1971).

Keener, Craig S., *Miracles: The Credibility of New Testament Accounts,* 2 vols. (Grand Rapids: Baker Academic, 2011).

————, *The Spirit in the Gospels and Acts: Divine Purity and Power* (Grand Rapids: Baker Academic, 1997).

Kelly, J. N. D., *The Epistles of Peter and Jude* (London: Black, 1969).

Kepler, Thomas, ed., *An Anthology of Devotional Literature* (Nappanee, IN: Evangel, 2001).

Küng, Hans, *The Incarnation of God: An Introduction to Hegel's Theological Thought* (Edinburgh: T&T Clark, 1987).

Kuyper, Abraham, *The Work of the Holy Spirit* (New York: Funk & Wagnalls, 1900).

Lake, Kirsopp, *Apostolic Fathers,* 2 vols. (Cambridge, MA: Heinemann, 1912).

Lampe, Geoffrey W. H., "The Holy Spirit in the Writings of St. Luke," in Nineham, ed., *Studies in the Gospels,* pp. 159-200.

————, *The Seal of the Spirit* (London: Longmans, Green, 1951).

Lane, William L., *Hebrews 1–8,* 2 vols. (Dallas: Word, 1991).

Levison, John R., *Filled with the Spirit* (Grand Rapids: Eerdmans, 2009).

————, "The Holy Spirit in the Gospels," in Lim, ed., *Holy Spirit,* pp. 52-56.

————, *The Spirit in First-Century Judaism* (Leiden: Brill, 2002).

Lim, Johnson, T. K., ed., *Holy Spirit: An Unfinished Agenda* (Singapore: Armour, 2015).

Lord, Andy, *Transforming Renewal* (Eugene, OR: Pickwick, 2015).

Lossky, Vladimir, *The Mystical Theology of the Eastern Church* (Cambridge: James Clarke, 1957).

Lowe, J., "An Examination of Attempts to Detect Development in St. Paul's Theology," *JTS* 42 (1941), pp. 129-42.

Luther, Martin, *Against the Celestial Prophets*, in idem, *Luther's Works,* 40.

————, *The Large Catechism* (Philadelphia: Fortress, 1959).

————, "Letter to Michael Stiefel," in idem, *Luther: Letters of Spiritual Counsel,* pp. 101-3.

————, *Luther: Letters of Spiritual Counsel,* ed. T. G. Tappert, Libraries of Christian Classics 18 (London: SCM, 1955).

————, *Luther's Works,* 55 vols. (St. Louis: Concordia; and Philadelphia: Fortress, 1955-86).

————, "On the Councils and the Church," in idem, *Luther's Works,* 41.148-66.

————, "The Sermons on Catechism," in idem, *Luther's Works,* 51.

————, *The Small Catechism* (Philadelphia: Concordia, 2005).

Luz, Ulrich, *Matthew 1–7: A Commentary* (Edinburgh: T&T Clark, 1990).

Macchia, Frank D., *Baptized in the Spirit: A Global Pentecostal Theology* (Grand Rapids: Zondervan, 2006).

———, "Groans Too Deep for Words," in *Asian Journal of Pentecostal Studies* 1 (1998), pp. 149-73.

———, "Sighs Too Deep for Words," *JPT* 1 (1992), pp. 47-73.

———, *The Trinity: Practically Speaking* (Downers Grove, IL: InterVarsity / Colorado Springs: Biblica, 2010).

Machen, J. Gresham, *The Virgin Birth of Christ* (Cambridge: James Clarke, 1930).

Martin, Lee Roy, "Hearing the Voice of God: Pentecostal Hermeneutics and the Book of Judges," in idem, ed., *Pentecostal Hermeneutics,* pp. 205-32.

Martin, Lee Roy, ed., *Pentecostal Hermeneutics* (Leiden: Brill, 2013).

McGee, Garry B., ed., *Initial Evidence: Historical and Biblical Perspectives on the Pentecostal Doctrine of Spirit Baptism* (Eugene, OR: Wipf & Stock, repr. 2007).

McGinn, Bernard, *Antichrist: Two Thousand Years of Human Fascination with Evil* (San Francisco: Harper, 1994).

McPherson, Aimee Semple, *The Four-Square Gospel,* compiled by Raymond Cox (Los Angeles: Heritage Committee, 1969).

———, *Give Me My Own God* (New York: H. C. Kinsey, 1936).

Menzies, Robert, *Empowered for Witness: The Spirit in Luke–Acts* (Sheffield: Sheffield Academic Press, 1994).

———, "Evidential Tongues: An Essay on Theological Method," *Asian Journal of Pentecostal Studies* (1998), pp. 111-23.

———, *Power: Foundations of Pentecostal Experience* (Grand Rapids: Zondervan, 2000).

Merrill, Eugene H., "The Samson Saga and Spiritual Leadership," in Firth and Wegner, eds., *Presence, Power, and Promise,* pp. 281-93.

Metzger, Bruce, *A Textual Commentary on the Greek New Testament,* 2nd ed. (London: United Bible Societies, 1994).

Miller, Donald, and Tetsunao Yamamori, *Global Pentecostalism: The New Face of Christian Social Engagement* (Berkeley: University of California Press, 2007).

Moberly, R. W. L., *Prophecy and Discernment* (Cambridge: Cambridge University Press, 2006).

Moltmann, Jürgen, *The Church in the Power of the Spirit: A Contribution to Messianic Ecclesiology* (London: SCM, 1975).

———, *The Coming of God: Christian Eschatology* (London: SCM, 1996).

———, *The Crucified God* (London: SCM, 1974).

———, "Preface," in Kärkkäinen, ed., *The Spirit in the World,* pp. viii-xii.

———, *The Spirit of Life: A Universal Affirmation* (London: SCM, 1992).

———, *Theology of Hope* (London: SCM, 1967).

———, *The Trinity and the Kingdom of God: The Doctrine of God* (London, SCM, 1981).

Montague, George T., *The Holy Spirit: The Growth of a Biblical Tradition* (Eugene, OR: Wipf & Stock, 1976).

Moule, C. F. D., *The Holy Spirit* (London: Mowbray, 1978).

Moulton, J. M., and G. Milligan, *The Vocabulary of the Greek Testament* (London: Hodder & Stoughton, 1952).

Müller, Ulrich B., *Prophetie und Predigt im Neuen Testament* (Gütersloh: Mohn, 1975).

Müntzer, Thomas, *Collected Works* (Edinburgh: T&T Clark, 1988).

Myers, Susan E., "Thomas, Acts of," in *NIDB,* 5.582-84.

Nida, Eugene A., *Understanding Latin Americans: With Special Reference to Religious Renewal Movements* (Pasadena: William Carey Library, 1974).

Nineham, D. E., ed., *Studies in the Gospels* (Oxford: Blackwell, 1967).

Noel, Bradley Truman, "Gordon Fee and the Challenge to Pentecostal Hermeneutics: Thirty Years Later," *Pneuma* 26 (2002), pp. 60-80.

Novatian, *Treatise concerning the Trinity.* In *ANF,* 5.611-44.

Ogungbile, David, "African Pentecostalism and the Prosperity Gospel," in Clarke, ed., *Pentecostal Theology in Africa,* pp. 132-49.

Olupona, J. K., "Africa, West," in *NIDPCM,* pp. 11-21.

Onoja, Adoyi, "The Pentecostal Churches: The Politics of Spiritual Deregulation since the 1980s," in Adekunle, ed., *Religion in Politics,* pp. 263-73.

Onyinah, Opoku, "Deliverance as a Way of Confronting Witchcraft in Contemporary Africa: Ghana as a Case Study," in Kärkkäinen, ed., *The Spirit in the World,* pp. 181-202.

Origen, *Against Celsus.* In *ANF,* 4.395-669.

———, *On First Principles.* In *ANF,* vol. 4.239-394.

Orr, James, *Revelation and Inspiration* (London: Duckworth, 1909).

Owen, John, *The Holy Spirit* (Grand Rapids: Kregel, 1954).

———, *The John Owen Collection: A Discourse concerning the Holy Spirit* (Rio, WI: Ages Software, 2004).

Pannenberg, Wolfhart, *Basic Questions in Theology,* vol. 2 (London: SCM, 1971).

———, *Basic Questions in Theology,* vol. 3 (London: SCM, 1973).

———, *Jesus: God and Man* (London: SCM, 1968).

———, "The Significance of Christianity in the Philosophy of Hegel," in idem, *Basic Questions in Theology,* 3.144-77.

———, *Systematic Theology,* 3 vols. (Grand Rapids, Eerdmans / Edinburgh: T&T Clark, 1991-98).

Parham, Charles F., *A Voice Crying in the Wilderness* (Baxter Springs: Apostolic Faith Bible College, 1902).

Parris, David P., *Reception Theory and Biblical Hermeneutics* (Eugene, OR: Pickwick, 2009).

Poloma, Margaret M., "Divine Healing, Religious Revivals, and Contemporary Pentecostalism," in Kärkkäinen, ed., *The Spirit in the World,* pp. 21-39.

Powell, Cyril H., *The Biblical Concept of Power* (London: Epworth, 1993).

Powers, Janet Everts, "Missionary Tongues," *JPT* 17 (2000), pp. 39-55.

Prenter, Regin, *Spiritus Creator: Luther's Concept of the Holy Spirit* (Philadelphia: Muhlenberg, 1953).

Procksch, O., "*hagios, hagiazō, hagiasmos, hagiotēs, hagiōsynē,*" in *TDNT,* 1.88-115.

Pulikottil, Paulson, "One God, One Spirit, Two Memories: A Pentecostal and Native Pentecostalism in Kerala," in Kärkkäinen, ed., *The Spirit in the World,* pp. 19-88.

Ramsey, Ian T., *Religious Language: An Empirical Placing of Theological Phrases* (London: SCM, 1957).

Reeves, Keith, "The Holy Spirit in Luke/Acts," in Lim, ed., *Holy Spirit,* pp. 62-66.

Reid, J. K. S., *The Authority of Scripture* (London: Methuen, 1958).

Ricoeur, Paul, *The Conflict of Interpretations* (Evanston: Northwestern University Press, 1976).

———, *Freud and Philosophy: An Essay on Interpretation* (New Haven: Yale University Press, 1970).

———, *Interpretation Theory* (Fort Worth: Texas Christian University Press, 1976).

Ringgren, Helmut, "*chāyāh, chai, chaiyîm, chaiyāh, michyāh,*" in *TDOT,* 4.324-44.

Robeck, C. M., "Seymour, William Joseph," in *NIDPCM,* pp. 1053-58.

Robinson, J. A. T., *The Human Face of God* (London: SCM, 1973).

Rogers, Eugene F., *After the Spirit: A Constructive Pneumatology* (London: SCM / Grand Rapids: Eerdmans, 2006).

Rorty, Richard, *Truth and Progress* (Cambridge: Cambridge University Press, 1998).

Rybarczyk, Edmund J., *Beyond Salvation and Classical Pentecostalism on Becoming like Christ* (Carlisle: Paternoster, 2004).

Sandmel, S., "Parallelomania," *JBL* 81 (1962), pp. 1-13.

Sandnes, K. O., *Paul — One of the Prophets?* WUNT/2 243 (Tübingen: Mohr Siebeck, 1991).

Schafroth, Verena, "1 and 2 Peter," in Burke and Warrington, eds., *A Biblical Theology of the Holy Spirit,* pp. 238-49.

Schlechter, S., *Some Aspects of Rabbinic Theology* (London: Black, 1909).

Schleiermacher, Friedrich, *The Christian Faith* (Edinburgh: T&T Clark, 1989).

———, *Hermeneutics: The Handwritten Manuscripts,* ed. Heinz Kimmerle (Missoula: Scholars Press, 1977).

Schnackenburg, Rudolf, *The Gospel according to John,* 3 vols. (Freiberg: Herder, 1965-75).

Schweizer, Eduard, "*Pneuma, pneumatikos, pneō, empneō, pnoē, ekpneō, theopneustos:* E.II. Luke and Acts," in *TDNT,* 6.404-15.

Scott, E. F. *The Spirit in the New Testament* (London: Hodder & Stoughton, 1924).

Sepúlveda, Juan, "Indigenous Pentecostalism and the Chilean Experience," in Anderson and Hollenweger, eds., *Pentecostals after a Century,* pp. 111-34.

Sibbes, Richard, *Works of Richard Sibbes* (Edinburgh: Banner of Truth, 1973).

Sjöberg, Erik, "*Pneuma, pneumatikos, pneō, empneō, pnoē, ekpneō, theopneustos:* C.III. Rûaḥ in Palestinian Judaism," in *TDNT,* 6.375-89.

Bibliography

Smail, Tom, Andrew Walker, and Nigel Wright, *The Love of Power or the Power of Love: A Careful Assessment of the Problems Within the Charismatic and Word-of-Faith Movements* (Minneapolis: Bethany House, 1994).

Smeaton, George, *The Doctrine of the Holy Spirit* (London: Banner of Truth, 1958).

Smitherman, G., *Talkin and Testifyin: The Language of Black America* (Detroit: Wayne State University Press, 1977).

Spittler, Russ, "Suggested Areas of Further Research in Pentecostal Studies," *Pneuma* 5 (1983), pp. 39-57.

Stendahl, Krister, "Glossolalia — The New Testament Evidence," in idem, *Paul among Jews and Gentiles,* pp. 109-24.

———, *Paul among Jews and Gentiles* (London: SCM, 1977).

Stephens, W. Peter, *The Holy Spirit in the Theology of Martin Bucer* (Cambridge: Cambridge University Press, 1970).

Stephenson, Christopher A., *Types of Pentecostal Theology: Method, System, Spirit* (Oxford: Oxford University Press, 2013).

Stowers, Stanley K., *The Diatribe and Paul's Letter to the Romans,* SBLDS 57 (Chico: Scholars Press, 1981).

Stronstad, Roger, *The Charismatic Theology of Saint Luke* (Peabody, MA: Hendrickson, 1984).

———, *The Prophethood of All Believers: A Study in Luke's Charismatic Theology,* JPTSup 16 (Sheffield: Sheffield Academic Press, 1999).

Sumney, Jerry L., "The Holy Spirit in Paul," in Lim, ed., *Holy Spirit* (Singapore: Armour, 2015), pp. 67-70.

Swete, Henry B., *The Holy Spirit in the Ancient Church* (London: Macmillan, 1912).

———, *The Holy Spirit in the New Testament* (London: Macmillan, 1909).

Taylor, Vincent, *The Person of Christ in New Testament Teaching* (London: Macmillan, 1958).

Tertullian, *Against Praxeas.* In *ANF,* 3.597-632.

Theissen, Gerd, *Psychological Aspects of Pauline Theology* (Edinburgh: T&T Clark, 1987).

Thielicke, Helmut, *The Evangelical Faith,* 3 vols. (Grand Rapids: Eerdmans, 1974-82).

Thiselton, Anthony C., *1 and 2 Thessalonians through the Centuries and Today* (Oxford: Wiley-Blackwell, 2011).

———, *1 Corinthians: A Shorter Exegetical and Pastoral Commentary* (Grand Rapids: Eerdmans, 2006).

———, *The First Epistle to the Corinthians: A Commentary on the Greek Text,* NIGTC (Grand Rapids: Eerdmans, 2000).

———, *The Hermeneutics of Doctrine* (Grand Rapids: Eerdmans, 2007).

———, *The Holy Spirit — in Biblical Teaching, through the Centuries, and Today* (Grand Rapids: Eerdmans / London: SPCK, 2013).

———, "'The Interpretation of Tongues': A New Suggestion in the Light of Greek Usage in Philo and Josephus," *JTS* 30 (1979), pp. 15-36.

————, *Life after Death: A New Approach to the Last Things* (Grand Rapids: Eerdmans, 2012; copublished as *The Last Things* [London: SPCK, 2012]).

————, *New Horizons in Hermeneutics: The Theory and Practice of Transforming Biblical Reading* (London: HarperCollins / Grand Rapids: Zondervan, 1992).

————, *The Two Horizons: New Testament Hermeneutics and Philosophical Description* (Grand Rapids: Eerdmans / Exeter: Paternoster, 1980).

Thomas, John C., "The Johannine Epistles," in Burke and Warrington, eds., *A Biblical Theology of the Holy Spirit,* pp. 250-56.

Thornton, Lionel S., *The Common Life in the Body of Christ,* 3rd ed. (London: Dacre, 1950).

Towns, Elmer, "The Holy Spirit and Church Growth," in Lim, ed., *Holy Spirit,* pp. 175-79.

Turner, Max, "Early Christian Experience and Theology of Tongues," in Cartledge, ed., *Speaking in Tongues,* pp. 1-33.

————, *The Holy Spirit and Spiritual Gifts Then and Now* (Carlisle: Paternoster, 1996).

————, *Power from on High: The Spirit in Israel's Restoration and Witness in Luke–Acts,* JPTSup 9 (Sheffield: Sheffield Academic Press, 1996).

Van Pelt, M. V., and Walter C. Kaiser, "*ruach*," in *NIDOTTE,* pp. 1073-78.

Vandervelde, George, "The Challenge of Evangelical Ecclesiology," *Evangelical Review of Theology* 27 (2003), pp. 4-26.

Vawter, Bruce, *Biblical Inspiration* (Philadelphia: Westminster, 1972).

Vriezen, T. G., *Old Testament Theology* (Oxford: Blackwell, 1962).

Waddell, Robby, "Hearing What the Spirit Says to the Churches: Profile of a Pentecostal Reader of the Apocalypse," in Martin, ed., *Pentecostal Hermeneutics,* pp. 171-204.

Wagner, Peter, "Third Wave," in *NIDPCM,* p. 1141.

Wainwright, Arthur, *The Trinity in the New Testament* (London: SPCK, 1962).

Warner, E. E., "Elim Fellowship," in *NIDPCM,* p. 598.

Warrington, Keith, *Pentecostal Theology: A Theology of Encounter* (London: T&T Clark, 2008).

————, "The Synoptic Gospels," in Burke and Warrington, eds., *A Biblical Theology of the Holy Spirit* (London: SPCK, 2014), pp. 84-103.

Watson, Francis, *Text, Church and World: Biblical Interpretation in Theological Perspective* (Edinburgh: T&T Clark, 1994).

Welker, Michael, *God the Spirit* (Minneapolis: Fortress, 1994).

————, *The Work of the Spirit* (Grand Rapids: Eerdmans, 2006).

Wesley, John, Sermon 10, from the *Christian Classics Ethereal Library,* http://www.ccel.org/ccel/wesley/sermons.

Westcott, B. F., *The Epistle to the Hebrews: The Greek Text,* 3rd ed. (New York: Macmillan, 1903).

Whiteley, D. E. H., *The Theology of St Paul,* 2nd ed. (Oxford: Blackwell, 1971).

Williams, Ronald R., *The Acts of the Apostles,* Torch Commentary (London: SCM, 1953).

Wilson, E. A., "Latin America," in *NIDPCM,* pp. 157-67.

Wittgenstein, Ludwig, *The Blue and Brown Books,* 2nd ed. (Oxford: Blackwell, 1969).

———, *Philosophical Investigations,* 2nd ed. (Oxford: Blackwell, 1958).

———, *Zettel* (Oxford: Blackwell, 1967).

Woodman, Simon P., "The 'Seal' of the Spirit: The Holy Spirit in the Book of Revelation," in Lim, ed., *Holy Spirit,* pp. 75-78.

Wright, N. T., "The New Inheritance according to Paul," *Bible Review* 14 (1998), pp. 16, 47.

———, *The Resurrection of the Son of God* (London: SPCK, 2003).

Yeago, David S., "'A Christian, Holy People': Martin Luther on Salvation and the Church," *Modern Theology* 13 (1997), pp. 101-20.

Yong, Amos, "From Azusa Street to the Bo Tree and Back . . . in the Pentecostal Encounter with Buddhism," in Kärkkäinen, ed., *The Spirit in the World,* pp. 203-26.

———, *Spirit of Love: A Trinitarian Theology of Grace* (Waco: Baylor University Press, 2012).

———, *The Spirit Poured Out on All Flesh* (Grand Rapids: Baker Academic, 2005).

———, *Spirit–Word–Community: Theological Hermeneutics in Trinitarian Perspective* (Burlington, VT: Ashgate, 2002).

Yun, Koo Dong, "Pentecostalism from Below: *Minjung* Liberation and Asian Pentecostal Theology," in Kärkkäinen, ed., *The Spirit in the World,* pp. 89-114.

Zizioulas, John D., *Being as Communion* (New York: St. Vladimir's Seminary Press, 1985).

Zwiep, Arie W., *Christ, the Spirit and the Community of God,* WUNT/2 293 (Tübingen: Mohr Siebeck, 2010).

Index of Authors

Index of Subjects
(patristic names are also included)

preservation of revelation, 110
presupposition, 169, 170-71, 174
pretending to supernatural revelations, 34
pre-understanding, 169, 180
priestly work of Christ, 67-68
Priscilla, 67
proclamation of the gospel, 37
promise, *172-73*
prophecy, 7-9, *33-34*, 43, 66-67, *73-75*, 79, 101, 142, 149, 188, 190
prosecuting counsel, 61
prosperity gospel, *148-50, 163*, 187
proto-Pentecostalism, 137
prototype in industrial language, 129
provisional way forward by negotiation, 130
public and rational, 114
purity and holiness, 16
purposive action of the Spirit, 12, 91
purposive sequence, 127
Pyongyang revival, 146-47

Quakers, early, 137
Qumran, 64

Radical Reformers, 16, 29
Radio 2 and *Radio 4,* 189
raised with Christ, 66
rapture, the, 166, 174
rationality, 16, 149, 176
reader-response theories, 170, 173, 179
readiness as disposition, 133, 181
reception history, 170, 174
reconciliation, 67
redemption of our bodies, 130
Reformation and post-Reformation periods, 120
Reformed Tradition, 90
relational being, 80, 88
renewal by the Spirit, 66
repeated endowments, 48, 52
repentance, 24, 41, 68, 180
repetitive chorus-singing, 187
repressed wishes, 185
reproduction of experience of Jesus, 186

resurrection, 62, 66-67, 127
with Christ, 31
by the Holy Spirit, 71, 125, 127
of Jesus and Spirit, 25-26, 30
return of Christ or Parousia, 75, 166, 181
revelation, *111-12*
Revelation, Book of, 73-75, 172
revival, 127
reward, 15
righteousness, 122
river of the water of life, 75
Roman Catholic traditions, 151, 177, 190

sacramentalism, 82
sacraments, 106, 109
Samaritan puzzle, 49, 51, *55*, 101
sanctification, *35-36*, 70, 106, *116-24*, 134
sanctification as process, not event, 117-18
schools and teachers, 151
Scripture, *110-15*
authority of, 115
credibility of, 115
Fathers and reason, 106, 114
inspiration of, 13, 69-70, 110-11, 114-15
meaning of, 115
and reason, 106, 123
as shaping community, 170
sealing of the redeemed, 75
second blessing, so-called, 48, 53
Second Epistle of Peter and Jude, 73-74
second-class Christians, 30
secretary, 65
secrets of the heart, 42, 185
secular vocations, 121
self-awareness, self-criticism, 153, *154-67*, 187
self-differentiation, 93
self-disclosure, 110
self-effacement of the Spirit, 23, 60
self-emptying *(kenōsis),* 22
setbacks and difficulties, 50
seventy elders, 7, 10
sexual and social sin, 117
shareholder *(koinōnos),* 100
Shema, 12

Index of Scripture and Other Ancient Sources